To: Micha[...]

Love + p[...]

from Oscar. 7x

Your Obedient Servant

YOUR
OBEDIENT SERVANT

The Story of Man's Best Friend

Angela Patmore

HUTCHINSON

London Melbourne Sydney Auckland Johannesburg

Hutchinson & Co. (Publishers) Ltd

An imprint of the Hutchinson Publishing Group

17–21 Conway Street, London WIP 6JD

Hutchinson Publishing Group (Australia) Pty Ltd
PO Box 496, 16–22 Church Street, Hawthorne, Melbourne,
Victoria 3122

Hutchinson Group (NZ) Ltd
32–34 View Road, PO Box 40–086, Glenfield, Auckland 10

Hutchinson Group (SA) Pty Ltd
PO Box 337, Bergvlei 2012, South Africa

First published 1984
© Angela Patmore 1984

Set in Linotron Ehrhardt by
Wyvern Typesetting Limited, Bristol

Printed and bound in Great Britain by
Anchor Brendon Ltd,
Tiptree, Essex

British Library Cataloguing in Publication Data

Patmore, Angela
Your obedient servant
1. Dogs—History
I. Title
636.7   SF422.5

ISBN 0 09 155310 5

CONTENTS

ACKNOWLEDGEMENTS

In order to research this book, I went to the highest authorities. I should like to thank them all for their help, and particularly the following:

Dr D. Abrahamson

Animal Aid

Mrs Clarissa Baldwin, National Canine Defence League

Mr Peter Boddy, Master of Reddyfield Bloodhounds

Mr Tony Blunt, Hearing Dogs for the Deaf

The British Small Animals Veterinary Association

The British Union for the Abolition of Vivisection

Mr Douglas Brodie MRCVS

Buckingham Palace and Her Majesty's Assistant Press Secretary

Mr Doug Burson, Quaker Oats Company, USA

Dean Leo Bustad, Professor of Veterinary Medicine, Washington State University, USA

PC Ray Cooper and Myra of the Metropolitan Police Force

Mr Andy Currant, Department of Palaeontology, British Museum of Natural History

Mr Bill Edmond, Secretary, Kennel Club

Mrs Janice Edmonds, Secretary, Alaskan Malamute Club

Inspector Simon Edwards, Officer in Charge, Police Dog Section, Kent Constabulary

Mrs Penny Evans, Secretary, Siberian Husky Club of Great Britain

Mr Mike Findlay MRCVS

Mr Bruce Fogle DVM, MRCVS

Mrs G. Glenister and Poppy

Mr John Gordon

The Guide Dogs for the Blind Association

Mr Brian Gunn, General Secretary, National Anti-Vivisection Society

Mr Bill Harman and Lady

The International Fund for Animal Welfare

The Joint Advisory Committee on Pets in Society (JACOPIS)

Dr Juliet Jewel, British Museum of Natural History

The Marquess of Tavistock

Dr Peter Messent, Honorary Secretary, Society for Companion Animal Studies

The Ministry of Agriculture, Fisheries and Food, Miss N. J. Hassall, Animal Health Division

Mr A. Mitchell, Staffordshire Bull Terrier Breed Council

Dr Roger Mugford, Consultant in Animal Behaviour

Ms Heather Pane, JACOPIS

Geoffrey Patmore, Yorkshire terrier to the author

ACKNOWLEDGEMENTS

Stanley Patmore, Mongrel dog to the author

Mrs Paddy Petch and the Rase retrievers

Chief Inspector Bryn Phillips, Officer in Charge, No. 3 Region Police Dog Training School, Staffordshire

Mrs Elin Richards, Bloodhound Club

The Royal Air Force Police Dog School, RAF Newton
Warrant Officer George Clapperton
Flight Sergeant Trevor Figgins
Civilian Dog Adviser Terry McHaffie
Flight Sergeant Al Murray

The Royal Army Veterinary Corps Training Centre, Melton Mowbray, Capt. Tony Rossell

The Royal Society for the Prevention of Cruelty to Animals:
Inspector Degenhard
Brighton Treasurer Philip Hale

Chief Superintendent Frank Milner
Executive Officer W. J. Pimm

Scott Polar Research Institute, Cambridge

Mr John Sherry

Ms Dorothy Steves

Mary Stewart DVM, MRCVS

Mr Mike Stockman MRCVS

Major Eric Stones, The Dogs' Home, Battersea

Des Thompson BA, MVB, MRCVS, 1982–3 President of the BSAVA

Ms Shirley Walne

Mrs Janet Ward, Secretary, Eskimo Dog Club

Mr G. S. Wiggins MRCVS, Veterinary Officer, the City of London

Chief Inspector Ray Wood, Officer in Charge, Eastern Region Dog Training School, Nottinghamshire

Mrs Barbara Woodhouse

PHOTOGRAPHIC ACKNOWLEDGEMENTS

The author and publishers wish to thank the following for permission to reproduce photographs:

BBC Hulton Picture Library; Bridgeman Art Library; Mary Evans Picture Library; Bill Harman; Hearing Dogs for the Deaf; Michael Holford; International Fund for Animal Welfare; Inspector Simon Edwards, Kent Constabulary; Keystone Press Agency; Mansell Collection; National Anti-Vivisection Society/Brian Gunn; National Canine Defence League; Popperfoto; Ann Ronan Picture Library; Frank Spooner Pictures/Gamma.

7

I

THE DOGFATHER

There are about six million domestic dogs in Britain and from fifty to eighty million in the United States. Why? The zoological name for these creatures, *Canis familiaris*, more or less sums up what we think of them. The dog has become familiar, an appendage some would say, a hygiene hazard, a defiler of parks, to be locked up, put down, wormed, neutered and pooper-scooped. Yet to live cheek by jowl with a dog is to take part in a prehistoric relationship, one that goes back 14,000 years in the fossil record.

That the creature should have been admitted to the house at all is astounding. A visitor from another planet might well fall down in a dead faint seeing a predator with forty-two lethal weapons for rending and grinding lying on the living-room carpet. The human head can only muster thirty-two pathetic pearlies. A fair-sized dog, so inclined, can exert a bite pressure of over 600lbs. He can outgallop and outlast a healthy man, trotting effortlessly for two days on end. His Cape Hunting cousins dispatch prey larger than ourselves cursorially: they eat it piecemeal as it runs for help.

Closely observed, the domestic dog is not 'familiaris' at all. He is rather odd. His nose has fifteen times the sensory area of ours, and yet he rolls in tremendous stinks. He chatters and chops at masonic messages laid down by his peers. He swells out his guard hairs, erects his hackles and lays back his ears in evil expressions that expose the buccal cavities on either side of his teeth. He leaves chemical identikit markings, saying God only knows what about us, by urinating and scraping interdigital glands. He seems to possess telepathic insight into human affairs, can read clocks and characters and predict the occasional death and homecoming. Yet among his own kind he must observe strange rituals – Uriah Heep gestures, regal gestures, stances and dances – to prevent self-genocide. He wags, whines, barks, bells and howls. After thousands of years of domestication he retains the ability to revert to the wild. And yet he stays with us. 'Faithful unto death' may be a cliché when applied to dogs, but it is no small thing in nature for a whole species to live and die for A.N. Other.

9

So how did this extraordinary business begin? When one of our prehistoric ancestors shouted 'Sit!' 14,000 or so years ago, what sort of creature was it that refrained from biting his arms off? To find out more about our first meeting with the family *Canidae* I went along to the British Museum of Natural History to look at a lot of bones. A skeletal 'Dire Wolf' of extinct viciousness stares ravenously at his visitors. He was one of over 1600 Pleistocene wolves who fell in the mud at Rancho La Brea near Los Angeles, and got preserved in a tar seep. Not quite so old is the 'Bone-Eating Dog', who was the most abundant carnivore in North America during the Pliocene, but who had perished by the end of the Biancan, perhaps unable to cope with the Dire Wolf. There were bits of 300 cannibalistic hyenas from a Devon cave dating from the last interglacial period; also the ulna of a wolf from one of the Thames terraces. Nothing, though, relating to domestic-dog fossils.

'It won't be easy to find anything on the earliest domestic dog,' said palaeontologist Andy Currant. 'There may be association with human remains, but then only because a dwelling like a cave, that would be suitable for a female wolf denning, tended also to be suitable for a man. You do get a morphological change (in the bones, etc.), but only after years of domesticated breeding. True dog fossils are common, but domestication is hard to prove.'

I talked with zoological historian Dr Juliet Jewel. 'It's a very complicated subject. There's a lot of controversy, for example, about the age of the dog remains at the Palegawra cave in Iraq, dated to 14,000 years ago and therefore Tertiary Pleistocene. According to some estimates they are only Neolithic. So it's inadvisable to be too specific about dates.' A German popular-science magazine refers to the 'oldest housedog' in the world as coming from the double grave in Oberkassel near Bonn.[1] This fellow lived 14,000 years ago, say the Germans.

Bearing this in mind, and that radiocarbon, fluorine and pollen dating are not always consistent, domestic-dog skeletons have turned up at Windmill Hill and Easton Down in Wiltshire, dated to 2000 BC. Another of the same period was found in the Neolithic flint mines at Grime's Grave, Norfolk. A much more ancient dog, resting beneath the hand of a human skeleton in what is now Israel (at the Natufian site) is believed to be 12,000 years old. And another was found at the Jaguar cave in Idaho and dated 10,500 BP (before the present). There are many domestic-dog remains scattered around the world: at Starr Carr, Yorkshire, dated 9500 BP; at Çayönü in Turkey, dated 9000 BP; prehistoric China: dogs buried in a human tomb at Wu-kuan-ts'un; north-west Alaska: dogs' teeth broken off artificially, perhaps to prevent damage to their burdens of caribou skins; prehistoric New Zealand: dogs' teeth used to make the points of composite fish-hooks; dog depicted in the Magdalenian frescoes of Spain from the Mesolithic era;

dog mentioned on an ancient Egyptian pyramid of 3733 BC, belonging to Cheops and called 'Abakaru'.

Old dogs, certainly, but of what sort, and with what ancestry? This question, of the dogfather, has caused taxonomists some hair-tearing, as we may judge from their vexing classifications of dogs, wolves and foxes. The grandfather of them all, some ten or fifteen million years ago, was a chap called 'Tomarctus'. He it was who founded the entire family of *Canidae*, including those now extinct and some thirty-five living species, divided (usually) into thirteen genera of tireless, galloping toe-walkers. Tomarctus and his sons were distinguishable from all previous creatures by a special toe arrangement to facilitate running, with a dew-claw in place of a fifth hind toe. If you examine your own dog (or somebody else's dog) you'll notice that he or she is abandoning the fifth fore toe as well, as the Cape Hunting cousins have done.

The general consensus among modern scientists is that all dogs, from mastiff to chihuahua, are descended from the wolf, or one of his sub-species.[2] Other wild and prototype dogfathers have been put forward from time to time; the jackal, for example, has had his day. Nobel prizewinner Konrad Lorenz argued for many years that the golden jackal was the dogfather of the 'little Spitz-like Turf dogs' who lived with nomadic Stone Age man when he finally settled in pillar dwellings along the Baltic.[3] These little fellows were short-muzzled and quite different from the local canine hoi polloi. Having confused everybody, Lorenz later modified his argument and acceded to the wolf. American professor Michael Fox is a newer wolf opponent. Studying canids all over the world, he believes the so-called link between the social behaviour of wolves and dogs, always a strong argument in favour of wolf ancestry, is tenuous. Most wild and feral dogs will form packs and 'be sociable' if their ecosystems allow them to, and even wolf packs split up when food is scarce. Chromosome counts, he says, are in dispute; in any case the wolf would scarcely have been suitable for man's requirements. The dog, says Fox, is descended from a dingo-like canid that was widespread across Europe in the Stone Age.[4]

One very cogent argument, though, in favour of the wolf is the size of his brain: 30 per cent larger than the equivalent-sized domestic dog. The jackal's, for instance, is much smaller. 'If the jackal had played any part in the dog's ancestry,' says wolf scientist Erik Zimen, 'this would be the only case in which enlargement of the brain followed domestication.'[5]

Let us suppose, then, that it really was the wolf. How did primitive man tame him? The majority view is that he killed the wolf and collared the cubs. Perhaps he knocked their teeth out, to be on the safe side. Some say he wanted them to help him hunt. Others think he felt sorry for them, raking over the middens or muckheaps, and adopted them. There have been many fairy stories suggesting how this may have come about; the truth is, we do not know. But once the cubs were reared, and these wolves mated, the next generation would have been slightly different from their peers; the next more so. One mustn't be put off the idea of a wolf dogfather simply because a Peke looks more like a wolf's lunch than his descendant; the isolation of hand-reared wolves from their kind would have been sufficient in itself to produce wide genetic variants fairly quickly. Curly tails, shorter muzzles, lackadaisical ears, floppiness and soppiness would have been selected. Vicious, prick-eared, burly customers would have got the chop. (One theory of the origin of the word 'dog' is that it derives from dug, since the early English breeders used to say 'that one's a dug' and 'that one's a bucket'.)[6] The notion that domestic dogs retain puppy characteristics in adulthood and that wild dogs do not, is still widely accepted.

At all events, the humans' wolves became, by degrees, less like their dogfather; more dependent, more friendly; and they evolved, according to prevailing local climate, conditions and local work, into every conceivable form.

Whether man originally wanted the wolf for a scenter or a sentry, or simply to howl back at the night that howled at him, he soon discovered himself to be the owner of a marvellous appliance. Why, there was simply nothing he couldn't do, a man and his new dog-job tool. He could shift heavy goods by loading them on the dog's back, or on a sled. The draught dog doubled as a draught-stopper and central heater, against those Ice Age winds lashing round one's portals. He could track and search for game, on a creeper leash, much more efficiently than his master. Then when he caught it, he could kill it, and, perhaps by means of a flint spear in the nose, be encouraged to give it up. If the worst came to the worst in a hard winter, the dog could be spit-roasted himself – some dog remains are chopped bones. He could guard the home, the heirlooms and the livestock, keeping the wolf from the door. His fur provided wool to make blankets and stuff bearskin mattresses. His skin made warm coats and, worn hair outermost, camouflage jackets for hunting. His gut, dried, made sewing thread, and his bladder supplied a window. He also supplied a friend.

For the first time in his life primitive man could progress from a hand-to-mouth existence, sleeping up trees, to a bijou cave, with livestock, grain and goodies on the premises. He'd never had an aide-de-camp before. Whatever the twentieth-century dog-haters may think, *Canis familiaris* was undoubtedly a major civilizing influence in the history of mankind.

The wolf, being the dogfather, has been studied in all his habits by a number of scientists: R. Schenkel,[7] J. P. Scott[8] and L. David Mech[9] have all produced seminal works. So has German wolf enthusiast Erik Zimen. Zimen has been up to his ears in wolves for a number of years, joining in howling concerts and watching captive and free-roaming packs in Germany, North America and Abruzzi, Italy. He began by interbreeding wolves and poodles to produce Puwos, which made delightful pets and came in fifty-seven varieties. Count Buffon, in his *Natural History* book of 1749, tells us that his attempt to interbreed a wolf with an Irish greyhound was a disaster. Mealtimes were not romantic. 'The wolf, instead of seizing the meat, instantly drove off the dog, then laid hold of the edge of the plate so dexterously as to allow nothing to fall, and carried off the whole. I have seen her run in this manner five or six times round the wall, and never set it down, save to take breath, to devour the meat, or to attack the dog when he approached.' There was a lot of 'dismal howling' and fierce fighting, but no Irish wolfcubs.

Taming wolves is no easy matter either, despite the cubs' instinctive love of Mother and Mister Alpha the 'pack-leader' (a contentious concept). Barbara Woodhouse had some success with hyenas in Gambia, but these are not, strictly speaking, canids. Actress Pat Phoenix had a Timber Wolf called Blackie that opened doors by knocking them down. Lorenz knew a Viennese policeman who tamed a wolf bitch called Poldi, but warns that males, especially, are liable to become 'biters from fear'.

Zimen started modestly with a she-cub, Anfa. He had no success whatever teaching her to sit or stay, despite prolonged walkies on a lead. Similarly doomed were his attempts to teach the wolves to pull a sledge, like Eskimo wolves of yore. One day a robin alighted on one of the team and caused a fracas, which ended with all the wolves in a blazing tangle.

In the enclosure that served as their home-base, the wolves formed a pack, and the females fought without warning or mercy, trying to kill any scapegoat who had fallen from grace in their ranking order. The males, within their own social system, were more matey. They did a lot of threatening and snarling but usually fought by Queensberry rules. When Zimen's studies were completed, his wolves were dispersed to small zoo enclosures. One day when he visited them, Anfa attacked him with something like personal hatred. So did another normally placid wolf, Alexander. 'If any of my wolves was real material for domestication – in the form in which it must have taken place 10,000 or 15,000 years ago – it was the friendly, unterrifying, titbit-loving Alexander,' Zimen said.

> At first I did not notice the change in Alexander, but one day when I entered the enclosure he suddenly jumped up at me and put both paws on my shoulders. He was so big that he looked down at me, baring his teeth. Whenever I moved he snarled more loudly, his big white teeth came alarmingly closer, and I did not feel at all comfortable. I tried to calm him, and spoke to him gently, saying 'Alexander, Alexander, be quiet, be quiet,' but it made no difference. He stayed there and went on snarling.[10]

Having made his point, Alex eventually got down, went to a bush and cocked his leg. So as not to lose face, Zimen did the same. He concludes that this is typical of 'tame' wolves. Tractable as cubs, they grow up dangerous. That Anfa and Alex might have borne him a personal grudge seems not to have entered his head. Anfa had a record, anyway, of biting men's trousers. Much more might be inferred from the behaviour of one of Zimen's other wolves, Mädchen ('Girl'), who weaseled her way into the house and could be regularly observed sitting beside his mother-in-law on the sofa.

What of the domestic dog's *Canidae* cousins? The family includes eleven species of fox (*Vulpes*), eight South American species of 'Dusicyon', mostly called foxes; the zorro, the crab-eating fox, the long-legged 'maned wolf' and the bush dog – all South American. There are three other types of fox, less like attenuated jackals: the bat-eared, the Arctic, and the Fennec; the Asian dhole, red-haired and savage; the nocturnal Japanese 'raccoon dog', imported to Finland for fur-production and now wild across Europe, hibernating in winter; and the spotted Cape Hunting dog, slinking over African savannahs. Then come the canids proper: nine species, including our own domestic dog, the wolf, and three species of jackal, the slender scavenger. Very like one of those (the golden) is the North American coyote, perhaps a product of parallel evolution. His solitary habits have succeeded, where pack-hunters – the wolves, dholes, and Cape Hunting dogs – have been driven to the edge of extinction by man. Then come the 'Simenian dog' of Ethiopia, a twin of the golden jackal; the extremely endangered 'red wolf' (whose zoological name means black dog), and the dingo of Australia. The dingo was once domesticated, arriving from mainland Asia with the Aboriginal settlers and then making shift on his own. All efforts to exterminate him have failed. A great fence has been erected across Australia to protect sheep farms, but the dingo is now apparently on both sides of it. He has been accused of just about everything, including the murder of a nine-week-old baby at Ayers Rock near Alice Springs.[11] And last, but not least, in the no-man's-land of classification, are the pariahs, eking out a living from human refuse in India and elsewhere. 'Pariah' is a Tamil word meaning drummer or outcast. Some scientists believe these creatures hold the key to domestication, but they are little known or studied.

Where may we find them, or any wild dogs for that matter, in Britain's eighty or ninety zoological collections? John Aspinall, a marvellous man who lets his wolves lick his face, has Canadian Timber Wolves, Cape Hunting dogs and even dholes among his collections at Howletts and Port Lympne (phone 022 778286 for details), but then his zoos are in many respects unusual. The volume concerning canids of the *International Zoo Yearbook* appears to refer to the 1960s; the London Zoo has Canadian Timber Wolves and Fennec foxes, a coyote who wouldn't show his face, a Cape Hunting dog equally shy, and the American Grey Fox. Dingoes? No. Dholes? Not likely. 'I have seen dingoes in the Duke of Bedford's private zoo at Woburn Abbey,' writes *Pan Book of Dogs* author Catherine Fisher.[12] I inquire there. 'I have looked back over our records at the Animal Kingdom and can find nothing in relation to dingoes,' the Marquess of Tavistock assures me. 'I certainly, personally, never remember us having any wild dogs, even before the Game Park.' I phone Longleat. Surely they'll have wild dogs there. 'No, they're not of great public interest,' a spokesman replies. 'Foxes? Nasty smelly things. You won't find many zoos with those.'

2

THE TASKMASTER

Whether the dog recognized primitive man as a pack leader, or simply someone large who appeared to be quartermaster of local rations, he was soon to find man a hard taskmaster. There was much to be done, and much whipping and whacking when it was not done to his liking. The time-honoured expression 'breaking a dog' is still used, and not always metaphorically. Without ever having made an undertaking to be dutiful, henceforth dutiful all dogs must be. One who refused his master's bidding was from now on a 'bad' dog or, in some cases, a dead dog. Man may have lost his own Paradise through disobedience; the dog was to lose his through doing as he was told. Suddenly a sharp divide appeared between what his instincts said he must do and what man said he must do. The old wolf days, the halcyon days, were gone.

The earliest races of domesticated dogs (as distinct from the wild things in chapter I) are usually divided by taxonomists into four types, all now extinct, descended from wolves and, ultimately, from Tomarctus. From these four – small, medium, shepherd and haulage – the 400-odd breeds we know today are thought to have divided and subdivided, according to their calling.[1]

Most of today's companion breeds were developed, or evolved, for a working life. With few exceptions, dogs were regarded as workers rather than pets. 'Toy' was a contemptuous term for a contemptible thing; writers from Tudor physician Dr Caius onwards poured scorn on women who had dogs rather than babies and attempted to find 'uses' for their little pets as pain relievers.

The Origin of Breeds

The origin of breeds has been the theme of many rambling discourses, charts and schemes, no two of which conform with each other, and I do not propose to set up another shambolic system here. Two of the earliest British books on dogs, George Turberville's *Noble Art of Venerie or Hunting* (1575) and Dr

Johannes Caius's *De Canibus Britannicis* (*c.* 1572) venture into the subject and venture out again without anything being decided. The Romans, who were sensible and sophisticated in their dog lore and may well have had rudimentary 'breeds', divided dogs mainly into three classes: *Pugnaces* for fighting, *Sagaces* for cleverness and *Celeres* for speed. *Sagaces* included nosework.

One of the more intriguing theories of dog-diversification concerns the need for endurance on the one hand (trotting, for shepherding and droving jobs) and speed on the other (racing, hunting by sight). Kennel Club Secretary Bill Edmond: 'When the single tracking dog puts its front feet down, its rear feet follow in the same pad marks, and this is a trait of great endurance. If the dog is going through snow or over rough terrain, the rear feet don't have to make new imprints. Whereas with the saluki, each paw makes a separate mark. This is a speed merchant rather than an endurance merchant.'

It is easy to point to ancient Egyptian and Assyrian tombstone work or to Roman mosaics and say, 'There's a greyhound,' and 'There's a mastiff,' and most people, including many in authority, do. But it is also misleading. The ancients may indeed have had dogs very much like modern greyhounds and mastiffs but it does not follow that these breeds have continued in an unbroken chain from 4000 BC until now. When a genetic pattern evolves it is filling a niche in its environment and, if this niche occurs in another place at another time, evolution is quite capable of repeating itself. Equally, when there is human intervention, breeding for giant size produces acromegalic features (the jowly look) and miniaturization produces pigmy features and achondroplastic features (the stubby look), and these are fairly consistent.

One has only to see some of the amorphous splodges confidently described in the literature as 'Maltese' or 'Tibetan spaniel' to grow dubious about the whole affair. The habit of discriminating by points and pedigrees is very new; our instinct now is to classify all dogs in terms of their appearance – mongrel when we don't know what it is – but, in the past, dogs were more often classified not in terms of their looks but in terms of their jobs. Their jobs were very important.

Ancient Egyptians

The ancient Egyptians were an exceptional people and exceptionally fond of dogs. The tombs of Cheops, Amten, Rameses II, Antefa II and Tutankhamen have yielded many tributes to favourite hounds, bodyguards and battle-dogs called Abu, Akna, Tarn and even Ken, and there is also a mottled alleged corgi belonging to Osertssem (Osertessen) in the XIIth Dynasty. One of the largest Egyptian cities, Cynopolis, whose citizens went to war with a neighbouring people for eating one of their pooches, was named after a dog. So was Sirius, the Dog Star that warned of Nile floods and the 'dog days' when passions ran high in the heat. The Egyptians worshipped a jackal- or dog-headed god, Anubis, embalmer and guide of the dead, and when a house-dog died, the men of the family shaved their heads and beards to show their grief. Cheops's own Abakaru was a house-dog, depicted wearing a fashionable collar and a little grin. Antefa II had four special favourites, one called Bahakaa, a white flop-eared gay dog with a bow tie. Some of these highborn animals are depicted as red, green or blue; perhaps they were powder dyed. What we call the pharaoh hound today, by reason of his evident ancestry (the *Cirneco dell'Etna* of Italy is another modern version), was known as the 'red-tailed dog' who glowed like a god when hunting. He was evidently very good at it; better even than the 'long-faced dog' or greyhound type.

Ancient Arabs

The saluki, or something very like him, existed possibly 7000 years ago. His gazing eyes, aerodynamic form and flat camel feet were made to go tearing after gazelles across the Sudan; he is a 'gazehound', for hunting by sight rather than scent. The Arabs would strap him under the loins to discourage his appetite, and hawks were released to blind his prey before he brought it down.

Ancient Persians

The ancient Persians, whose king Cambyses invaded Egypt in 525 BC with battalions of war dogs trained for formation attack, revered all canines – shepherd, house-dog or vagrant. The Zoroastrians regarded strays as local cleansing officers and it was considered a bad sign if they turned their noses up at one's corpse. Persian strays were protected by religious ordinances as we may see from the *Zend-Avesta*. The dog was created by the god Ahura, 'self-clothed and self-shod, watchful, wakeful and sharp-toothed, born to watch over man's goods'. Indeed, 'no house could subsist on earth but for two dogs, the shepherd dog and the house-dog'. Persians were adjured to 'bring ye unto him milk, with meat and fat' because 'it is the dog of all creatures of the good spirit that fastest decays into age . . . watching over goods none of which he receives'.

Babylonians

Some of the earliest Babylonian carvings show 'mastiffs' or at least 'massives' chained to aristocratic owners as bodyguards. Such dogs were allowed to roam locally to greet lunatics, lepers and beggars. Herodotus writes that four cities were required to provide food for the Babylonian governor's kennels, in lieu of tax. Ashurbanipal, living in 625 BC, called his own dogs Mischief, Barker, Boss-dog, Grabber and Gnasher. The Babylonians may not have troubled about breeds as such, but markings, size and colour were important. To be bitten by a brown dog, for instance, was 'lucky'. Some of the royal massives, of which terracotta figures remain, would grab and gnash lions and wild horses.

Assyrians and Hebrews

The Assyrians of ancient Iraq had a large canine workforce. The royal households had the obligatory massives for fighting and swift saluki types for hunting, a century before Christ, and much earlier still palace friezes depicted hunting scenes with huge dogs, beaters and nets. The Hittites of ancient Turkey buried dogs in their royal tombs. The Hebrews, on the other hand, hated dogs, partly because the Egyptians revered them, though not one of the oppressors' curs barked on the night of the Exodus to give the Jews away. For this forebearance God apparently told them to give unto the dogs their unclean meat, which by degrees came to be interpreted as meaning dogs were themselves unclean. There are many scriptural references to scavenging dogs as loathsome and dirty. Still, they were good enough to be used as shepherds: Abraham, by all accounts, had 4000 tending his flocks and in the Apochrypha we find one story of a faithful dog, in the Book of Tobit. Otherwise, references are of the spiteful sort. The Moslems despised dogs too, regarding them as unclean eaters of refuse. Nevertheless, they came in handy. Mahomet allowed them to be used in the chase, and you could eat what they caught for you provided the name of Allah was uttered as the dirty beasts were slipped.

Afghans

In Afghanistan there are rock paintings depicting hirsute greyhounds with trousers dating from 2200 BC. They look like Alfie, 1983 Crufts Supreme Champion, so perhaps Alfie's ancestors were used in the chase 4180-odd years ago. Like the saluki and greyhound, the Afghan hunts prey by sight. In vast arid expanses, sniffing is too slow to catch a cold, much less a hot dinner.

Ancient Greeks and Romans

We know that the classical canine was important because the Greeks and Romans tell us so much about him. The Romans were probably the first people to develop what we would call breeds, according to Dr Jewel of the British Museum of Natural History. She quotes a Roman authority on agriculture describing, in the first century AD, the science of selecting sheepdogs: 'As guardian of the farm,' says Columella, 'a dog should be chosen which is of ample bulk with a loud and sonorous bark.'[2] He prefers black for a farmyard guard, but white for a sheepdog, to distinguish him from a wolf. The Romans introduced several Swiss breeds of mountain dogs some 2000 years ago as sentries for their military posts and trading stations in the Alps, and they took herders, probably ancestral Rottweilers, into Germany. Their hunters and warriors were legion and they greatly respected 'macho' dogs that would put on a good show in the arena. Cicero speaks of the dog's 'extraordinary scenting ability in following a track', and Marcus Varro, who bred dogs himself, tells us they had two separate kinds for hunting and shepherding, and that it's not a bit of use buying one's sheepdogs from huntsmen or butchers because they would either be bone idle or chase hare. We should buy them 'ready trained', he said.

With their armoured war dogs and diverse training methods, the Romans probably thought they had the dog business sewn up. But in 55 BC, they invaded Britain and were attacked by even more massive mastiffs than their own. Gratius told fellow Romans, 'Forget the form and colour, which in British dogs are the worst points. When the tug-of-war is on and their blood is up, just watch them go!'

Many of the British towsers were shipped off to Rome and slaughtered in the amphitheatres, as the conquerors believed in glorious death. They considered their gods to have dogs and sacrificed them accordingly, and they also ate dogflesh themselves, especially pups in whey. They were unforgiving taskmasters. In memory of the Gaulish invasion of Rome, when their canine sentries were derelict in their duty, the Romans annually crucified dogs on elder trees.

Like the Romans and Egyptians, the ancient Greeks favoured dogs as incorruptible temple guards. These welcomed visitors, killed thieves and saw revellers home at night. 'If the drunkard misbehaved himself on the way home, then the dogs tore his clothing to pieces and he arrived home very scantily attired.'[3] There were small dogs in Greece which have been identified as 'Pomeranians'; they had curly tails, were called 'table dogs' and were depicted on vases, playing with children. As early as the fall of Cnossos (c. 1400 BC) the Greeks evidently had dogs for hunting and herding. Homer thought highly of the Hellenic hounds that coursed boar. These would have worn hunting spikes, leather doublets and armoured collars for protection, and there are many fine examples of hunting collars from medieval Germany, which give some idea of the ironmongery, in the Leeds Castle dog-collar museum in Kent.

The Greeks also had armoured battle-hounds called Molossians, long dogs for coursing hare (Arian gave lectures on coursing), and guards and sentry hounds, one of them called Soter, that reportedly saved Corinth when their handlers were drunk on patrol. Socrates in *The Republic* tells Glaucon the dog is 'a true philosopher' and Plutarch felt strongly about dogs being ill-treated, exhorting citizens not to regard them as mere possessions to be discarded like old shoes. Lucretius writes very movingly of the faithful Athenian dogs that lay strewn in the streets dying of plague.

Indians and Tibetans

Among the Parsees of India the dog was treasured and it was considered a crime to neglect him. The fame of ancient Indian dogs spread far and wide. Alexander the Great used four of them to bait a lion, and Xenophon recommended them for chasing wild boar, fawn and stag. The Babylonian governors liked them too. Who knows but that the Indian dhole, now furtive and dangerous, was once a prized domesticated dog? Tibetan breeds were relied on for protection from wolves, for shepherding and, according to one source, for disposing of the monks' bodies in the monasteries. They also turned prayer wheels. The Tibetan wrote his prayers out on parchment and put them in a revolving box. Every time the wheel turned, his prayers were considered said, and the Shih Tzu and Tibetan spaniel have both been credited with the job. The small dogs doubled as muffs, carpet slippers, hot-waterbottles or peace-offerings. Centuries before Christ, they were a precious tribute paid annually to the emperors of China by the ruling dynasties of Lhassa, who also bred another fellow, the Apso, for similar purposes.

Chinese Take-Aways

The Chinese have few dogs left; they've eaten most of them. Yet according to early travellers they once used huge dogs to pull sleds and wonderful swift hounds, with hardly any scenting powers, to hunt. A massive breed called the 'Ngao' was used for manhunts and dogfights – which also featured the Shar Pei, that 2000-year-old fellow with all the wrinkles who appears to have descended in a fast lift. But in northern China especially, the people ate dogs. Butchers dragged or carried canines to the slaughterhouse with neighbourhood dogs barking and biting at them as they went. Skinless dogs and joints hung from butchers' hooks between the dried rats and the live birds with their eyes put out. Yellow dog was thought more tasty than black dog, especially for soup, but black dogs were better for frying. Notices went up in the Buddhist temples urging their congregations to stop dog-eating, but it was to no avail.

21

Skins fetched good prices; chow furs were worn by officials. The dogs were felled with clubs and then dropped in boiling water to have their hair scraped off. The poor chow, when it arrived in England, was nicknamed the Edible Dog as a joke ('chow' isn't much of an improvement). Yet Confucius was telling his followers in 551 BC to save their old chariot hoods 'to cover the dear house-dog in his grave'.[4] Watchdogs guarded the halls of the singing girls, fierce as tigers and none too well-disposed towards the punters. But one canine who escaped both the fleshpots and the cooking pots was the palace Pekingese. Mention of 'square dogs' in China goes back to 1760 BC, but it was in the first century AD that Chinese emperors began to use a short-legged midget called the 'Pai' to vet handshakes from voluminous sleeves. (Ironically, in Peking Municipality, a ban is now in force, with the capital's 400,000 dogs being clubbed and drowned by owners and extermination teams. The Chinese Government considers pets a personal indulgence.)

Meanwhile, the Eskimos were crossbreeding their ex-wolves with fresh ones for better-spirited sledging, and on the opposite side of the globe the Aborigines and their hunting dingoes were combing Australian wastelands for food, perhaps 30,000 years ago, according to one estimate. When Europeans arrived in the Americas they found at least twenty varieties of dog, and the Indians used them for food and as beasts of burden. The Dakotas collected the bones after a meal and buried them respectfully. The Iroquois burnt them. The Huancas, before they were conquered by the Incas, worshipped the dog as an idol, ate his flesh, and made a trumpet out of his skull to play at festivals. The Xoloitzcuintli, or Mexican hairless dog, was the Aztec pork pie.

The story goes on and on: there has scarcely been a civilization on earth where dogs have not performed some service, even if only to clear refuse or provide food. Indeed the Filipinos were tucking in quite recently until discouraged by the International Fund for Animal Welfare; their custom had been to truss the dogs live for market by tying their front legs behind their backs and muzzling their faces with wire and jagged tincans; there are still many equally horrifying markets in South-East Asia and Polynesia, if anyone is interested. The IFAW recently discovered dogs being prepared for the table in South Korea by slow hanging. While still conscious, their fur was removed with blowtorches. Others were thrown into boiling water. No one seemed to care.

International Fund for Animal Welfare (IFAW)
Tubwell House, New Road, Crowborough, East Sussex TN6 2QH. Tel. (08926) 63374;
or PO Box 193, Yarmouth Port, Massachusetts 02675, USA

The Isles of Grief

To misquote that great doglover, Byron, Britain very quickly became the Isles of Grief so far as its canine labourers were concerned. Our reputation as animal-lovers must be of very recent date because fear of rabies and general callousness led to all manner of persecutions. Official dog-whippers in churches, and London's annual Dog-Whipping Day, were the norm for a very long time. Britain's dogs have been used for every rotten job imaginable, from turning spits to hunting witches. They have a chequered history. Alfred the Great exacted fines from the owners of dangerous biters. King Arthur, if he existed, had a dog called Cavall; Fionn MacCoul of the Fenian Princes, had a 'small-headed, sleek-haunched' hound called Bran, who met his death by leaping from Coeggy-y-Bran in Ireland. Many dogs have been named in his honour, including one of Queen Victoria's beloved pets. Hywel Dda (Howell the Good) of Wales, leaves us record of the ancient Welsh 'breeds': they were the buckhound, greyhound, tracker, watchdog, shepherd, peasant dog and 'colwyn', named after the bay in Denbigh and possibly used for fishing.

Perhaps the most famous and legendary British dog is Gelert, whose monument has drawn many a tourist to Beddgelert valley beneath Moel Hebog in Wales. His master Llywelyn, the Welsh chieftain, came back to the tent one day and ran the dog through, thinking it had killed his infant son. Too late he found the live child and a dead wolf under the bedclothes, and was so sorry for what he had done that his remorse passed into a Welsh adage and many poems. There has been scholarly argument over whether the dog was a wolfhound or a greyhound.

Britain exported dogs to Rome, including 'dogs of superior breed for the chase' according to one of Caesar's contemporaries. The second-century Greek poet Oppian suggests that, as early as the Roman occupation, the British terrier had 'gone to earth'. Rather later, the dog breeds in England were listed as: 'your greyhounde, your mungrell, your mastiffe, your lemier, your spaniell, your hennets, terears, butchers' dogges, bloodhoundes, dunghill-dogges, trindle tails and prick-eared curres'.[5]

In 1016, Cnute passed his famous Game Laws, permitting small dogs to be kept near forest lands but ordering all other freemen's dogs, large dogs and especially greyhounds, to be maimed to prevent them from chasing game. Villeins were forced to maintain royal hounds for His Majesty's hunting. This was the first of many such edicts to control dog ownership and ensure that the poor had smaller and humbler dogs than the hunting aristocracy. Under Edward I a dog gauge was introduced, shaped either like a stirrup or a seven-inch ring, and any dog that could not pass through it would be hamstrung or have its feet or knees mutilated.

The Game Laws were in force until after the Restoration and, although shepherds and swineherds were still permitted their herders and drovers for fear of wolves, this was the dawn of the dog snob: one dog for the rich and another for the poor. Under King John (1199–1216) dogs 'trespassing' in the forests were destroyed, to deter the uninvited from hunting for food. The monarchs, nobility and clergy maintained sizeable hound and greyhound packs; Henry II's were fed on bread, paste and flesh, and kennelled on the Isle of Dogs. The hound, that canine nobleman, was extolled in 1406 by the second Duke of York in his famous treatise, *The Master of the Game*, as having great goodness, knowledge, memory, diligence, perception, obedience, hardiness and 'smelling', 'and he would sooner die than anything be lost in his keeping'.

Under Edward III you could be fined 'forty pence' as then for allowing your dog to stray in the London streets, 'gentlemanly' dogs always excepted. The freedom of the metropolitan mungrell, dunghill-dogge and trindle tail was henceforth curtailed.

In the Middle Ages many beggars' mutts could be seen dancing on their hind legs in the markets, grubbily dressed as fine ladies and gents, some in plumed hats and others with collecting caps. They danced the more deftly for being welted with canes. Baiting was considered excellent sport. Tudor maps of the capital show two bear-gardens and amphitheatres by the Thames with the unfortunate contestants tied under a shed. Elizabeth I maintained packs of harriers, buck, hart and otter hounds. Her physician Dr Caius deplored other British women doting on tiny 'comforter' dogs. Meanwhile we have another list of 'breeds', detailed by Tom (Edgar) in *King Lear*. 'Avaunt, you curs!' he tells the 'mastiff, greyhound, mongrel grim, hound or spaniel, brach or lym, or bobtail tike or trundle tail'. The king himself is more worried about little Blanch, Tray and Sweetheart, *chiens de luxe*, taunting his poverty.

Many dogs turned waterwheels and spits. A kitchen at the Hanbury Arms in Caerleon, Wales had a turnspit wheel still attached to the ceiling in the nineteenth century, operated by a short-legged dog in a cage. The more he ran, the more he ran, despite the roasting heat. Crueller than spitwheels were waterwheels, imprisoning teams under the whip. There were truffle hunters searching the loamy soil of Hampshire, driven wild by the toothsome scent yet never allowed to eat what they dug up. Dogs were widely used as beasts of burden, of course. Butchers' carts and milk carts were drawn at speed by teams, and there were fashionable traps and buggies, sometimes with three or four grown men in them, dragged by gasping mastiffs and Great Danes in harness. The rat catcher had his terriers; the poacher his lurchers and silent alarm dogs, some of them with ingenious lanterns on their heads that winked when the dog turned towards a noise. Matthew Hopkins, witch-finder general, found an infallible guide to local witches by watching to see if the poor old women consorted with animals, which they usually did. He called the creatures by spirit names like 'Vinegar Tom' and said they were obviously witches' familiars, rather than Fidos or Rovers.

Even better sport than witch-hunting was the duck hunt. Many a tavern near a pond is still called the Dog and Duck, where hunters once assembled with their dripping 'retrievers'.

There was always a brisk trade in dogskins, dried and cured, and dog furs for hats, coats, gloves and muffs. The merchants employed lusty chaps rather like Canadian seal-cullers to bludgeon passing beasts, throw them in sacks and convey them to the tanners' yard where nasty things happened to them. Concerned individuals were prevented from interfering on the grounds that the dog-knockers would be put out of their jobs. Carts drawn by mastiffs rattled along to the docks, taking to the manufacturer the skins of their distant relations fastened in neat bundles. Dogs and their by-products, particularly pit-dogs from Ireland, were a major British export, and kennels were kept by tradespeople in the city. The butchers teased up bulldogs on their own livestock for baiting, the greengrocers' delivery teams were a familiar sight, trundling on the cobbled streets, threading through crowds and past pickpockets and cutpurses, trained to whip out a wallet before you could say Fagin's den.

In 1830 another gallant attempt was made to classify the breeds, this time by Colonel Hamilton Smith. He came up with: wolf strain, watch and cattle dogs, sight dogs, scent hounds, cur dogs and mastiffs. That seemed to take care of everything, with 'cur dogs' a useful miscellany without specific tasks. In 1890, thirty years after Darwin's *Origin of Species*, yet another valiant investigation was made by a Mr Windle, and details were published in the Proceedings of the Zoological Society (London). After a good deal of measurement and weighing of skulls, skeletons and teeth, he abandoned the project as 'a hopeless task'. The most recent and interesting classification is by an American, John McLoughlin. McLoughlin departs from the usual 'dog a job' pattern to examine breeds on the basis of Tolkienous mutation: neoteny (retardation), giganticism, miniaturization and dwarfing, as well as the more usual groups such as polar dogs, pariah dogs, gazehounds, etc. *The Canine Clan* (Viking Press, New York, 1983) is less a genealogy, more an attack on breeders through the ages.

It is not necessary, however, consciously to breed a dog for a particular task. The dog is not a teapot; little by little he will evolve over many generations, the better to fit his vocation, without the need for genetic engineering. In fairness, the last word should go to the Secretary of the Kennel Club, whose library of old and rare dog books yielded much of the foregoing information. Bill Edmond: 'The breeds have developed over the years, and certainly there have been changes, just as there have been changes in all species. Human beings are today taller and they live longer. That's not through selective breeding; it's a natural mutation, and dogs are presumably subject to similar changes. The breeders have tended to use the best mutations, where they can direct them, to develop the dog.'

3

THE ACCOMPLICE

Whatever the dog's many and varied services, the one that made him positively indispensable to man was as accessory to murder. The dog's nose has been steeped in blood for centuries to satisfy man's hunger and bestiality. Long after the need to hunt for food had passed, the wish to vaunt over the animal kingdom and terrorize creatures in their natural habitat has driven man to discover more sophisticated ways of exploiting the dog's predatory talents. To display man's cunning, the dog must outflank and outwit the fox. To express man's vanity and nostalgia the dog must drive the noble stag. To satisfy certain unacknowledged appetites the dog must course or scent and kill the hare, called 'puss' and 'cunny'.

There are at present in the British Isles 242 packs of hounds hell-bent after the fox and foxcubs, six packs berserk for the stag and deer, five packs set on punishing the otter, seven for massacring the mink and coypu, and to murder the hare there are fifty-one packs of harriers, 111 packs of beagles, eleven packs of bassets and twenty-seven coursing clubs of greyhounds, as well as innumerable private and affiliated clubs of salukis, deerhounds, borzois, Afghans and lurchers. To murder 'madam' hare or anything else popping up from its nook or cranny, there are untold droves of individuals with guns and gundogs. And, finally, there is the whole wagon-train of humans on horseback, in cars, in landrovers and on foot, with blood-coloured vestments, blooded children, horns, staves, spades, whistles, whips and guns, that follow in the wake of the dogs who do most of the dirty work. Using the dog's natural instincts distances the human killers from their quarry and removes any qualms they might otherwise have felt about seeing a disembowelment for which they themselves are responsible.

> The chase, the sport of kings,
> Image of war without its guilt

wrote William Somerville (1675–1742) in the unlikely event of anyone feeling a bit squeamish in those days; the concept of a crusade or 'war', punishing guilty or naughty animals, dies hard. The Duke of Beaufort, late president of the British Field Sports Society, in his book *Foxhunting*, calls the fox an 'opponent', as though 'Charlie' were in the blue shorts coming out at the bell and liable to do some damage. The BFSS, in a booklet for children called *Would You Like to Go Hunting?*, describes the fox as a 'villain' who shows no signs of fear or panic as its executioners home in. The rotter is blamed for stealing poultry, 95 per cent of it bricked up in factory farms, even though the fox's main diet consists of voles, mice, rabbits and insects ('*and* blackberries' adds one man I spoke to who spent much of his pre-war life in foxhunting). Most mysteriously of all, the human hunter likes to steep himself in a fantasy of conservation and ecology. He is doing his bit for the quarry (otters and hare are in decline, and there is now a fugitive urban-fox population) by being somehow mystically involved in its life and death. Why, even if the hunted animals haven't *done* anything, they probably enjoy it. The dogs do.

The number of breeds that have been invented by man for putting the boot in is formidable. To name but a few, the foxhound, southern hound, basset, beagle, Talbot (the white bloodhound), Bracken (the European pursuit dogs such as the Kopov for lynx, wolf, bear and boar), the harrier, terrier, dachshund, otterhound, boarhound, deerhound, elkhound, pharaoh hound, wolfhound, bloodhound, greyhound, saluki, borzoi, Afghan, basenji, Rhodesian ridgeback, lurcher, Weimaraner, plott hound, coon hound, Akita and Great Dane. Setters and pointers are trained to spy and 'grass' on the quarry by giving away its hiding place; the spaniel busybodies it out and the retriever goes and fetches the dead, or escapees trying to get away with a mere bullet-hole. Impressive cohorts, every one of them, and magnificently bred.

Clearly, there are two distinct types of canine assistant, the one who trots and uses his nose, and the one who sprints and uses his eyes. The gazehound has a deep, spacious chest for lung-room, long, thin muscly legs, flexible lumbar vertebrae worked by powerful loin muscles coiling and galloping, and a long-headed (dolichocephalic) profile with extended nasal cooling equipment. He also has sad, staring eyes and a remote wistfulness, hoping to spot something moving in fields afar. Like humans of similar body type he is usually thin, melancholic and anxious.

The scenting hound is of acromegalic bloodhound ancestry. He is jowly and fleshy-faced, with sagging ears and sometimes sagging eyes. He is a marathon dog, capable of trundling and trotting over mighty distances, unswayed from his One True Purpose, nose to the ground, a canine vacuum-cleaner drawn by an invisible lead over invisible-smelling landscapes. Even if he is bent, spiral-legged and deformed, like the digging Monsieur Basset or Herr Dachshund, nothing can deter his busy nostrils, or dismay his unwavering appetite for Getting Things Done, Getting to the Heart of the Matter, and Finding the Whippersnapper for Master.

There is also a third sort of hunt assistant, much favoured by the peasantry for small quarry, whom we shall be looking at in a later chapter: a fiery little fellow whose job is to go muck-to-the-wind after anything buried, boled or holed up underground, and either bark at it or attack it with a lot of shaking and snapping, which he prefers even to barking set-outs. The terrier is a sharp-eyed, bossy, cussing, explosive personality who will fight to the death anything he finds remotely irritating.

A journalist, Andrew Alexander,[1] recently attacked heartless abolitionists who say foxhunting should be outlawed: why 'thousands and perhaps tens of thousands of hounds would be put down' he railed, if bloodsports were discontinued. (There is no danger of this happening, by the way; both Commons and Lords are full of hunt sympathizers.) Sadly, hunting dogs are rather accustomed to being put down. As Mr Jack Chudley, with many years' hunt service in South Devon behind him, explains: 'I've *known* them hunting at eight, but on average they're finished at six.' Mr Brian Toon, of the MFH Association: 'Most people would like to think they'll get six or seven seasons out of the hounds; of course it varies with the terrain, the length of the season and the size of the pack.' And then it's goodnight sweet prince. 'They're all put down,' says Mr Chudley, because they can't be turned into house-dogs overnight. Former MFH Major Harding Cox, writing before the war of his favourite hound Landsman: 'I ran the old fellow in his fourth season but he could not go the pace with his flying companions. . . . His death warrant had been signed.'[2] But then all but a few foxhounds in Britain were put down during the world wars; they are put down for being insufficiently game, and a foxterrier of Lord Lonsdale's was put down for over-enthusiasm. 'Dead game!' retorted the Earl to Harding Cox. 'Why hang it man, he would have killed every fox in the country if I had let him live!'[3] And lest we should become, like Andrew Alexander, mawkish, it must be remembered that hunting dogs are not treated with much sentimentality anyway. They of all dogs have traditionally been 'broken', and huntsmen have not been shy of using the 'ash plant' on their behinds. Hunts employ 'whips' and 'whippers-in' who carry the articles of their trade as they exercise their dogs, whereas you or I or Andrew Alexander would be hauled off to court for so doing.

A whipper-in of the Berkeley Hunt, Patrick Martin, was recently cleared of allowing his hounds to savage a cat on a caravan site at Berkeley, Gloucester. Residents could not save Budgie the cat, but they tried to save the fox by attacking the hounds with broomsticks. This incident shows how blame is generally apportioned in the business.

Hunting with dogs may be very savage; it is also very old. Even Aristotle's

Treatise on the Chase is by no means the earliest record, as we have seen. The Egyptians used both sight and scent hounds for catching their dinner, and killing animals has long been used to train men for killing in war. The Athenian Xenophon, who had beagles and basset packs and called the dog the invention of the gods, subscribed to this 'war-games' idea in 390 BC. But he also laid down a code of conduct for sportsmen to allow their quarry grace or 'law'. Using dogs this is difficult to do, unless they are slipped, as in coursing. The fox that goes to earth is rarely permitted harbour there: it is baited with a terrier, dug out and destroyed, or bolted again for the hounds. The stag that fords a river or runs into the sea is permitted no sanctuary; and the same ruthlessness applies both to the mink and the otter. Badger-digging gave no quarter whatsoever to the badger. So it is difficult to discover in what sense the activity of hunting them could be described as 'sport', where an element of chance is involved. True, the *mustelidae* such as the badger and otter will give a good account of themselves in their death throes, and attempt to take the odd dog with them; perhaps this is the 'sporty' part referred to.

Philip Windeatt in his splendid little book, *The Hunt and the Anti-Hunt* (Pluto Press 1982), traces sportsmen and their game to the ancient Gauls who 'coursed for sport rather than what they got', as Caesar put it. In France the hunting horn first blew, and William the Conqueror, who probably brought St Hubert bloodhounds to Britain, brought organized hunting too, levelling whole villages for the chase. His son, William II, actually met his death while hunting in his New Forest. Alfred the Great, of course, had hawks and hounds; King John had foxhounds in 1213; so did John of Gaunt and the Black Prince – a beagle fan[4] – 200 years later. In the fourteenth century Edward II produced his *Treatise on the Craft of Hunting* concerning the buck deer, doe, fox, marten and roedeer. The fox he described as a sort of poacher: 'the thief in the wood'.

In the sixteenth and seventeenth centuries the stag was preferred, fenced in parks and pumped full of crossbow bolts. Elizabeth I, no squeamish lady, once watched sixteen bucks torn down by greyhounds, and she would administer the *coup de grâce* herself, slitting the animal's gizzard. The hounds of the period were big, Talbot-like and clumsy, slowly trundling in the confines of their lords' enclosures and belling tunefully when they'd found yet another one. The bucks weren't very fast either; many were tame, and some were deliberately hobbled to give the dogs a sporting chance.

James I preferred the cinemascope 'super slay' of the Norman hunt, using a 100 couple of Irish greyhounds to ambush a valley of deer. James spent most of his time hunting; he and his court would descend like a swarm of locusts on the countryside and hunt or eat everything in sight. One day His Majesty's best hound Jowler went missing. When he eventually turned up he had a note tied round his neck:

Good Mr Jowler, we pray you speake to the king for he hears you every day and
so doth he not us, that it will His Majestee to goe back to London, for els the
country will be undoon, all our provision is spent already, and we are not able to
intertaine him longe.[5]

James, who took little notice, was a likeable fellow notwithstanding. He
named his wife 'Beagill', Lord Buckingham 'dogge Steenie' and most of his
friends after dogs. He sent for a lot of animals by mail order, and was so
overwhelmed by a gift of beagles from Buckingham that he sat down and
wrote a thankyou note in his own hand, saying 'Blessing blessing blessing' for
'so fyne a keenel of yong howndes'; they were delightfully pretty 'and all of
thaime runne together in a lumpe'.

Sadly, the country was fast running out of juicy big animals to massacre;
James V of Scotland wrote urgently to the Archdeacon of East Riding, hoping
to procure bloodhounds that could ride on horseback.[6] What he wanted them
for we can only surmise, since bloodhounds are quite capable of keeping up
with horsemen anyway. Perhaps he wished them to go out alone and form a
posse. Meanwhile landowners of the period began keeping packs of hounds
for the hare and fox. Probably the earliest foxhunt proper was the Charlton
near Chichester, drawing coverts in 1687. One of the meaner little practices
of stag hunts then (and until very recently) was 'carting' a tame stag to a
convenient place in a crate, tying a ribbon on its de-horned head and then
setting after it with dogs. And the less said about deviant orgies with hunters
and deer in fancy dress, the better for the reader's stomach.

In the early eighteenth century, most large things worth hunting had been
attended to. Now it was the fox's turn. Aristocrats spent their winters chasing
him from staging posts in their domains, and London Bridge and Westminster Bridge were built to afford access to meets. Deer being now in short
supply, even the rich were having to make do with fox and hare, and clearly
a new type of hound was called for. Gone were the lumbering great nin-
nies of the Tudors; hounds were now fleet afoot, or 'Charles' and 'Madam'
would show them their heels. Subscription packs shot up during the Golden
Age of 1820–90, and to be MFH was *the* éclat. Jack Mytton of Shropshire
was so intimate with hounds that he would challenge them to bite-ins, seizing
his rivals on the nose. Thomas Assherton-Smith, another hound man, kicked
a sheepdog for witnessing a kill.[7] There was a good deal of ill-feeling at the
time about what actually constituted a 'hound'. Major Harding Cox, MFH
and Victorian *éminence grise* of the dog world, tells an amusing story about a
huntsman of his acquaintance giving his pack road exercise. Apparently on
turning a corner they suddenly came upon the kennelman of a famous
greyhound trainer, airing his 'long-tails'. The foxhounds raised their hackles,
sidled up to the greyhounds and showed their teeth. 'Guard away back!'

shouted the huntsman, 'Ware cur-dogs!' The kennelman made rejoinder, alleging that it took the other 'lumbering knock-kneed blighters' God knows how long to 'roll over any fox as isn't lame or mangey'. The matter was settled at the height of the season at Copstone Briars, when a brace of greyhounds shot out from a gorse patch and seized the pack's own quarry in their teeth.[8] A 'hound', though, was indeed generally designated a scent hunter after Turberville's book on hunting of 1575.

With all his new-found celebrity, the fox was in decline. This would not do. It is one thing to complain the fox is a cunning pest, and quite another to eradicate him from one's catchment area. So in 1794, working hounds were laid off in Leicester to 'enable a stock of old foxes to get up again'. Foxes were brought into Shropshire and Cheshire for the hunt, as Philip Windeatt tells us, carried by 'bagmen'. By the 1820s the 'bag fox' trade was an organized affair, operating from London's Leadenhall Street. Some dealers got their supplies from Holland and France (importing about 1000 French Reynards a year) and this practice continued until the twentieth century. The risk of importing rabies in this fashion was staggering. Harding Cox describes an outbreak in his hunt kennels which affected his puppies being 'walked'.[9]

In the latter part of the twentieth century, otter-hunting has been suspended in England and Wales, perhaps to enable a stock of old otters to get up again, though the mink, occupying the same territories, is hunted in the same way, by the shaggy otterhounds themselves, by foxhounds and by labrador-foxhound crosses. But foxhunting and beagling are more popular. Even before factory farms in 1927, an ex-secretary of the Poultry Keepers' Protection Society said that twelve years of investigation showed foxhunting to be a hindrance to agriculture and poultry-keeping.[10] Countryman W. H. Hudson, in his classic *A Shepherd's Life* of 1910, tells us that his shepherd friend 'Caleb'

> considered that the hunted fox was a great danger to sheep when the ewes were heavy with lambs and when the chase brought the animal near if not right into the flock. He had one dreadful memory of a hunted fox trying to lose itself in his flock of heavy-sided ewes and the hounds following it and driving the poor sheep mad with terror. The result was that a large number of lambs were cast before their time. . . .[11]

A modern foxhunt may cover ten miles after one gasping fox. If the pack 'checks' (loses the scent) the huntsman will cast them in a wide arc to pick it up again. Then they will either run the fox to ground, to be baited and dug out, or the hounds will 'bowl it' themselves. Huntsmen prefer to kill above ground; they say the hounds administer a quick nip in the neck. 'What is more likely,' says Windeatt, 'is that the quarry is brought down by the lead hound, then disembowelled by the pack. . . . The Huntsman, if he is on the scene, will encourage the hounds with cries of "tear 'im" and "eat 'im". The horn will be blown for a kill.'[12] Trophies are taken: the mask, brush and pads are distributed. The hounds, maybe fifty couple of big hardworking dogs, get what's left. Foxhunting and cubbing go on throughout the year except in May, June and July while the crops are ripening.

Scent-hunted hare that go to ground are luckier: they may be 'given best' or at least destroyed before the dogs get them. In coursing they may shelter in a sough, or reach the adjoining field if they are fast enough. Greyhounds used in coursing have more speed on the straight but less cornering adroitness.

> When a greyhound catches a hare, it grabs any part of the animal. . . . Once it has hold, it will not drop the hare, and may even run away with it. Or both hounds may grasp the hare and the much-disputed but well-documented tug-of-war will ensue. Hares scream.[13]

Or there's wolf-coursing, Russian style. Harding Cox describes a typical tame wolf-course on the estate of his friend Prince Scherinsky Shihmatoff, where the wolves were driven into a level enclosure by human beaters and then torn down by borzois slipped in threes, before being muzzled by a mounted *chasseur* with a leather thong on a staff. Borzois were more beefy then. 'Coursing' comes from the Latin *cursus*, running.

Stags? Stags are singled out as 'warrantable' (unlucky) by the 'harbourer', whose job is to select a stag that has settled. Four or five couple of reliable hounds called tufters are then called to flush the animal from its harbour before the rest of the pack is laid on. The hunted deer will try everything it knows to save itself. It will gallop, lie down among other deer, leap streams and even impale itself on a fence, run into buildings, sharp gorse, or the sea. When the animal is exhausted and can find no refuge, it will turn and stand at bay to the dogs. These days stags are generally dispatched with a gun, but Windeatt refers to hounds bringing deer to the ground by hanging on their hindquarters.[14] The venison is given to local farmers to sweeten their tempers; the heart, feet and liver are distributed and the hounds, who have done all the work, get the offal. They used to be fed on horses, slain, skinned, and left to stink in the woods near Winterbourne Bishop, according to W. H. Hudson's farmers.[15]

The otter hunt, still rampant in Scotland and Ireland, is less merciful. Otters take refuge underwater but leave telltale bubbles. Eventually they must come up for air. If they hide in bank fastnesses they are poked out with staves. Otterhounds are equally adept on land or in water. If the otter gets into a holt it can be dug out with spades or flushed with a terrier, but the kill is by the hounds and it usually takes quite a time as the otter is tough and leathery and very brave. Its paws and bones make trophies for the human conquerors.

Gundogs

There are other kinds of sport using dogs. Gundogs have traditionally helped to win glory for their owners in field trials. The first Kennel Club affair was in 1873, but two American writers have found records of much earlier ones. The first trial in Central Europe was apparently organized by Holy Roman Emperor Rudolf II in about 1603 on his estate near Prague: 480 dogs, some from as far away as Spain, competed, together with their owners, for eight days.[16] In 1865 there was a British field trial, with the following scoring system: nose 40, pace and range 30, temperament 10, staunchness before 10, staunchness behind 10. In October 1898 there were field trials for bloodhounds on the Yorkshire Moors near Ravenscar.[17] In 1899 a 'retriever test' for spaniels was organized by Mr S. Smale on the Hampshire–Sussex borders.

The modern field trial takes various forms but in the Royal Brierley Crystal Stakes, for example, a team of beaters with spaniels drives the game to the guns, and the competitors shoot sufficient birds to test the dogs' ability to retrieve. Fallen birds in a field trial must be fetched in the order required by the judge; sometimes the dog gets confused. His master whistles and signals where each bird lies, calling 'I lost, I lost.' Hard mouths and chomping on the quarry are penalized but birds are not always immediately recovered. They may lie up in tree roots, wounded, until somebody comes to look for them.

The bustling spaniel (cf. *Español*) probably reached England from Spain. John of Gaunt and the Black Prince are thought to have returned with some from their Iberian peninsular campaign, in the fourteenth century, although a 'spaniel' is mentioned as existing in Britain by a sixth-century poet.[18] The spaniels of 600 years ago were rather *too* bustling. Their wagging tails irritated the hunters, but the dogs were taught to flatten their bodies to the ground so that nets could be dragged over their backs. A peg was fastened either in the dog's collar or mouth to stop it fidgeting during this operation; it was no easy matter restraining it from poking its nose into everything. The dog also put up heron, pheasant, partridge and duck for the hawks and falcons. Spaniels swam to retrieve fallen waterfowl, fetched crossbow bolts, and started up hare for coursing with greyhounds. Often, spaniels were scatty.

At first they were called simply 'land spaniels' or 'water spaniels' depending on their territory. Later they diversified. The old field spaniel, a canine caterpillar, was slow. The Welsh springer, the Clumber, Sussex and Norfolk became popular (Sussex and Norfolk were later called English springers). The pointer is mentioned in 1530 as a retrieving dog, but when a fowling-piece evolved from the old flintlock gun in the seventeenth century, the pointer was singled out for freezing in midstep over game in stubble. By

1790 the spaniel had been crossed to establish a 'setting spaniel', one that could show the position of the quarry and await the nod to flush it. The pointer and setter were stealthy and slow, to give the cumbersome gun time.

Meanwhile smaller spaniels were crossed with Japanese imports. The new little 'cocker' bustled woodcock from dense cover; the 'springer' sprang anything into the open, and might retrieve it too. As guns evolved, so did gundogs. The original pointer, from Spain and Portugal, had a superb nose, strong on air scents. He would indicate game for human beaters, who then drove it out for the archer, gazehound, hawk or even cheetah. This slow pointer was speeded up by crossing with foxhounds. The new dog could quarter the ground at speed, then turn to bronze, aligned like Eros. This extraordinary chap was then crossed with the spaniel to produce the English and Irish setters, who could both set and flush. But brilliant gundogs like these faded from popularity during the era of the Big Bag when birds fell like rain and dogs were largely redundant. What we are seeing now is a sort of renaissance. The modern continental gundog (the German short-haired pointer, Hungarian Vizsla or the Italian Spinone) can theoretically do it all: hunt, point and retrieve. The only thing they can't do is fire the gun. These days the rule of thumb seems to be a pointer of some sort, or a setter, for sparse, open heathland, a bustling spaniel for rough country with thick cover, and a retriever (which may also hunt or point) for grousebutts and easy pickings. Favourites of the past and present are the labrador, a trusty, stalwart, clever dog who for some reason finds humans inordinately wonderful, the golden, the Chesapeake Bay, the flatcoated ('wavy') and curlycoated.

But the retriever is particularly interesting: it is unnatural, after all, for a predator to fetch grounded game, dead or alive, rather than eat it. A hundred years ago a leading authority was advising his readers not to take their retrievers to their friends' shoots because it wasn't good form to be seen racing round after the dog trying to tear the game out of its mouth and 'hitting it on the nose with a stick'.[19] To pick up a corpse or a 'runner' and not mangle it beyond recognition the retriever needs a soft mouth. 'If on the contrary', says Harding Cox fifty years on, 'a young dog shows signs of possessing a hard mouth, the only thing to do is to make him retrieve a stuffed hedgehog skin or a worsted ball stuck full of needles'.[20]

'I've never used a hedgehog skin in my life,' says Jack Chudley, who now trains gundogs. 'Apparently it was meant to stop them biting down, but in any case the opposite happens. They get so annoyed with the hedgehog, they'll try and kill it. I think training as we know it now didn't dawn until about the 1920s. In the old days it was all done with a stick, or one in the ribs.' What about eating the game? 'Any dog if he's really hungry will eat a bird or anything else, but if he's well fed, he'll retrieve it. One good meal a day.'

Labrador breeders will often use a little rubber ball, or food pellets, to get the pups hunting and fetching. Then they're introduced to clay-pigeon shoots to accustom them to the noise. The clay saucer is launched and simultaneously a canvas dummy is thrown for the dog to retrieve. It soon gets the idea. It also learns the noble art of aloofness by having rabbits bustled round it – a great temptation on the job.

According to 'Idstone', writing in *The Field* in its heyday, deer stalkers have used retrievers for centuries. 'No one thought of losing a crippled stag,'[21] though the modern retriever dates from the 1850s. It needed 'great delicacy of nose and power of stooping, cleverness in following the wounded bird' as well as 'love of approbation' to prevent the dog 'venturing to break out when game is before him', says 'Stonehenge', *Field* editor. A small dog was cheaper: it could live on scraps in the house to save keepers' expenses. Stonehenge thought it a good idea to have one in your punt, for waterfowl. C. Wentworth Day disagrees. 'They get in the mud, and bring it into the punt. They are swept away on the tides, and may have to be retrieved themselves. They shake the water all over you, and then they lie and shiver for hours.'

Last but not least, the poodle (German *Pudel* from *puddeln*, to make a puddle) reputedly acquired his clip for buoyancy and temperature control. Yet in 1607 Topsell, in *The History of Four-Footed Beastes*, was writing, 'In a really hot summer there may be some excuse for doing this, but surely not at other times. Nature provides the dog with the equipment it needs and the coat of the water-dog protects it against the icy effects of the water. Take away any part of the coat by shaving and the dog will not be too keen to swim. . . . Any ordinary land spaniel, unused to the water, will tire any twenty overshaven dogs in water.' Perhaps the poodle was originally clipped to save mud-dispersal or 'puddling', but there is a much more likely explanation. In Belgium he was used to smuggle Mechlin and Brussels lace over the frontier, with his body shaven, the lace wound round, and a false poodle coat over the top.[22] A bit of smuggling was small beer, after all, compared with some of the dog's 'accomplicements'.

4

HAIRS TO THE THRONE

Frederick the Great of Prussia summed it up: 'The more I see of men,' said the scholarly king, 'the better I like dogs.' Monarchs and potentates are, by the nature of their work, lonely people, surrounded by flatterers of every sort of whom they are understandably chary. It is no accident that a great many royals and rulers have rejoiced in the company of their dogs. Frederick's dog Gengesk was made a prisoner-of-war at the Battle of the Soor and his return was included in the terms of the peace treaty. In his cloak Frederick carried a small Italian greyhound, whose death he mourned by building a tomb at his castle of Sans Souci at Potsdam. Another Great, Alexander, remarked, 'If I were not a man, I would like to be a dog.' He so mourned the loss of *his* favourite that he built a city in the dog's honour.[1] Queen Elizabeth II, when asked as a child what life she might have preferred for herself, replied that she'd like to have been 'a lady living in the country with lots of horses and dogs'.[2] David Rivault, tutor to the young Louis XIII, complained that the lad paid more attention to his dog than his lessons. When Louis grew up he walked about the audience chamber with a basket over his shoulder containing one of his tiny spaniels, which he would talk to between petitioners. The dog had the beauty of not asking for anything.[3] Henri III of France spent more than 10,000 *ecus* a year on dogs, and he also wore one of these fashionable dog baskets round his neck, tied with a blue ribbon. His three best little spaniels were called Liline, Titi and Miani or 'Mimi', who took turns to guard him at night. Henri was stabbed to death by a Jacobin monk in his bedchamber at St Cloud. Tiny Liline had attacked the assassin's ankles on his arrival but had been told off and put in an antichamber by the unsuspecting King.[4]

Lodbroc, King of Denmark, was also assassinated; his murderer would have escaped detection without the intervention of his dog. William of Orange awoke to find his small pooch leaping up and down on his face as he lay on his back in a tent in 1572 during the Dutch war of independence. Outside, the Spaniards of Julian Romero and the Duke of Alva had killed his two secretaries, and William would have snored on. He went on to found the monarchy of the Netherlands, and often said that 'but for his dog he had been taken', to quote Somers's account, 'and untill the Prince's dying day he kept one of that dogges race . . . white little hounds with crooked noses, called camuses' – probably pugs.[5]

Thisbé, the small spaniel of Marie Antoinette, didn't jump on her face but she did try to get into the carriage that took her mistress to prison in the Concièrgerie, and, when prevented, ran behind. Young Madame Royale's spaniel Mignon smuggled messages that helped her to escape, but Thisbé was definitely banned. She was taken home by a sympathetic dressmaker, Arnaud, but couldn't seem to get over it, and, jumping out of the window one day, fell into the Seine.

In 1100, Bouchard IV, then Duke of Montmorency, was defeated by Louis, son of Philip I, and turned up at court with all his noblemen to pay homage, wearing a collar inscribed, 'Faithful as the dog'. This became known as the Order of the Dog. Another order once revered but now injuriously referred to as the Order of the Elephant, was instituted in honour of a dog. Denmark's highest chivalric order was founded in 1463 by Christian I. The king had fallen ill during a plague epidemic and his courtiers dispersed, leaving him alone with his spaniel Wild Brat. The king recovered and his courtiers trickled back, shamefaced. He had initials engraved on their insignia which stood for 'True is Wild Brat'.[6] Charles V of France, in 1371, made another dog very famous. A knight had been murdered and the victim's dog kept attacking a particular courtier, Richard de Macaire, and, as it were, dogging his steps. The king ordered a trial by ordeal and Macaire, with a cudgel, was pitted against the furious dog of Montargis, by report an enormous greyhound and by legend called Dragon. Macaire was permitted no armour and the dog was provided with a barrel as a refuge from the blows. (One engraving shows the barrel open at both ends.) The duel was witnessed by thousands in the Ile Notre Dame and the dog won on a split decision.[7]

Apart from the 'greyhounds' of the Pharaohs, the borzois of the Tsars and the Pekes of Imperial China, there have been royal dog courtiers in Britain since Beli Mawr and Fingal. Alfred the Great was a respected dog-trainer and falconer, who, in common with most of his successors, loved the song of hounds. The Saxons, Danes and Normans all loved hunting; so did the Plantagenets. Edward IV was loath to keep his hounds outside in the cold, so brought them indoors. When his queen Elizabeth Woodville could stand the smell no longer he created the post of 'dog butler' to muck out the royal apartments. King John kept his dogs outside; just as well, since he had 240 greyhounds.

The ruling Tudor dogs suffered a setback during Henry VIII's reign. They were banished from the court. Henry was as fond of dogs as the next king: an inventory of his effects included such items as 'six dog collars of crimson velvet embroidered with pearls, the swivel of silver'. He also sent war dogs to Charles V of Poland and 'greyhounds, hounds and great dogs' to the French Queen. But he drew the line at having his personal apartments fouled by every passing court canine, and issued a proclamation that all 'greyhounds, mastiffs, hounds or other dogs' must be kennelled outside, 'so as the premises duly observed, and the houses abroad, may be sweet, wholesome, clean and well furnished'. He made an exception for 'small spanyells' for whom he had a soft spot. When one of his own went missing he rewarded the finder five shillings, and his household disbursements included those of his spaniel keeper for such items as 'a hair-cloth to rub the dogges with'.

There was one dog of Henry's acquaintance who altered the course of history. She belonged to Henry's emissary to the Vatican to procure an annulment of his marriage to Queen Catherine. As he bent down to kiss the Pope's toe (as protocol then dictated) the Pontiff moved his foot forward. The dog saw this as an attempt to kick her master in the face and set about the papal foot. A 'riotous' scene ensued. Henry VIII, unable to secure his divorce, founded the Church of England. Compared with this, Franklin D. Roosevelt's German shepherd, Major, biting Prime Minister Ramsay MacDonald scarcely ranks as an international incident.

Elizabeth I kept a pack of pocket beagles called 'glove' or 'singing' beagles. Her physician Dr Caius produced one of the world's earliest dog books and her godson, Sir John Harrington, wrote a long letter to 'Prince Henry' in 1608 recommending his remarkable dog Bungey, explaining that he had borne Her Majesty's mail from Bath to Greenwich with discretion and secrecy. On one dispatch, bearing two charges of sack wine from Bath, the cordage slackened, and Bungey delivered one to the house in his teeth, returning later for the other. His struggles were witnessed by farm labourers who refrained from interfering and later told Sir John of the business.

But the most famous Tudor dog was not Bungey, but the tiny black-and-white pet of Mary Queen of Scots; according to biographer Lady Antonia Fraser this was a Skye terrier and according to other commentators a spaniel (again the problem of classifying early dogs by 'breeds'). The dog, whatever it was, shared the Queen's last years in prison and went with her on her execution walk at Fotheringhay in 1587, hidden in her skirts. As her body was being removed from the block, the dog was discovered. This account is endorsed by Lord Burghley's hand:

> Then one of the executioners, pulling off her garters, espied her little dog, which was crept under her clothes, which could not be gotten forth but by force, yet afterwards would not depart from the corpse, but came and lay between her head and her shoulders, which being imbrued with her bloode, was caryed away and washed.

The Stuarts escaped from their worries and fears into a world of dogs, surrounding themselves with loyal canine subjects who cushioned them from unkindly reality. They had dogs at court, dogs in kennels, dogs in their banqueting halls and dogs in their beds. James I, who named most of his immediate family after dogs, liked to take his mind off things with a lion – mastiff fight. In one such after-dinner entertainment the lion badly mauled two dogs, and a third was sent in which hung like grim death onto the lion's lip and saved itself. James was a huntsman and sent home to Scotland for his own terriers soon after his accession. He favoured cairns, or something like them, for their derring-do.[8]

Charles I seldom ventured forth without a few 'toy' spaniels, though he admired greyhounds for their dignity and gentleness. Alexander Pope tells us a story he got from Sir William Trumbull of the doomed king discussing the merits of dogs with his courtiers. Charles said he preferred the greyhound to the spaniel because it had all the good nature of the other with none of the fawning – a pointed reference to some of his court boobies. But it was a spaniel, Rogue, who accompanied Charles on his walk across the park to his execution at Whitehall. When the king was dead, a guard exhibited the dog for a few shillings to the goggling multitudes. Eleven years later, Charles II found out and issued a warrant for the man's arrest.

Charles I had instilled in his children his own great love of dogs, especially little spaniels. Henrietta of Orleans introduced a red-and-white one to court which her brothers crossed with their black-and-whites. Even Charles's cousin Prince Rupert was a spaniel-fancier, as we know from an advertisement in the *London Gazette* of October 1667, offering a reward for his black-and-white spaniel 'with red eyebrows', lost in Dean's Yard, Westminster. Rupert was a soldier, not given to mushy outbursts, but he was very upset when his poodle, Boy, was killed at the Battle of Marston Moor. He wrote, 'I would rather have lost the best horse I own.'[9]

James II was frankly dog potty. While being rescued from a sinking ship, he insisted the crew put about to get his dogs off the wreck. James had dozens of small spaniels in every nook and cranny of the royal apartments, overrunning the dining halls and going in and out of the Council Chamber as they pleased. His courtiers got rather fed up with it. Still, his brother Charles II had been, if anything, worse. So obsessed was he with the family spaniels that his name has been attached to them ever since. Our 'King Charles spaniel' probably looks more like the monarch than the dog he favoured, which had a pointed muzzle and the headshape of the Cavalier. But whatever the dogs looked like, and wherever he got them from, Charles adored them and didn't mind what state his chambers were in so long as they were with him night and day. One he was especially concerned about was a 'black dog, between a greyhound and a spaniel' which went missing and for which he offered a reward. The king was upset. He believed the dog had been stolen; it would not otherwise have left him and, besides, it wasn't English.

Charles used to walk his troupe every morning in St James's Park, to the annoyance of Londoners who thought he should be poring over the affairs of state. The king defended his dogs' freedom vigilantly, ordering 'cushions for ye dogges' and suffering the odd one to take a lump out of some unpleasant detractor, like the varlet who said, 'God rest your Majesty but God damn your dogs.' Critics generally stayed mum, at least to the king's face. John Evelyn complains:

> He took delight in having a number of little spaniels follow him and lie in his bedchamber and where he often suffered the bitches to puppy and give suck, which rendered it very offensive, and indeed made the whole court nasty and stinking.[10]

The Lord Chief Justice was required by His Majesty to introduce a charter giving the king's dogs the right to be admitted to the Privy Council, and admitted to palace or court when they scratched at the door. Whether or not the Stuarts' admiration for little spaniels made them popular in the public eye, their royal patronage ceased with the demise of James II. William and Mary were pug people. All that remains of the King Charles era is a spaniel who appears on the terrace at the rear of Ham House, a mile south of Richmond, home of one of Charles II's ministers, the Duke of Lauderdale. The dog appears and disappears and has been seen many times, even in broad daylight.

The Age of Reason does not abound with royal dog records although Alexander Pope did present one of the King Georges with a collar inscribed, 'I am His Majesty's dog at Kew; Pray tell me sir, whose Dog are you?' and George IV hunted a pack of dwarf beagles over Brighton Downs. But Hanoverian royal dogs really came into their own in the 1830s, when an eleven-year-old girl was painted by R. Westall RA with 'dear little Dash', variously described in the literature as a dachshund, a tricolour spaniel and a Manchester terrier. According to the child's diary Dash was dressed up in 'scarlet jacket and blue trousers'.

Queen Victoria lived and died with dogs in her company; a white pom was at her side at the end of her days. She would defend them stoutly from criticism. When Lord Melbourne accused Dashy of having crooked legs the diminutive Queen sent for the creature and put him on the table, demonstrating his soundness of limb. Of all British monarchs it was she who gave her canine subjects real respectability in the public eye. Whatever they may have thought of the marauding hunting dogs and lapdogs of the Tudors, or the Stuarts' foreign 'comforters', Victoria's dog empire was quite another matter. Here was a collection of individuals of every sort and size, and the public knew them by name and saw them taking prizes in the dog shows.

Bully, the fawn pug, was permitted when he was old and grumpy to sleep in his keeper's bed. Darnley, the collie, was exhibited at Crufts in 1891; he was a genuine working sheepdog of the type Victoria had seen in the Highlands. (One of the first dogs ever to fetch £1000 was a collie, because of the Queen's approval.) The brace of magnificent 'Russian fantailed greyhounds', presented by the Tsar, started a society boom in borzois. Marco the golden pom – not a dinky 'toy' but a big handsome keeshond-type dog weighing 30lbs and called a 'spitz' by the Queen[11] – set off a boom in poms of all sizes. Victoria showed six 16-pounders herself: Fluffy, Nino, Lulu, Gilda, Mino and Beppo. The Queen received many dogs as gifts from abroad. Dachshunds arrived from Germany, one of which Albert sketched in 1840, showing remarkable flair. The Prince Consort, who loved greyhounds and kept beagles also, used the little Fritzes as retrievers on pheasant shoots at Windsor. They had legs in those days. A dachshund boom began. Another gift was a rare Tibetan mastiff, sent by the Viceroy of India, Lord Hardinge, in 1847. And in 1860 came the most famous gift of all, presented by General Dunne and christened Lootie. The fawn-and-white Pekingese had been found by looting British soldiers in the Summer Palace of Peking, barking frenziedly with four others over the body of the Emperor's aunt. Lootie lay full-length in a forage cap, huffed and puffed, and clearly wasn't going to put up with anything except a palace. She is said to have weighed 3lbs, and lived until 1872.

Although Victoria showed her dogs, she put their welfare before ridiculous fashion. Her standard poms, unlike their miniature contemporaries, suffered no whelping fatalities; she gave all her dogs the best veterinary care and mourned them when they died. She would have nothing to do with tail-cropping. Modern breeders, standing by with their tourniquets and styptic pencils and listening to the squeals, would have won no kudos at all with Queen Victoria. (Edward VII waxed rather fierce on the mutilation of ears and effectively put a stop to it in Britain, as we shall see.) Victoria's concern extended beyond the welfare of her own lucky pets; she realized that the vast majority of her canine subjects were still flea-ridden menials to be kicked about and cracked over the head as anyone thought fit. In 1840 the prefix Royal was added to the Society for the Prevention of Cruelty to Animals. The tide was beginning to turn.

Edward VII, my personal favourite, and Queen Alexandra were both dog enthusiasts. The Queen was in the fancy, entering a St Bernard and a basset at Crufts in 1893. She showed and bred a variety of dogs, from her own Japanese spaniels to her wonderful Alexander, who won three shows in 1897. Champion Alex was a borzoi from her ill-fated nephew the Tsar. The Queen

also showed Pekes, her own world-class bassets and a samoyed. She founded
a strain of black labradors in 1911 which became very famous. When she died
in 1925, King George V changed the royal kennel prefix from Wolferton to
Sandringham.

Edward VII, who was a standard-bearer for dog rights, was suspicious of
certain 'fancy points'. The dogs he loved and kept about him were friends
whom he regarded as beautiful on their own account. His Majesty's attitude
is a breath of fresh air to anyone bored rigid by canine aesthetics. It first
came to light in the matter of royal Peter.

The then Prince of Wales had what Kennel Club judge Major Harding
Cox described as 'an alleged French Bulldog'.[12] The Prince thought Peter an
altogether breathtaking specimen of the breed. He was a brindle, 'weighing
quite 30lb'. Harding Cox relates what happened:

> The first time the Prince of Wales appeared with the redoubtable Peter he
> sought my opinion of the animal, whereupon, despite the frowns and winks of
> my hostess and other guests, I proceeded to demolish all Peter's claims to being
> within measurable distance of even a passable French Bulldog. This seemed to
> sadden the dog's royal master who, addressing his favourite, said in his
> somewhat guttural voice, 'Ah well, Peter, beauty is only skin deep, and if you
> are not beautiful, you are at any rate good,' emphasizing his words by patting
> the dog affectionately.

Peter's attention, meanwhile, was entirely taken up by the arrival of afternoon
tea, and especially the lowest shelf on the cake-stand. Helping himself to an
item, Peter felt a sudden reproof from the boot of Harding Cox, 'whereupon
the brute gave me away by voicing a sharp yell of anguish and attempting to
give me a taste of his teeth'. The Prince, sitting out of view of the fracas, asked
who had hurt his dog and, being told by Harding Cox of the cake raid,
addressed Peter solemnly: 'I am afraid you have been playing the thief. That
was very naughty.' And then the Prince turned to the Major. 'But you must
not kick Peter!' he said.[13]

The next of Edward's favourites was a 'so-called Irish terrier' to whom
HRH was very attached, and who died in an accident. He was succeeded by
Caesar, who survived the King. Caesar was an old-fashioned wirehaired
foxterrier, bred by the Duchess of Newcastle. He hurled himself in the air for
titbits, slept in an easychair by the King's bed, and travelled with him to
foreign parts. His hobbies were listed in the dog *Who's Who* as 'hunting and
motoring'. He preferred a front seat and, where vacant, the King's. On one
occasion His Majesty got in and sat on him.

King Edward entered many of his 'alleged' breeds in shows, considering
them fine dogs, worthy to stand among champions. Judges like Harding Cox

may have been secretly appalled, but racked their brains for courteous remarks. The Fakenham show judge was put to the test with two 'Rampur hounds' and two 'Indian tail-less dogs'. The Rampurs were 'like small deerhounds, but for the characteristic that they had no hair'; one was 'of a mouse colour, the other spotted a sort of pink-and-blue, rather similar to young plum pudding coloured pigs'. They did not take prizes. His Majesty's large and very savage Tibetan mastiff didn't win anything either, except possibly Most Sullen in Show. Better received by the fancy was Luska, a black-headed Siberian husky. Author of *Royal Dogs* Macdonald Daly tells us the King 'hit the right note with that one'.[14] Another specimen was Vulcan, a bloodhound, who in 1869 didn't win anything but looked suitably bored and contemptuous. Two mastiffs, Druid and Duchess, not numbered but given the customary royal letter-code, A and B, evidently failed to impress in 1867. A little better success was had with the King's 'Molodetz' Tsar borzois,[15] for who could question dogs of such descent? And then there was the King's fine batch of sporting dogs, of whom the slightly undershot Clumber, Ranger, impressed even Harding Cox as 'the only really good dog exhibited by King Edward'.[16] 'A Clumber can do the work of three beaters,' said the King, who used them in teams over Sandringham's bracken.

Poor Edward suffered the slings and arrows of outrageous fancy to an extent, but he drew the line at mutilation and instructed Francis Knollys to write to the Kennel Club as follows:

> I am desired by the Prince of Wales to acknowledge the receipt of your communication, and to inform you in reply that he has kept dogs for many years, and frequently sends some of them to exhibitions, but that he has never allowed any dog belonging to him to be 'mutilated'. His Royal Highness has always been opposed to this practice, which he considers causes unnecessary suffering, and it would give him much pleasure to hear that the owners of dogs had agreed to abandon such an objectionable fashion.

Ear-cropping became a punishable offence in Britain in 1895. Elsewhere in Europe and in the USA, ears are tailored still.

Whatever showgoers may have thought of King Edward's 'sorry lot' as Harding Cox called them, they were mightily chastised in May 1910 by the sight of an unhandsome, non-prizeworthy but immensely noble wirehaired foxterrier marching in His Majesty's funeral cortège ahead of nine kings and innumerable princes, wearing his collar medal, 'I am Caesar, the King's dog.'

The House of Windsor has carried on the proud tradition of royal dog-owners in Britain. King George V entered his splendid labradors at Crufts. The King was a crack shot and his gundogs, such as the Clumber Sandringham Spark, and his Wolferton labradors, were cracking dogs. Jet was a Crufts champion; Ben won six Kennel Club challenge certificates.

Several of the King's own dogs were called 'Bob', notably a cairn who raced after His Majesty's pony round the Sandringham estate. Then there was Heather the collie, Happy the foxterrier, and Jack the sealyham – who lived to a combined age of thirty-eight. Jack was one of several sealyhams beloved of the King, and Jack himself was so fond of his royal master that he would literally faint with excitement at reunions.

King George VI, apart from his family's fondness for corgis, was a labrador man, and his half-dozen or so yellow labs were peerless retrievers. In 1948 he entered his Windsor Bob at the Kennel Club's retriever trials, where the dog defeated twenty-two rivals, and Sandringham Glen was a constant shooting companion. As Macdonald Daly recalls, George VI spent his last days out shooting, and twice visited the kennels on the evening before he died to examine the injured paw of one of his gundogs.

The Duke of Windsor liked cairns, pugs and Alsatians (called GSDs or German Shepherd Dogs now). His Claus of Seale was a prizewinner of sound deportment. Even in darkness, kings have their dogs. When Edward VIII abdicated and left the country, a cairn terrier went with him. This was his own Cora, who slept on his bed and who had special steps made for her to climb up when she was too old to jump.

And, finally, we come to Dookie, Jane, Crackers, Carol, Susan, Bee, Foxy, Tiny, Heather, Buzz, Rikky, Choo-choo, Sugar, Mimsey, Stiffy, Rowley, Bill, Whisky, Sherry, Scrummy, Honey, Ching, Johnny, Brush, Geordie, Smoky, Spark, Shadow, Myth, Fable, Diamond, Pipkin, Piper and Chipper, and also Blackie, who happens to be brown. All of these have changed guard at Buckingham Palace under HM Queen Elizabeth II and her family. There is no doubt that these royal dogs have done a great deal to popularize not only corgis, dachshunds, labradors and Shih Tzus, but also dogs in general. The public imagination does not easily forget the sight of Crackers, the ageing corgi, wheeled in a pushchair to take the air when his legs could no longer carry him, or Rikki, dachshund to the Queen Mother, motoring to Inverness for an emergency x-ray. Not all of the royal dogs are of recognized breed. In several cases the Queen has mated a corgi bitch with Princess Margaret's dachshund Pipkin, to produce a little race of 'dorgies'. Piper is a dorgi bitch and Chipper a dorgi dog. Of more linear credentials was Choo-choo, whom the late King described as 'the animated dishcloth'. His forebears, Shih Tzus or Tibetan 'sons of lion', had been sent as tributes to the emperors of China. Choo-choo made a noise like a train; Dookie, the late King's inaugural corgi in 1933, made a much louder noise, especially if he was accidentally shut out of the Royal Lodge at Windsor which he guarded jealously, along with another of his properties, 145 Piccadilly. Dookie would admonish passing dogs through the railings, herd guardsmen and dinner guests by nipping at their heels, and herd the chairs, gnawing the legs if they proved obstinate. King George called him 'the greatest personality of a dog that I have ever known', though he was putty in the young Princess Elizabeth's hands and would allow himself to be carried about baby-fashion, with his legs sticking up in the air.

Prince Charles's earliest dog was Sugar, a corgi with fetching white ankle socks. The Queen's own Susan, who lived from 1944 to 1959, was an eighteenth birthday present. The present corgis are Susie's descendants. They don't have licences because the Queen isn't mentioned in the relevant law. Buckingham Palace also make the point that:

> The Queen takes a very great interest in the Sandringham Kennels. Since her accession to the throne in 1952, the breeding programme has gone from strength to strength culminating in the training of four Field Trial Champions, namely, Sandringham Ranger, Sandringham Slipper, Sherry of Biteabout and Sandringham Sydney. The most recent Field Trial Champion, Sandringham Sydney, has become very well known and popular in the field trial world.

The labradors royal accompany the Queen in her leisure hours. *Majesty* author Robert Lacey: 'Jumping in and out of Land Rovers with great wet labradors is her idea of a perfect afternoon.' When you are invited to Sandringham, he says, an equerry tells you to come inside and meet the Queen.

> And in a small sitting room you find her enjoying gin and tonic before lunch in an orange pullover, among a lot of other people dressed in tweeds. 'I'm afraid there are rather a lot of dogs', she says, and for the next few days you find yourself with uncanny frequency encountering a figure in a headscarf in one of the corridors, chopping up meat, and you are not quite sure how you should address the Queen of Great Britain and Northern Ireland in such circumstances.[17]

Apart from royal dogs, there have been many other canines in positions of international influence: Adolf Hitler's Blondi, the faithful German shepherd whose pups Hitler hand-reared himself in the Berlin bunker; US Presidential dogs, standing beside their masters through thick and especially through thin: Richard Nixon's cocker spaniel Checkers, and King Timahoe, his Irish setter; Gerald Ford's golden retriever Liberty; the Kennedys' Pushinka, daughter of a Russian spacedog who bore four pups at the White House; and Fala, Franklin D. Roosevelt's famous Scottie. Fala was thought to have been retrieved once at great expense, by a destroyer from the Aleutian Islands. Roosevelt responded, 'I think I have the right to resent, to object to libellous statements about my dog.'[18] Then there was Heidi, the Eisenhowers' Weimaraner, Peter Pan, a fiery terrier belonging to Calvin Coolidge, and

Grits, a merry mongrel friend of Amy Carter. But having a First Dog is also a heavy responsibility, as some Presidents have learned to their cost. Possibly the worst piece of P R work L. B. Johnson ever did was to lift one of his two beagles, Him and Her, by the ears in front of a press photographer. The dogs remained loyal; many erstwhile supporters didn't.

Dogs do not judge presidents or princes by their greatness; they do not care whether their masters or majesties are loved or despised, rising or falling. Samuel Pepys, one of those people irritated by Charles II's fondness for his little spaniels, records a visit to the Council Chamber in September 1666. He writes, 'All I observed was the silliness of the King playing with his dogs all the while, and not minding the business.'

All things considered, perhaps Charles the King was minding the business better than Pepys the diarist.

5

THE SEVEN DWARVES

In this chapter we are going to look at the table dog, fist dog, lapdog, sleeve dog, bedwarmer, comforter and 'toy'. These are the seven main types of ambiguity for referring to a dog which is very small. There are two processes of miniaturization. One results from selection of the runt of the litter over many generations, producing pituitary hormonal changes and small but proportional representations of the original. The other is due to achondroplasia, a condition affecting cartilage of the bone-ends, producing stunted limbs and foreshortened faces. If you are feeling pedantic the latter are true dwarves and the former midgets, but they are, at all events, little 'uns. Both types of mutation occur in man, but by accident. Achondroplasia happens perhaps once in 10,000 births.[1] In dogs the mutation occurs by design, to produce creatures of permanently infantile appearance.

Some people find such mutant dogs appalling and the bantamizing cruel, particularly where it prevents normal whelping, walking or eating. Miniature black-and-tans or English 'toy' terriers almost died out during the nineteenth century because the craze to reduce them to 2–4lbs in weight made them 'no longer viable'.[2] The compression of the Peke's face has resulted in a skull so altered from the norm 'that the teeth are barely rooted in the maxillary bone, and the dog must eat artificially pre-chewed food or die'.[3] During the 1900s Pekes with so-called 'strangle tongues' fetched higher prices and dealers pulled pups' tongues in an effort to lengthen them.[4] On the other hand, the human desire to lavish affection on something little and helpless goes beyond mere sentimentality, and breeders of dwarves have catered for this need.

Women have generally been blamed for canine shrinkage, though men are not immune to tiny dogs. Augustus the Strong (of Poland) tarnished his reputation slightly by adoration of a little white Italian greyhound, whom he immortalized in ivory and encrusted with jewelled collars. The dog had fashionably cropped hippo ears and was enormously fat. It may have reminded poor Augustus of his childhood. Emperor Claudius had a Melitan dog, like a tiny white lamb. Two such creatures, wee woolly blobs of the sort one always imagined artless dabs in early paintings, are on display at Tring Zoological Museum; they are labelled 'Maltese' but are probably not Maltese and definitely not 'terriers'. Pliny mentions them in the first century AD as 'the pretty little dogs that our dainty dames make so much of, called *Melitaei*', and one authority thinks they came from Melita, the Dalmatian island, rather than 'Melita' – Malta.[5] If you visit the museum (it's well worth a trip – Tring Zoological Museum, Akeman Street, Tring. Tel. 044 282 4181), you might like to look at some microscopic 'lapdogs' too: one is Mexican and rat-sized, the other Russian and hamster-sized. Both are white and furry. They are mentioned in Mivat's *Monograph of the Canidae* of 1890 and they inspire in museum visitors a respectful silence.

Women of ancient Greece and Rome had lots of baby dogs. Julius Caesar saw so many in the streets, he inquired whether women had ceased to have children. Apart from Pliny, many writers have associated dwarf dogs with women. Some have been rude. Oppian refers to the dogs as 'pampered'. Religious leaders, along with Elizabeth I's physician Dr Caius, write scathingly of British women doting on small dogs, especially 'pretty kind of dogges called the spaniel gentle, or the comforter . . . curled and rough all over, which by reason of the length of their hair, make shewe neither of face nor body'. These spaniels were 'sought out far and near to satisfy the nice delicacy of dainty dames; instruments of folly to play and dally withal in trifling away the treasure of time'.[6] People suggesting such dogs could serve no useful purpose, though, annoyed the doctor equally: 'I dare say, by their leaves, they be in a wrong box,' he says, because of course they could draw the bellyache and, worn like a mustard plaster, could absorb disease. Why, some of his own patients' comforters had actually snuffed it, Dr Caius assures us. A Dr Smithe of later date would order 'rubbed dog' for a child with colic, and this was an acknowledged cure. Even Pliny, writing centuries earlier says of the *Melitaei*, 'if they be ever and anon kept close unto the stomach, they ease the pain thereof'.

Cnute's Game Laws in 1016 refer to lapdogs ('which dogges are to sit in one's lap') as being the only ones generally permitted near the forests and Henry VIII, as we have seen, allowed 'small spanyells' at court during the great dog ban. Titian's Venus, with not a stitch on, nevertheless has her lapdog in the picture, and this caused the author of *Women of the Renaissance*[7] to remark, 'A lady much preferred her one little lapdog, which she carried on her arm against her heart, took to bed with her, and had painted in her own portrait.' Lapdogs are mentioned in eighteenth-century satire as being favoured to the detriment of husbands; Pope, a dog-lover, nonetheless uses the joke. Thomas More's wife, in the sixteenth century, had a terrible row with a beggarwoman over the ownership of a lapdog, which the Chancellor had to sort out.[8]

What exactly is the fascination exerted by tiny dogs? A BMNH zoologist thinks they have been bred to look 'babyish'. Although the Peke is still a relative of the wolf and true to type in basic physiology, 'The word babyish is actually the clue to the way in which the wolf has been transformed into this other creature because it is the retention of juvenile or even foetal characteristics in the adult that is responsible for the change.'[9] Many of the achondroplastic breeds (e.g. the pug and the Griffon Bruxellois) even have quasi-human faces. In the wild such mutants would not survive and the human owner's understandable protectiveness towards them has convinced the 'mites' of their own importance. Many become spoiled and surly, and some are required by their breed standards to have a noble mien, an emboldened demeanour or stage presence not required in normal-sized canines.

It is not, of course, the dogs' fault. They become little Napoleons and give little nips. The tiny black-and-tan terriers which were so fashionable in the 1800s (and have recently been revived) were prick-eared, brawny little fellows, their heads held back sternly in case of any bother. The common Yorkie (my own, as distinct from the lustrous show tot in his scratch-preventing stockings) is noted for his fearless, bustling air. He was bred originally for ratting. A pugnacious pug I met once at the College of William and Mary in Virginia (how appropriate – they loved pugs) was running for President of the students' union and would patrol the campus and refectory on his own, a sort of diminutive bursar. His name actually was Napoleon.

Pugs are worldly wise; they have probably been around a long time. Their ancestors were evidently called 'fist dogs', from the latin *pugnus*, a fist.[10] Elizabethan Dr Caius refers to a little dog called the 'fisting hound' or 'fisting curre', and boxers whose faces have enjoyed a lot of fist are called 'pugs' because their noses get squashed in. One is rather suspicious of suggestions that 'pug' was, in earlier times, a term of endearment like 'pet'. Lexicographers are male and pugs have endured more derision from jealous men than most breeds.[11] In Shakespeare pugging meant thieving, and before that the noun meant goblin, or little devil. The dog may well have been named sarcastically after the huge Roman gladiatorial dogs, *Pugnaces*.[12] They were also sometimes called 'Dutch mastiffs' and *camuses*, or flat-noses.

In Britain the show pug suffered further indignities. He was exhibited in necklaces and allotted points for having three hairs in each mole on his cheek. By the mid-nineteenth century demand for pugs outstripped supplies. 'Pug breeding became profitable; much was bred that ought never to have been bred, and any pug-like dog was at once operated upon, its ears removed, and as soon as the wounds were healed, was sold as one of that breed,' says one historian in 1934.[13] The redoubtable Major Harding Cox (he of Peter-kicking fame) judged them and, unlike many colleagues, made 'the puggies move around' to their owners' dismay. He thought even pets should be able to walk. A similar plea for perambulating pugs comes from Dr Cryer, in a monograph on the breed in 1891:

> It is said by some writers the smaller the better, which is good, provided the shape and other general characteristics are in proportion, along with health and vigour. As a rule, however, when they are very small they have been stunted, and hence lose their symmetry and good health. If the Pug-dog is simply for a house or lady's lapdog, have him small by all means, but if he has to run three, four or five miles a day with a gentleman, then he should be of a larger size.[14]

The furless dwarves seem to have enjoyed particular favour as bedwarmers, perhaps because they had less fleas. Fleas were undoubtedly a consideration. In a book on rural sports dated 1486, and attributed to an English prioress, a list is given of existing dogs of the realm together with the postscript, 'And smale ladies popis that beere a way the flees'.[15] A bare bedwarmer was perhaps preferable to one that was forever scratching itself in the night. Even Queen Victoria's pug Bully – another small pugilist – slept in his keeper's bed, and the barer Xoloitzcuintli was apparently a favoured Aztec hot-waterbottle.[16] In colder Neolithic climes, woolly polar dogs were bred down to make footwarmers, and little dogs have traditionally doubled as cuddly muffs. When Queen Elizabeth II and Prince Philip departed for their honeymoon, their open carriage to the station contained rugs, several hot-waterbottles and Susan the corgi.[17] ('Corgi' *means* 'dwarf dog', from the Welsh 'cor' – dwarf, and 'gi' – dog.)

The poor Xoloitzcuintli warmed the Aztecs in other ways. He provided body-heat when they ate him. Table dogs have generally been of tender years, plump and small. Ancestors of the Chihuahua, whose appearance ought to melt a heart of stone, were served up by the ancient peoples of Mexico; Aztec priests sacrificed them and 'Colima dogs' – clay figures of fattened midgets – were common in burial sites of AD 800–1500.[18] The Greeks and Romans (who ate hot dogs in whey) had many 'table dogs' patrolling at mealtimes. Small canines walked under their low tables as well as being served up on top of them. Patrocles had nine as pets and two were cast into the flames of his funeral pyre to join him for dinner in another place. Oppian writes disparagingly of 'pampered domestic table dogs' at home, and contrasts them with little British hunting midgets, presumably terriers.

The term 'table dog' is one thing; the term 'toy' quite another. A small animal is not 'a plaything, a trifle, a thing for amusement or look; a matter of no importance', and the sooner this reprehensible misnomer is banned in polite society, the better. This is not a new criticism. Sixty years ago Major Harding Cox of the Kennel Club was writing, 'The word "toy" I have always deprecated, even as regards the tiniest of ladies' pets.'[19] Yet still the pejorative is applied to miniature dogs by breeders and show authorities who either do not care or actually regard such an animal as a mere bagatelle compared with normal-sized dogs. Those who breed and popularize 'toys' should be the last to begrudge them the common dignity of sentient creatures.

A roll of honour of small breeds testifies to their usefulness throughout history and throughout the world. They lower blood-pressure, raise the alarm, rout the verminous, relax the tense and requite the lonely, and they provide, out of all proportion to their size, companionship and fun. The Chinese Happa dog, the probable progenitor of Pekes and pugs, known in China since 1700 BC, is a short-furred, flop-eared, triangular fellow with narrow hindquarters. The Japanese spaniel or 'Chin', another ancient, oriental, noble dog related to the Peke, was first shown in England in 1862. The Tibetan spaniel, treasure of the monasteries, was reputedly a gift from the ruling dynasties of Lhassa to Imperial China. The rare Assyrian sand terrier, or African hairless dog, a naked soul, came from the same stock as the Mexican hairless and Chinese crested dogs. The specimen at Tring is dark grey and glossy with small pink splodges and a hairy crest down his face – this is probably the mysterious 'Rampur hound' exhibited by Edward VII at the Fakenham show; his kind were probably eaten. The Griffon Bruxellois, fiery-eyed and facially like a pug with whiskers, descended from the Teutonic Affenpinscher, and was latterly a Belgian royal favourite. The Butterfly dog, Papillon, with its aerial earholes, was probably familiar in medieval Europe and is known to have paraded at the court of Louis XIV; it has a drop-eared Continental cousin of evident dwarf spaniel ancestry. The 'toy' bullterrier is another tiny pugilist: just forty-six of them were registered with the Kennel Club in 1968. The Yorkshire terrier, a bonny ratter, is bred down from the miners' dogs. The Italian greyhound, reputedly of ancient Rome and depicted in medieval German and Flemish paintings, is an exotic precursor of the whippet, a twentieth-century British dog. The 'toy' poodle is an entertainer descended from water-dogs. The King Charles and Cavalier we met in chapter 4. The Maltese or Melitan dog, cottonwool pet of Claudius, is now renowned as a silken showpiece.

Not included above but not forgotten: the miniature Pinscher, so fashionable in the nineteenth century in Germany; the pug, introduced to England by the Dutch East India Company; the miniature Manchester or black-and-tan terrier; the Shih Tzu, mentioned in China as early as AD 624 as the treasured 'son of lion'; the wee Chihuahua, who once tickled the Aztec's palate. There are also the mini-versions of utility dogs like the miniature Dobermann in America and the Shetland sheepdog; the Peek-a-poo, the Cock-a-poo; pocket beagle and pocket cocker; the French bulldog Harding Cox calls 'a half-baked bull terrier'; and the pom, Queen

Victoria's friend reduced to infinitesimal size from an ancestor like a keeshond (some beholders see him depicted on Grecian urns if they really put their minds to it). Responsible modern pom breeders aim for a small dog which is also sturdy and sound: one that can give birth without the enormous expense of Caesarian section. But history tells a sadder story:

> When show days started the difference in size made it difficult to judge them fairly. The small dogs were in great demand. This led to smaller and yet smaller Pomeranians being bred. At last a truly appalling situation developed. Pomeranian mothers were far too small to have their families, and the mortality at whelping was extremely heavy.[20]

Pre-war chairman of the Kennel Club, A. Croxton Smith:

> The bantamizing craze did not set in until after they were first exhibited in 1871.... In fact I am inclined to think that the bantamizing craze has been pushed too far, for many of the minute specimens weigh from 3lb to 4lb, lose in type and coat, and have legs like cedar pencils.[21]

And finally we come to the doyen of dwarves, the Sleeve Dog who ruled the diminutive rulers of ancient China. The carriage and demeanour of the Pekingese are those of a dog contriving to live beneath its dignity. Its sensibilities were not meant to suffer such outrages as apartment living and canned food, and it is really a testimony to the animal's patience that it does not set about the lot of us.

Orientals have had a fixation about breeding little dogs; the Peke is but one example. Palace dogs are first mentioned in Chinese literature in AD 618 but they are undoubtedly much older. A bronze *tazza* dated to 1200 BC depicts quite a few of them. The Lion Dogs of the Imperial court were, like the Tibetan spaniels later, paid as annual tributes by the Dalai Lama of Tibet. When Buddhism swept China a symbol was needed for the sacred lion of Buddha, and Chinese mythological painters, who had never seen a lion, depicted something resembling the Pekingese.

He lived in a sacred temple at the Summer Palace of Peking, was bathed and perfumed daily by slave girls, bore the hem of the royal ceremonial robes in his teeth and announced the Great One's arrival by barking, to signal underlings to fall flat on their faces. One emperor raised the Peke to the rank of viceroy (*K'ai Fu*). All his dogs wore ceremonial hats 8¾ inches high at the front to denote their exalted rank. Human officials did not take kindly to this and the emperor was obliged to post a guard on the new viceroys to deter reprisals against their sacred persons. Pregnant bitches, sorry, expectant 'wives', were taken to look at carvings and paintings of lovely dogs to imprint them on their minds, and stealing a Peke was a grave offence carrying the death penalty and imaginative tortures. Until 1860 when the Summer Palace was sacked and Lootie and her fellow-captives taken to England, only two Pekes are known to have gone abroad: in A D 900, it seems, the emperor gave a brace of palace dogs back to the Dalai Lama at Lhassa, and from these black-and-white Tibetan spaniels are reputedly descended.[22] Believe it or not, the Peke is *definitely* the product of a liaison between a lion and a squirrel. The littler version was often borne in the emperor's sleeve to vet callers and 'bite foreign devils instantly', to quote Empress Tzu-Hsi. His markings had religious significance, but the Empress Dowager in her famous 1902 poem 'The Pearls' (which begins 'Let the Lion Dog be small . . .') decreed that there be 'dogs appropriate to every costume in the Imperial wardrobe' – perhaps for camouflage.

The Empress made a lot of specifications, not all of them designed to please a vet:

> Let its eyes be large and luminous. Let its ears be set like the sails of a war-junk. Let its nose be like that of the monkey god of the Hindus. Let its forelegs be bent, so that it shall not desire to wander far, or leave the Imperial precincts. . . . Let it be dainty in its food, so that it shall be known as an Imperial dog by its fastidiousness. . . . Thus shall it preserve its integrity and self-respect, and for the day of sickness let it be annointed . . . so shall it remain – but if it die, remember thou too art mortal,

she adds, warning the flunkies responsible. Yet it would be wrong for Westerners to call the Peke 'spoiled'. It was not, after all, a dog but a lion metamorphosed, a magic creature of the Buddha who symbolized both Himself and the holy emperors' dynasty. When the lion dogs departed the palace, the emperors would perish, and so it proved.

Besides, any Westerners believing the Pekingese to be a useless toy are mistaken. During the First World War the Pekes of England, unable to join up, rallied to donate the combings of their coats to the Red Cross, to make bedsocks and waistcoats for the wounded in hospital. Which toys could never do.

6

THE GLADIATORS

This chapter must needs be gruesome. Reading it after dinner might not be a good idea, though anyone who claims to like dogs should try to read it. There are enough blind eyes being turned to the subject already. Dogs have been officially employed as gladiators since the Roman Empire, and in Britain, Australia and America today, despite animal-protection laws, business is on the up and up. US police have, in the past, published forthcoming contests in their gazettes; in a raid on Rhode Island in the 1970s a policeman was arrested for protecting the dog pit.[1] Animal charities hand over information, but few arrests are made. Two magazines, *Texas Pit Dog Reports* and *Pit Dogs* are mailed to secret subscribers' lists. *Pit Dogs*, a Florida comic, gives delightful accounts like this:

> Lou gets into the shoulder deep and throws Missy and bites hard, making Missy cry out, but Missy gets on the nose and starts biting hard. Lou stays in hold as Missy is biting the nose very hard and busts an artery on the side of the cheek of Lou . . . Lou is getting weak from loss of blood, having a hard time breathing. She is swallowing a lot of blood from the mouth. . . .[2]

Two American authors who have gone into the subject warn 'the fans are often pistol-packers with short tempers. Two persons prominent in Texas dog-fighting were found murdered in gangland style in 1973, and even dogs have been shot to death.'[3] Fighting takes place in makeshift plywood pits, and ends when one dog 'curs out' (shys away) or dies. Losers do not generally last long on account of their own maulings and their owners' disgust.

To give you some idea of a really good 'do', here is an account of one 'historic' encounter in 1881, the result of a challenge issued in the columns of the *Police Gazette*, between cockney Charlie Lloyd's 'Pilot' and the very famous 'Krieger's Crib'. The venue was Louisville, Kentucky and by 5a.m. all roads leading to the pit hall were jammed. The dogs were weighed in at 7.15a.m. and rinsed off in warm milk, in case of poisoned embrocations.

At 9.20 they were let go. Crib caught Pilot by the nose. Pilot shook him off then both took leg holds, Pilot loosing to go for the throat, but Crib took Pilot by the ear and threw him hard. While down, Pilot secured a breast hold, then changed to a hard leg bite. This incensed Crib, and he threw Pilot five times then took his nose. Crib began to look favourite and bets changed hands. Pilot got another leg hold and set in. After 42 minutes the battle was even; they were still on their feet, but Crib was limping now. Pilot downed him, but Crib got up and threw Pilot hard. Crib seemed the better wrestler but with a weaker bite, and the going got steadily against him because up or down Pilot was still biting hard. Pilot threw Crib twice, and Crib made a turn for the side of the pit but Pilot was on him, and dragged him back without need of human intervention. Crib turned again and jumped clear of the pit, but Pilot jumped out after him and got his nose again. Both dogs were picked up and returned to the pit. Pilot was on top now, and he held Crib down and began to shake him. At 1 hour and 25 minutes Pilot was declared the winner, and the stakeholder paid over about $6000.

Both these dogs were imported from Britain. In the UK today, smartly dressed purseholders and the odd vet, with hoods on to protect their reputations, sit amongst punters in barns and garages and collect match fees of up to £10,000. One respectable Plymouth breeder of Staffordshire bullterriers recently closed down her kennels after twenty years to protect her dogs from the clutches of the fight buyers.[4] *Daily Mirror* reporter Frank Palmer went undercover in 1978, receiving a punch in the chest. One chap he talked to who had been among a 100-strong crowd at a gipsy convention dogfight, said, 'I don't know what all the fuss is about. Sheepdogs shepherd sheep. Alsatians guard things. These dogs are bred to fight anything.'[5]

Which of course they are. When Trajan returned to Rome after crushing the Dacians he put on a jambouree in the amphitheatres that lasted 123 days, during which 5000 animals died, most of them domestic, many of them dogs, and the best of them British. A Roman consul, Symachus, mentions ferocious British dogs, especially seven Scottish ones, which 'were shown at the Circensian Games, to the great astonishment of the people, who could not judge it possible to bring them to Rome in other than iron cages'.[6] Britain has been rather prominent in the gladiator business. The bulldog, bullterrier and Staffordshire are all British inventions, designed to maul, maim, bait and kill. In fact, the more one inquires into the history of animal exploitation, the more this nation of animal-lovers seems to stand head and shoulders above others in the muck-heap.

Bull-baiting, though popular in Spain, Germany and France, was probably a British invention too. In 1209 a nobleman, standing on the parapet of Stamford Castle, saw bulls being driven through a meadow by butchers' herders, and thought what a topping wheeze it would be to have them battle it out on the village green.[7] Baiting with dogs of the bear, boar, bull, badger, lion, horse, mule, etc., have all been popular in the UK; badger baiting continues, as it were, unabated, despite legal sanctions. In 1978 Frank Palmer was offered a badger for a 'do' for £10. One baiter enthused: 'Dogs are put in against it and get points for pulling it out of a barrel or corner. I'd back a good, fit, field-fresh badger against a dog any time.'

When bull and bear baiting were legal the crowds flocked in. Sometimes events were on a raised platform surrounded by fireworks or burning oil. The bill would often include a dog burnt alive as an *hors d'oeuvre*.[8] This is an account given by John Houghton, Fellow of the Royal Society, in 1694:

> I have seen a dog tossed by a bull thirty, if not forty feet high – and the men strive to catch them on their shoulders lest the fall might mischief the dogs. I must tell you that the famed dogs have crosses or roses of various coloured ribbon stuck with pitch upon their foreheads: and such like the ladies are very ready to bestow on dogs that do valiantly. . . . The true courage and art is for the dog to hold the bull by the nose till he roars, which a courageous bull scorns to do.[9]

The bull wore a collar fastened to a rope or chain, attached to a stake,

> so that it will turn around – thus the bull circulates to watch his enemy, which is a mastiff dog with a short nose, that his teeth may take the better hold. This dog, if right, will creep upon his belly, that he may if possible get the bull by the nose, which the bull as carefully strives to defend by laying it close to the ground, where his horns are also ready to do what in them lies to toss the dog; and this is the true sport.

Medieval baits were held on the frozen Thames, using bulls and mastiffs, but these dogs were gored so often that the government had to send agents to look for fresh stock. A Mr Alleyn was a famous dealer and supplier of bears and mastiffs to royalty. 'It was not altogether easy to give satisfaction, for sometimes a bear would by no means take kindly to having its eyes burnt out.'[10] Another dealer, William Fawnte, specialized in 'sporting boles' that could 'throw up your dodges in to the lofts'.

Mastiffs, though brave, were really too heavy and slow, and their ears were vulnerable. It was thought best to remove them altogether beforehand, and this practice continued long after baiting ceased, with leading dog experts testifying in court that no dog could live without cropped ears.[11] Baiting the bull was believed to tenderize his beef, which is why butchers kept dogs in their yards for the purpose. As the slaughterhouse was the butcher's castle, he baited his cattle as he pleased, and could train his dogs better than common street fighters. Butchers' dogs were therefore much sought after;

they became more specialized, and were called 'beast dogs', 'bullbaiting dogs', 'bullmastiffs', 'bulldog terriers' or just 'butchers' bull dogs'. With a little outcrossing to terriers and pugs, faster, more athletic dogs of great tenacity emerged, some with a 'lay-back' to allow the dog to grip limpet-like and breathe while being tossed about and profusely bled upon. They were powerfully built, at around 45lbs and upwards, and their jaws were gin-traps.

The fame of these dogs grew. Neither mutilation nor death appeared to scare them, as they hung on grimly to the agonized bull's face and ignored all his powers of retribution. One bulldog owner at Bury St Edmunds cut off his bitch's legs one by one, yet still she would not let go. Edward Ash describes a typical holy-day bait in England. I quote him at length because he writes so beautifully:

> The bull, little aware of the fate awaiting it, its horns covered with tow, was led to the stake, the ring fastened in the roadway. The indignity and pain to which its body and organs were subjected drove it into a condition of madness. The chain fastened from the ring to the stout leather collar about its neck prevented it from getting to the hissing, shouting crowd, and the men that ran in to strike it with their sticks and twisted its tail did to it whatever opportunity allowed them. It no longer mattered if the bull was seriously injured, for in any case it had not long to live. When it was sufficiently maddened two or three dogs were let in upon it. We read of the frenzied attempts made by the bull to toss the dogs, and to protect his nose from them. A bull which had been frequently baited [in the butcher's yard] would scrape a hole with his feet and put his nose down into it. Great was the screaming and yelling when the unfortunate bull, roaring with pain and fear, was pinned by one or other of the dogs. Then the bull was entirely at the mercy of the crowd, and they could do what they liked to it. At a bull-baiting in 1801, a baiter, armed with an axe, hacked off all four hoofs, so that the bull was baited on bleeding stumps. There of course came a time when, its nervous energy exhausted, a bull no longer cared what was done to it. If bulls could pray they would pray for death. Many were the ways to wake it up again: a fire lit beneath its stomach or boiling water poured in its ears.[12]

There were two kinds of bait: the 'turn loose' match and the 'let go' match. In the former, two or more dogs were released simultaneously and in the latter the dogs took turns, with their seconds goading the bull on. To be fair, the bull had a second as well, who would shout 'Halloo!' to warn the animal of a dog being set on. Most baits degenerated into a free-for-all, with dogs and dog owners all joining in, and the butcher delivering some extravagant *coup de grâce* to advertise his meat.

Meanwhile, galas were held in the pits, where dogs were torn limb from limb by their own kind, and either tortured, or were tortured by, other 'opponents'. In 1799 there was a fight between a monkey and a cross-mastiff.

Very cross indeed, by all accounts. The bookies reckoned the monkey would last six minutes. To spice things up, the monkey was given a thick foot-rule with which to defend himself. The monkey leapt three feet off the ground and came down on the dog's back, biting into the scruff of his neck and pulling his ear to wrench his head round. With the edge of the ruler the monkey began to whack the dog over the head until it yelled, and continued whacking patiently until it keeled over with a fractured skull. Another contest in 1801 featured a man and a bulldog. The dog actually got the man down and was looking into his intestines when taken off. To show how history repeats itself, in 1983 RSPCA officials in Barnsley, Yorkshire, appealed for information from the public to help them track down the organizers of bouts between men stripped to the waist and Staffordshire bullterriers. Inspector Tony West told reporters, 'We can only assume the winner is the one who lasts the longest.'

Despite the rather obvious cruelty, governments of the period failed to introduce legislation to stop the baiting or the pits. Animals have had few friends in Parliament and successive bills were voted down. MPs were influenced by a lot of prattle about toughness and the Bulldog Breed, and by breeders who feared their dynasties might not continue. They were quite right. When the ban affecting bull baiting (1835) was eventually expanded to embrace the pits, bulldogs and bullterriers became unprofitable relics. Seventy-lb bullterriers like Young Storm and Old Storm were redundant and worthless. So was that veteran of 104 fights, Belcher the bulldog, a scarred, sad reminder of dirty deeds. The pits, which had been the elegant snooker halls of yesteryear with chandeliers and seating for hundreds, stood empty. The dogs themselves were considered passé, dense and horrific-looking.

They did not, however, look anything like the bulldogs and bullterriers of today. Most had 'tiger-tails' or whip-tails; some were coarse coated. The bulldogs were of rational head-size, much more like our present day bullmastiffs, boxers and Staffordshires (the boxer evolved from the German Bullenbeisser, another specialist baiting dog). The old gladiators were more actively built and higher on the leg than now. Bulldogs, the real ones, were not disproportionately bowed or chesty. Nor did they look like Winston Churchill. The modern bullterrier and bulldog are idealized versions of fighting dogs. They are products of the fancier's imagination rather than of the pit. The white bullterrier's wedge-shaped skull is new; so are his shifty triangular eyes and want of a stop. Despite his big new ears (a tasty target to Young or Old Storm) he has frequently suffered from deafness, a congenital complaint.

But the more radically altered beast is the bulldog. No one need doubt his bite capabilities. The only canine to have seriously injured Barbara Woodhouse[13] has also blotted his copybook on the show bench. Harding Cox, who owned and bred many a 'Bungo' as he called them, speaks of an effusive, slobbery, loving nature, which, once roused, becomes indiscriminately savage. At one show he stood helplessly by as an attendant, trying to remove from the bench a bulldog angered by its neighbour, leant over to unhook the dog's chain. This was the last anyone saw of the man's face. The bulldog's jaws shut on it like a vice, and were only prized open with the greatest difficulty. I am a great fan of the modern bulldog and can think of few sights more cheering than his merry naval roll and wondrous countenance, but the bulldog suffers cruelly from his show points. He is the victim not only of achondroplasia but of another condition, brachycephalicism, in which the skull is enlarged and the nasal area compressed, to give the required Desperate Dan protrusion of the lower jaw, like certain reverse-beaked birds of prey and piranha fish. The deformity often results in the soft palate impinging on the entrance to the larynx. Not only would the modern bulldog be unable to breathe whilst hanging from the bull's nose; in many cases, without the intervention of a veterinary surgeon, he cannot breathe at all.

> The bulldog, which was designed by selection to be able to breathe satisfactorily while hanging on to the bull which it was attacking, was less undershot in its working days than it is at present; breeders have chosen to stress by selection the very factors which militate against its chances of survival if it was left to its own devices and not attended by veterinary surgeons capable of coping with the problems of respiratory embarrassment and dystocia peculiar to the breed.

So says a widely respected authority on canine maladaptations, Mike Stockman, in the veterinary magazine *In Practice*.[14] Mr Stockman is very sympathetic towards breeders in general and believes most are sensible people who love dogs and would never deliberately harm them. But, as he told me, 'The bulldog has enough problems to sink a battleship. The Kennel Club is doing its best very slowly to get this altered but it is up against a very conservative element in the bulldog world.'

Mind you, Bungo's problems now are as nothing compared with his treatment by fanciers of yore. 'I was faced', says show judge Harding Cox, 'with an objection to Bumble, on the ground that he was faked, i.e., that he had been "manipulated" like Sheffield Crib and others, by having the frenum of his upper lip cut, and his nose forced back by an implement resembling a thumbscrew.'[15]

A different kettle of fish is the Staffordshire bullterrier, recognized by the Kennel Club in 1935. Why, you may ask, should such a dog rise to prominence 100 years after dog fighting was banned? The answer is that the Staffordshire is no idle dream of pit-dogs gone by. He is the real Macoy. John Gordon, who breeds them now, explains, 'The *name* may have been

Above : Bertram Mills' Signings Spurn League Offer

Left : 'Give me strength.' Performing dogs in general give the RSPCA a headache

The very first electric-hare race meeting at Belle Vue, Manchester

1912 bulldogs battle it out

DOG FASHIONS FOR 1889.

DORGUPINE, CROCODACHSHUND, POMME-DE-TERRIER (BLACK-AND-TAN), VENTRE-À-TERRIER (SCOTCH), HIPPOPOTAMIAN BULLDOG, GERMAN SAUSAGE DOG HEDGE-DOG.   (*By Our Special Dog-fancier.*)

George du Maurier's famous *Punch* cartoon on breed deformation, 1889

Above : Adjudged 'The Ugliest Dog in the World' at the Petaluma 80 show, San Francisco

Right : Who are we to judge dog beauty?

Once a ratter. Two Yorkshire terriers in paper bangers

A terrified dog awaiting vivisection. In Britain alone in 1982,
13,146 experiments were performed on dogs

Laika. The worlds' first space traveller in her seat in Sputnik II

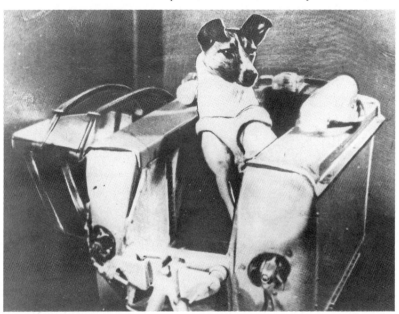

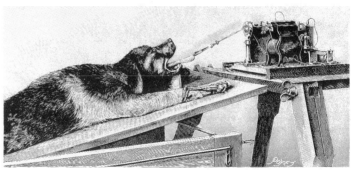

Before and after. Dog dragged along motorway restored by the
National Canine Defence League

Hearing dog Chum with Mr and Mrs Chapman

'Lady and I travel all over on the railways.'
Bill Harman with his second sight

Penning in Hyde Park sheepdog trials, 1955

The Old Shepherd's Chief Mourner. Landseer sums it up

recognized in 1935 but the breed itself evolved round about 1820, by putting a terrier to the bulldog. Not the bulldog of today, which is a monstrosity, but an earlier kind. The Staffordshire bullterrier is the *real* bullterrier.'

The modern Staffordshire is a genuine fighter-unto-death – a real gladiator. This is not my opinion so much as the view of those in the trade. White bullterriers, cross-Dobermanns, GSDs, lurchers, bullmastiffs, boxers and others are used, but the Staffordshire is the modern pit-man's fancy. In the US, despite competition from nightmarish 'pit-bulls', bandogs and other creations, the Staffordshire holds sway, and his fights are watched by several hundred spectators at a time, ringed by lookouts with walkie-talkies.

In Britain the threat of a £500 fine or three months' imprisonment does not deter enthusiasts of 'the Bloods', who told Frank Palmer, 'Staffordshires are born killers, but you can train them to be that little bit keener.'[16] One pitman had seen two Staffordshires fight for two-and-a-half hours, until they could no longer stand. True, they may be brutally treated to make them 'game', starved, tethered and baited. One West Country fan explains: 'Once they have turned, you can never make them lose that savagery.'[17] Much photographed with his proud owner was Butcher, of Yorkshire, a scarred Staffordshire of immaculate pedigree and fight-record. His manager, a general dealer from Wombwell, boasted, 'Since I have had him he's had six fights, two of them fatal. He never loses.' And he added, 'It goes on all over. You are not going to stop it.'[18] Lightweights check in at around 30lbs. Heavyweights, like 'Sullivan', tip the scales at 55lbs. In his last bout near Mansfield, Sullivan redistributed so much of his opponent's anatomy that the dog's remains had to be shot.

Training methods vary. One fight-man renowned for throwing cats into his backyard described another method he'd seen, in which a Staffordshire was teased up with a cat in a cage suspended from a revolving clothes-line. A favoured American variation is to remove a kitten's claws and suspend him in an onion bag from a spring, with his paws hanging out. Ordinarily, pit-dogs are given 'tasters' of a cat as a puppy, a Jack Russell at nine months and a mongrel for a 'roll' as an amateur. In the real thing, 'The dogs get a lock on, screaming at each other. If they don't break flesh, their faces come out in a big blood blister.'

It isn't always easy to induce dogs to fight, whatever their breeding. Canids are ceremonious in avoiding mutual destruction, and some scientists refer to a bite inhibition. One method of overcoming any canine qualms is to tether the dogs in the pit and throw a bitch on heat just out of their reach. This irritates them slightly, and when they are in a reasonable lather the dogs are released to take their spite out on each other. They are very fit, from roadwork and millwork (in a treadmill). Some are injected with drugs such as novocaine to mask the pain barrier and push them into the cloud of rage from which many do not return.

Mr A. Mitchell, of the Staffordshire Bull Terrier Breed Council, believes the fight-men are a 'lunatic minority' and that 'organized dogfighting for money is practically non-existent'. In any case, he says, dog-fighting is old, international and sophisticated. 'There were actually three or four different schools of breeding among the original Staffordshires; some rangey, some heavy. The breed standard changed in 1938; they're much more "bully" now. The Darlaston men wanted a small dog that was fast in and fast out. The Cradley Heath men liked wide-spaced fronts. A third variety – big reds – were tall dogs with long necks that could reach down on an opponent.' He says there are one or two 'revival style' pit-bulls in England. 'Some odd bod in Devon has one, and I believe there's another in London.' In fact, in the past six years approximately 300 pit-bulls have passed through UK quarantine kennels, and MP Janet Fookes recently spearheaded a move to put a stop to large-scale pit-bull importation from America, where the pups are starved and released on kittens and weaklings slashed with a razor. This will not deter pit-bull breeders. A Canadian living in Lincolnshire advertises his wares in the *Exchange and Mart*. Pit-bulls have been known to chew concrete.

A chemist in the Glasgow area in June 1983 developed a roll of film and was so shocked by what he saw, he took it to the police. The film showed Staffordshires and other dogs pit-fighting, some with important bits hanging off. RSPCA Inspector Degenhard: 'On several occasions we've come very close to prosecuting these people and fallen short at the eleventh hour because of tip-offs. Journalists could be a help if they waited until we got a prosecution before blowing the story. Otherwise all our lines of investigation go suddenly cold and these characters disappear like rabbits down rabbitholes.' Inspector Degenhard refers to a chap breeding pit-bulls here. 'I wouldn't like to have to separate two of those.' How is it that such dogs are being bred in the UK in the 1980s? RSPCA Chief Superintendent Frank Milner: 'I suppose they use the same excuse [i.e. historical interest] that the rare poultry breeders give when they breed birds for cockfighting. These barbaric "countryfied" sports have got to be stamped out.'

Before the last war, R. H. Johns, associate secretary of the National Canine Defence League (NCDL), went undercover to watch organized dogfights in a colliery town. The experience affected him so deeply that he produced a booklet, *Smash Dog-Fighting and Badgering*,[19] calling for something to be done about evasion of the law. Posing as a Blood fan, he went along to watch Killer, a white dog with a prominent jaw, do battle in the host's backyard where pups were having their heads rubbed together to give them the general idea. 'For thirty minutes he bounced a big dog about the shed, leaving him in a very sorry state.' The trainee was thought to be showing promise, though, and was christened Jack the Ripper. Jack was rested for two months and then built up with mill and roadwork, and 'paunch', a macho mash prepared on the kitchen range. Then he was taken out of his private box and electric lights rigged in the shed. Jack was very cordial with the human visitors; many of the dogs were. An improvised pit was made with boards, and a sparring partner, the white-and-brindle Grip, was introduced. Grip had disgraced his owner in a previous fight by refusing to go the thirty-minute distance, and was considered cannon fodder.

Jack and Grip flew out of their corners. The fight was silent. Jack, a throat-and-chest fighter, seized Grip's throat and munched on it for five minutes. 'Grip was able to chew on Jack's legs from time to time, and then had him down on the floor.' At twenty minutes they were separated. A fresh dog was brought in for Jack: a heavier 'spar'. This dog bounced him about the pit and the boards were bathed in red. After twenty minutes they were pulled off and permitted three seconds' rest. Jack, 'with his nose appearing almost sawn off, was released to see whether he was still game. He went straight over to start the fight again.' He would now be backed against any dog of his weight in England for a high match-fee. If he lived. Iodine was dabbed on his wounds and he was bathed and put before the kitchen fire. 'Grip was lying dead on his chain in the yard. His master laughed when he saw it, and went and sank the body in the midden. He always showed signs of satisfaction when he was able to add another fallen gladiator to that muckheap of his.'

7

GOOD SHEPHERDS
AND HEELERS

When the sheep were feeding quietly and there was little or nothing to do for hours at a time, he would not lie down and go to sleep like any other sheepdog, but would spend his vacant time 'amusing of hisself' on some smooth slope where he could roll over and over, then run back and roll over again and again, playing by himself just like a child, or he would chase a butterfly or scamper about over the down hunting for large white flints, which he would bring one by one and deposit them at his master's feet, pretending they were something of value. . . .[1]

The sheepdog is perhaps the most human of all canines. He takes the imprint of man, spending his life in tune with man's requirements, detailing in his mind the shepherd's wishes with the help of a whistle, or a hint of a whistle, from across the hill. As Rochester tells Jane Eyre, '. . . it is as if I had a string somewhere under my left ribs, tightly and inextricably knotted to a similar string situated in the corresponding quarter of your little frame'.

The flint-collector is called Badger, one of the dogs referred to in W. H. Hudson's classic, *A Shepherd's Life*, based on the recollections of James Lawes and other nineteenth-century shepherds on the Wiltshire Downs. Many such canine personalities emerged. Another 'stump-tail', Sally, would take umbrage. If her master 'spoke too sharply to her, or rebuked her unnecessarily for going a little out of her way just to smell at a rabbit burrow, she would nurse her anger until an opportunity came of inflicting a bite on some erring sheep. Punishing her would have made matters worse: the only way was to treat her as a reasonable being and never speak to her as a dog – a mere slave.'[2]

Bungtails were common in many parts of Britain; Westmoreland had a breed said to be born with short tails after seeing a Manx cat. Curtailed sheepdogs are supposed to have escaped the dog tax, but they were probably docked in the belief that a lack of rudder would prevent them from turning sharply near the sheep. They had to run in an arc. Many modern shepherds prefer what they call a 'dead tail' that does not wag. The dogs vary according to climate and local terrain: short coats for the lowland rain; tousled thick pile for the Highland cold; darting speed for the mounted shepherds of the Weststonedale. Before enclosures, and especially for swineherding in the oak and beech forests, the dogs had to contend with wolves, so they were fierce and burly.

Perhaps the oldest British sheepdog, until recently unknown beyond the crags of his native Highlands, is the bearded collie, the probable ancestor of the Old English Sheepdog. He is believed to have been brought to Britain in 2000 BC from Western Europe,[3] where several such shaggy tykes may have descended from the Komondor of the Magyars. Sheepdogs are mentioned by the tenth-century Hywel Dda of Wales. 'Whosoever possesses a cur, though it be the king, its value is fourpence. A herd dog that goes before the herd in the morning and follows them home at night is worth the best ox.'[4] Gradually, the dogs became more specialized. The Highlands needed a rock-climber and barker; the south of England, with heavy, stiff sheep, also required a fairly aggressive if less hirsute dog. The Borders produced a dog with 'eye' that could hold the sheep with his gaze. Cows were more dangerous. Sheepdogs have been used for cattle but are occasionally kicked in the head, receiving tumours.[5] The Welsh dwarf dog (Cor-gi) could nip the cow's heels and duck smartly, and the Ormskirk heeler of Lancashire was similarly skilled.

By Tudor times, the wolf was gone. 'Our shepherd's dog is not huge and vast and big, but of indifferent stature and growth, because it has not to deal with the bloodthirsty wolf,' says the Elizabethan dog author, Dr Caius. This English dog, 'either at the hearing of his master's voice or at the wagging of his fist, or at the shrill and hoarse whistling and hissing, bringeth the wandering wether and straying sheep into the selfsame place, where his master's will works to have them, whereby the shepherd reapeth the benefit, namely, that with little labour and no toil of moving his feet, he may rule and guide his flock according to his own desire'.[6]

There have probably been as many local sheepdogs as dialects and early engravings and photographs reveal a motley lot. The collies, though, were widespread: bearded, smooth, rough, border, Shetland (originally called a 'collie')[7] and probably a few others – perhaps named after the black-faced mountain sheep of the Scottish Highlands rather than 'coaly' or 'collied', meaning black. As wolves disappeared from south to north, large guard-dog types could be bred down, punished for biting and taught to reinforce the shepherd's authority by barking and running up and down. Sheep would take more notice of a dog than a crook. And gradually the dogs became small and skilful, actively shaping the flocks themselves.

Collies are highly sensitive animals and do not take kindly to being pulled about. One savaged a child some time ago, so that it needed 100 stitches. Barbara Woodhouse commented, without generalizing, that *some* working collies were like this and didn't like being mauled about by children and having no work to do.[8]

Many shepherd dogs have a distinctive gait, an elasticity and smoothness of the rear axle that gives the impression of grace and endurance. The border collie's hindlegs are longer than its forelegs, for slinking, skirting, spurting and slowing. The shepherd must be able to turn his dog's speed up and down like a gas jet without jolting or alarming the sheep. If one considers a list of dogs whose ancestors have been used for shepherding, this power and poise become especially noticeable. The Abruzzi shepherd dogs of Italy still wear 2-inch iron-spiked collars against wolves in the mists and mountains, but they have the distinctive free loping gait. So does the Italian Maremma of the Tuscan farmers, scrambling smoothly up crags. The English 'bobtail' (Old English Sheepdog), despite his size, retains the graceful springy trot of his droving forefathers. Sheepdogs spend much of their time ambling and trotting, single-tracking in their own footmarks. The Pyrenean mountain dog has a powerful rolling gait; the modern German Shepherd, an alchemy of Teutonic sheepdogs, could balance a glass of water on his rear before it became fashionable to slope his back like a ski-jump.

The roll of honour for this vital job includes an impressive number of European breeds: the shaggy Polish lowland sheepdog; the giant Schnauzer, once a drover; the Komondor, Kuvasz and Puli of Hungary (the 'doormat dogs' with the Rastafarian dreadlocks); the long-haired Briard and smooth-coated Beauce of France; the Tervuren, Malinois, Groenendael and other herding dogs of Belgium; the Tibetan mastiff and terrier, both used by nomadic tribesmen with their mountain herds; the huge northern Indian sheepdogs, for seeing off wolves; the Bouvier des Flandres, a cowherd and butcher's dog; the Italian Bergamaschi; the Rottweiler, believed to have driven livestock before the Roman legions; the Maremma, Pyrenean and Appenzell of the mountains; the Norwegian Buhund, the Armant of Egypt and innumerable others have all seen service as sheepdogs. The oldest of the Europeans, apart from the Komondors and Kuvasczok, may well be the Russian herdsman's Aftscharka, perhaps a remnant of the Neolithic shepherd dogs, woolly and crossed with narrow gazehounds for speed. He was a familiar sight in the Crimea. One came to England with a circus, got lost, and was found, starving, by James Lawes. He took it home and mixed a feed in a bucket, emptying it on the turf:

The dog hurled himself down on the food and started devouring it as if the mass of meal had been some living savage creature he had captured and was frenziedly tearing to pieces. He turned round and round, floundering on the earth, uttering strange noises like half-choking growls and screams while gobbling down the meal; then when he had devoured it all he began tearing up and swallowing the turf for the sake of the little wet meal still adhering to it.[9]

Lawes had never seen such a rage of hunger, yet this dog had been roaming all the time among flocks of sheep. It looked like nothing on earth but it had to be a sheepdog and Lawes used it for a time on the Wiltshire Downs, where somebody recognized it as a 'Rooshian'. In its native country the dog would have sat on a coat with two or three others, watching for wolves and bears. Sheep were sacrosanct and not to be touched.

Homer refers to faithful mastiff-sheepdogs repulsing the wolf, and Lucretius mentions the 'lightly sleeping shepherd dog with its faithful heart'. The Roman agricultural authority Columella wrote a book explaining that sheepdogs wore large wooden collars where he came from, and could not be classed with dumb animals because their bark was full of 'eloquence and meaning'. A sonorous bark was needed in a farm guard to terrify the 'crafty plotter'. A sheepdog should be white, solid white to distinguish it from predators, and a farmyard dog solid black for a more 'alarming appearance'. Dogs of broken colour, says Columella, are no good. (Many modern shepherds say just the opposite.)

Some of these early sheepdogs were enough to turn a funeral up an alley. Albanian ones were known to attack passersby while the shepherd puffed on his pipe, and a seventeenth-century Turkish traveller refers to Greek sheepdogs 'the size of asses', in double or triple chains, that could bring down a man on horseback. 'The shepherds look on these as their companions and brethren, and do not object to eat out of the dish with them.'[10] They doubled as war-dogs and guarded the mountain passes, livestock being a very valuable commodity in wartime. The Hebrews despised their good shepherds and heelers and said so in many scriptural references like Job XXX, i, but the ancient Persians were warned in the *Zend-Avesta*:

> Whoever shall smite a shepherd dog, or house dog, or trained dog, his soul shall fly amid louder howlings and fiercer pursuings than the sheep does when the wolf rushes upon it.[11]

The Persian sheepdog, considered near-human, could be held morally responsible for murdering a sheep. On St Hubert's Day (3 November), shepherds all over christendom would go to church to ask for a blessing on their near-human helpers and get wafers said to protect them from rabies.

In parts of Canada the stockmen employed a dog very like the modern sheltie, called a Hare Indian dog. Two were once exhibited in cages at the London

Zoo but proved to be tame and friendly. The early American sheepdogs were trained to go out with the flocks and bring them back at dusk, unaided. Puppies would be put to ewes, following their foster-mothers and worrying them home at night for a proper feed. The other sheep, having no pressing engagements, would follow. In Australia the dingo was crossed with sheepdogs, sent over from the Lammermuir Hills in the nineteenth century, to breed the 'kelpie' or little helper. Dingo blood has been used to make superior herd captains, and one famous kelpie won several trials.[12] Australian sheep are a disorderly mob and require a bit of barking and a firm paw.

Despite their astonishingly human faculties, sheepdogs have not always been treated kindly. The oracle in these matters, Phil Drabble, writes, 'Many shepherds and farmers are unimaginative men who too often regard their dogs as mere tools of the trade, expendable when their useful life is done.'[13] Even at the end of the 1800s in Britain, farm dogs had to find their own food and, because of the ambiguous attitude of shepherds towards their masters' game, sheepdogs would often be thrashed for catching a hare or walloped for not catching one, depending on who was looking. The sheepdog was broken with hard words and hard blows. 'Caleb' (James Lawes) killed a dog called Tory for chasing a swallow, and his brother Dave killed a dog called Monk for disobedience. Yet they do not appear as unusually cruel or thoughtless men in Hudson's book, *A Shepherd's Life*. Hudson himself remembers the custom back in Argentina for a dog even suspected of sheep-worrying to be hanged from a gallows.[14] A more modern attitude is demonstrated by shepherd and trial judge Tony Iley. He recommends leaving the stick at home, but grasping the dog round its neck and lifting it off the ground. One of his dogs, Jim, fell limp after such treatment.[15]

British shepherds have used their dogs for a variety of extra duties, such as killing adders, retrieving lost spectacles and hynotizing the odd hare while the shepherd goes behind to give it a blow. Bitches occasionally foster lambs and some collies have been specialists at recovering 'coupies'. A coupie is a Scots ewe that has rolled over on her back and can't get up. Shepherd William Caig (1881–1968) writes of his brother George's dog, Tyne, winner of the Bargrennan trial in 1921, whose masterpiece was coupies. He could 'wind' them from two miles off and show his master where the sheep lay, kicking her heels in the mist.[16]

There is a lot of disagreement about training. Some shepherds insist that sheep will attack a young dog and that, in any case, the pup will not have their speed, work itself to a standstill and become cowardly and 'broken-hearted'.[17] On the other hand a pup will already have all its skills – blocking, turning, driving, etc. – locked away in its head. 'The word "training" applied to a puppy jars on my ears,' says Tony Iley.[18] 'It implies something that you put into it and perhaps rub it well in with a cleckie – all wrong of course. It's all there already, bred in that wee brainbox.' Pups will round up ducks and hens instinctively, and many an old sheepdog, deaf and blind, has returned to this last round-up. Iley prefers to train the dogs young, 'holding up' sheep to them at four or five months. At eight months his pups have the speed and begin their out-run lessons. At ten to eleven months they may gather at 50–100 yards and do a little drive, however imperfectly. They learn left and right whistles and, finally, the blowback and the shed. By thirteen months they can manage a small trial. Iley prefers a rough diamond with some stubbornness to a slick 'fancy' dog.

Other shepherds differ. They say you should never let a pup run on the sheep before he has their speed or he'll learn to bark. A traditional method, as with coupling hunting hounds, is to let the pup watch a mature dog and associate signals and actions in its mind. Of course, if this is overdone the pup will lose initiative and begin to rely on the dog rather than the shepherd. Some shepherds insist that the pup's magical learning period is over at a year old and that, thereafter, he becomes just another dog. Others say you shouldn't even begin breaking him until he's mature.

Despite recent reports of commercialization and corruption in the trials world, sheepdog trials do raise standards: competition inevitably does. Border collies have been granted Challenge Certificates by the Kennel Club since 1982, a development lamented by some countrymen who fear for the future of the breed in exhibitors' hands. Trials, though, are controlled by the International Sheepdog Society. Early competitions are described by William Caig. 'There was an exhibition given of two dogs working by Joseph Moses, Brogntyn, Wales, with his two small grey coloured dogs. All his directions were given by whistles which they obeyed with remarkable intelligence. I had never seen anything like it,' he writes in April 1900 of a trial at Castle Douglas.[19] These days every Tom, Dick and Harry can discuss the finer points of penning and shedding, thanks to television. Iley quotes a timely plea from the editor of the *Scottish Sheepdog Handler*, Matt Mundell, criticizing what he calls 'table-tennis' trial fields:

> The collie can still be improved in the hands of good shepherds and farmers, through breeding. But never turn it into a machine. We can never do without their inborn intelligence and initiative.

There are many recorded instances of collies guarding their flocks all alone, while master is over the hill or in the tavern, and many a tale of their individuality and conscientiousness. One of James Lawes's dogs, Watch, would ask to go for a drink in a pond a quarter of a mile away, and return promptly to his duties. Collies watching other competitors performing in trials will often register admiration or contempt, and every individual dog, according to Hudson's Wiltshire shepherds, has a 'kink' or personal idiosyncracy. Iley believes you have to look deep into the creature's character at the outset to discover the 'true dog' underneath, be it never so ugly or unprepossessing on the surface. Handsome is as handsome does.

This chapter would not be complete without mention of James Hogg, the Ettrick Shepherd, and his extraordinary dog, Sirrah. You may have heard the story before. One night a flock of lambs in Hogg's charge pushed down a hurdle and escaped, bleating for their mothers. Hogg and his human assistant went among them in the pitch darkness but the lambs panicked and scattered. Sirrah had also vanished. A fine state of affairs this was. Knowing the ewes were to the south, Hogg picked his way there, whistling for his blessed dog. He had lost the lot: 700 head of sheep. Next morning the moors were bare. Hogg and his lad were making their way to report the dreadful news when, chancing to look over a narrow ravine, they spotted the flock tightly packed at the bottom, with Sirrah blocking the only exit, looking round for help. Not a lamb was missing. By and by, Hogg trained a younger dog and gave Sirrah away. 'I told the old dog to go,' he explains, and the dog went off obediently with his new master. 'Once he came back, but, being told to return, went off again, knowing that he was no longer wanted by me. He never came back. He lost all his interest in his work, and his new master could do nothing with him and finally got rid of him as useless.' The string situated in the corresponding quarter of his little frame had evidently broken.

8

TRANSPORT AND
GENERAL WORKERS

If ever dogs needed a trade union, the TGWU would have been it. Canines in the transport and haulage industry, in exchange for the highest productivity, have received the worst pay and conditions in the world. Here is Apsley Cherry-Garrard providing a humorous episode in the otherwise sad story of Captain Scott's last Antarctic expedition. It concerns a workers' collective formed somewhere near Biscuit Depot, sometime in 1913.

> The most hardened trade unionist might boil with rage at the sight of 11 or 13 huskies dragging a heavy load including their idle master over the floe with every appearance of intense joy, but truth to tell, there were signs that they were getting rather sick of it, and within a few days we were to learn that dogs can chuck their paws in. . . . They combined readily and with immense effect against any companion who did not pull his weight or against any one who pulled too much.[1]

The dogs would sometimes get a 'down' on a particular individual and try to murder him or her, 'without our being able to discover their doggy reason', but one dog, Dyk, was singled out for special attacks. Whenever a team, of which Dyk was a member, was halted, he would whine and tug at his harness, eager to get going again; this spoiled his workmates' rest period. 'They were justifiably resentful,' says Cherry-Garrard.

The dogs on Scott's expeditions had probably the least justification for restrictive practices, and I am grateful to the Scott Polar Research Institute, Cambridge, for allowing me to see books, private papers and letters in Scott's own hand that tell the story of their fair treatment. 'Fair' in the context of polar exploration, of course, where all animals are scientifically expendable – and Scott's were no exception. He wrote to Sir Douglas Haig that, should he fail to reach the Pole in 1911–12, he would try again 'provided fresh transport can be brought down: the circumstances making it necessary to plan to sacrifice the transport animals used in any attempt'.[2]

Scott felt for the suffering of his dogs and ponies. The *Discovery* expedition 1901–4 had not been successful in dog terms, and he attributed their failure on his southern march 1902–3 to fish which had gone bad. (Dr E. A. Wilson described their condition as a kind of scurvy or dysentery.) Having limited experience of dogs, Scott saw their lacklustre pulling as a sign of boredom:

> A dog must be either eating, sleeping or interested. His eagerness to snatch at interest, to chain his attention to something, is pathetic. The monotony of marching kills him. This is the fearfullest difficulty for the dog-driver on a snow plain, without leading marks or objects in view.

They may well have been bored to death; Sir Douglas Mawson, on his Australian Antarctic expedition, used front-runners to lead the dogs, but this was not the point. The real reason, says one authority on Scott's transport, was that they were underfed.

> The expedition had dog biscuit, but they were not given it: for that, he put the blame on a man whom he did not name. They were given stock fish only, which contained no fat or carbohydrate. Over the whole period, he gave them no more than 14oz of dry fish per day, and on the day that Barne went back he was giving them only 8oz. He expected them to work on that, beat them when they would not work, and was surprised when they died one by one.[3]

Scott sincerely believed that he was treating the dogs correctly; 'I do not think it would be possible to take more care of the dogs than we do,' he writes, and his journals show how he studied them and tried to fathom their behaviour.

> What lingering instinct of bygone ages can impel them to this extraordinary custom is beyond guessing; but on these calm, clear, moonlight nights, when all are curled down placidly sleeping, one will suddenly raise his head, and from the depths of his throat send forth a prolonged, dismal wail.... If one is sentimentally inclined... it touches the lowest depths of sadness.

On the fateful *Terra Nova* expedition of 1910–13, Scott was beaten to the Pole by Norwegian Roald Amundsen and died, with four of his men, trying to get back. Just what difference might have been made had Scott taken more dogs, better dogs, or managed his dogs more effectively, we can only speculate. But we *can* speculate.

Amundsen combed Greenland for over 100 dogs and began his journey south with fifty-two of the best and five men, reaching the Pole on 14

December 1911. Scott had engaged Cecil Henry Meares to collect dogs from Siberia, and started his own march with twenty-four dogs, sixteen men, ten ponies and two motor sledges, but arrived at the Pole a month later. He had originally set out with thirty-one Siberian huskies, two Eskimo dogs and a collie called Lassie, but lost some from a Nematode parasite and the rest at sea. They had been chained on top of the main deck-cargo of the *Terra Nova* with little shelter because there was no room. In the gales some were washed overboard, others were very ill, and at least one hanged by its own chain. Scott describes their plight:

> They must perforce be chained up and they are given what shelter is afforded on deck, but their position is not enviable. . . . The dogs sit with their tails to the invading water, their coats wet and dripping; it is a pathetic attitude deeply significant of cold and misery. Occasionally some poor beast emits a long pathetic whine.[4]

A fresh supply of fourteen dogs delivered in January 1911 proved of no sledding value except for 'Snowy' and 'Bullet'. At Hut Point there were no tents for the dogs even in the severest weather, such as Amundsen pitched on the Barrier. The gales would not permit it. The dogs dug their own holes and waited for the blizzards to bury them. Eleven dogs pulled 500lbs – Scott describes the load as 'backbreaking' – at a 'smart pace'. They usually got on well except at mealtimes, when 'the smallest circumstance starts a fight'.

Amundsen's dogs were all permitted to run loose, muzzled. They were given seal-flesh pemmican and dried fish, and fed dog to dog. 'I do not know whether *we* could have fed dog to dog,' says Cherry-Garrard, 'for ours were Siberian dogs which I am told will not eat one another.' Scott's dogs were fed (this time) on 8oz Spratts biscuits containing meat and cod-liver oil. Meares made seal-flesh pemmican, for variety, and when ponies were killed on the drive south they had horsemeat. At first Meares gave the dogs 10oz of biscuit only, later increasing to 1lb or, 'at most', two-and-a-half biscuits. (Oates was reluctant to feed them on seal flesh.) Scott left Meares to get on with it. The pemmican oil and the oil in the biscuits caused 'purgation'. The dogs ate their own excreta and also their harnesses. They were pulling their loads well, sometimes twenty-three and thirty miles a day, but, if they were slow, their provisions had to go further. They ate less and pulled less. It was a vicious circle. Dogs that did not pull (e.g. an American husky and an Eskimo dog called Peary) were killed but not used for food.

Scott records the suffering of his dogs in the severe weather. 'The main trouble that seems to come on the poor wretches is the icing up of their hind quarters; once the ice gets thoroughly into the coat the hind legs get half paralysed with cold.' The balls of snow between their pads made their feet bleed, Lappy's in particular.

Despite their hard work Scott was ambivalent and never liked to rely on the dogs. As his disillusionment grew he gave the teams minor tasks and feared Amundsen's dogs would forge ahead. 'If he gets to the Pole, it must be before we do, as he is bound to travel with dogs and pretty certain to start early.'[5]

In their third season, when the polar party had gone, the dogs seem to have fared better. The remaining men set up a hospital for them and let all but the vicious ones run loose, so they hunted their own seal meat. They were given 1½lbs a day of biscuits with pemmican for variety, and two teams were now pulling 'splendidly', 600lbs each, up to twenty-nine miles a day, 'half with loaded sledges!' enthuses Cherry-Garrard; and though they were now sick of it, they had already done 1500 miles on the Barrier alone.

Whereas Amundsen had put his money on his dogs and skis, Scott had, from the beginning, hedged his bets. His letters in the Institute, for example to 'Skelly' Skelton,[6] reveal his hopes of relying on motorized transport and include a sketch in fountain pen of 'the motor' he had in mind: 'The key to everything'. He was quite emphatic. 'Without it, we can do little more than retrace our footsteps' (on the *Discovery* expedition). A typewritten paper on transport, presumed to be Scott's, refers to the necessity of motor sledges to cover the round trip of 1466 miles to the Pole and back. 'Except with very large numbers of animals such a distance could not be approached.'[7] In the event 'the motors' let Scott down. A. G. E. Jones noted,

> If the money spent on motor sledges had been used to buy more dogs, he could possibly have taken them up the Boardmore Glacier and on to the plateau. He may not have reached the Pole before Amundsen, but he would have given himself a greater chance of returning alive with his four colleagues.[8]

Amundsen evidently admitted from the outset his ignorance of dog transport and asked for help. Otto Sverdrup was the man to give it. He had been with Nansen in Greenland and on the drift of the *Fram*, and he knew first-hand about dog psychology on cruel expeditions. 'The relation between dog and driver had to be that between equals. A dog was not a horse; he was a partner, not a beast of burden, and the Eskimo dog was a comfort in the Polar wastes.'[9] The transport policy of Nansen and Sverdrup was the one adopted by Amundsen: dogs, intelligently used, and men on skis to complement them, with no 'idle master' sitting atop the luggage. Sverdrup even gave Amundsen his own dog team as a nucleus.

Another South Polar drive of 1912–13 by Sir Douglas Mawson, with Xavier Martz in charge of the dogs, ended in tragedy because provisions and the best animals went down a crevass. The surviving dogs were shot for food. They had lived on a meagre fare of hide and worn-out gloves, and their flesh was stringy. ('We were to get little nourishment from these starving creatures,' Mawson lamented.) Martz, a semi-vegetarian, became ill. One morning the men breakfasted on a dog skull, scooping the brains out with a wooden spoon. All the men were to die, except for Mawson, and he suffered Vitamin A poisoning from the dog liver. The soles of his feet came away and lumps of skin and hair began falling off, a condition he mistook for scurvy. He barely reached safety. In 1983, twenty-three-year-old explorer Benedict Allen, of Newton Valence, Hampshire, killed and ate his faithful dog in the South American rain forests 'for his vital proteins'. He had adopted the nameless stray in an Indian village and they travelled hundreds of miles together. Allen survived.

Sir Ernest Shackleton favoured half-bred Canadian huskies crossed with collies, St Bernards and wolves. His second Antarctic-expedition dogs were quarantined at Hackbridge, Surrey. Siberians were preferred by Rear-Admiral Richard Byrd, who took fifty-odd with him to circumnavigate the Antarctica coastline in 1933. Admiral Robert Peary of the US Navy could scarcely have managed without his huskies on the North Polar expedition of 1893–5, and one Eskimo dog, 'Furthest North', taken by Peary across Greenland, stands handsomely stuffed in Tring Museum. Peary pays his dogs the following tribute:

> And never were dogs or men more faithful than these poor brutes. Day after day they struggled back across that awful frozen desert, fighting for their lives, and ours. Day after day they worked till the last ounce of strength was gone from them, and then they fell dead in their tracks without a sound – 41 of them out of 42 with which I left the last cache.[10]

To realize just how little Captain Scott's dogs had to complain about, one really needs to look at accounts of early explorers and travel-writers, like McClintoch, Hayes, Hooper, Kane and Ledyard, and delve into books like *Tents of Tuski* and *Arctic Boat Journey*, for references to *Esquimaux* and dogs in their native environment.[11] Gruesome records emerge, *viz*: a ravenous team tear the harness off each other and run off into the snow, staggering in a frenzy. Fed some days on air pie or on frozen walrus hide like iron plate that had to be chipped with an axe, the dogs are savage. They tear at everything in sight, even bits of wood protruding from the snow. Those that fall down are torn at by the others. The men wait with swords and bludgeons to see them off. These are kissing cousins to wolves after all. Some of the dogs, too weak to attack, stand howling among their tangled traces. One or two drag themselves into the hut and fall into the fire. Ordinarily they sleep outside in the pelting sleet and snow, crying frenziedly when they see a light or sparks flying from the chimney.

Discipline is severe. If the dogs will not pull, they are whipped. 'They throw themselves down in the snow, howl vigorously at first, their cries gradually subsiding into a short moan at each blow.' One traveller says he has seen dog drivers

deliberately dispose themselves to the task, place one foot upon their sledge, and throwing back their arms to clear their dress, rain blow after blow upon the wretched creature, sometimes for 10 minutes or a quarter of an hour continuously.

Usually this worked but, if it didn't, there was worse to come. A hole would be made in the snow for the dog's nose, to be pounded remorselessly, or else there was the method of one driver, who 'quietly drew out his knife and stabbed the dog in two places'. W. C. L. Martin in his *History of the Dog*, 1845, sums it up. The Eskimo dog 'is a slave, ever toiling, and hardly used, subjected to want and blows, to cold and extreme fatigue'. Until the IFAW fought for a recent prohibition, worn-out huskies were still hanged in Greenland.

Nineteenth-century travellers referred to anything pulling a sledge as an 'Esquimau dog', though wolflike dogs of the Arctic circle are even older than the Eskimos, and various shapes and sizes of strong, hardy, double-coated, prick-eared, display-ruffed, long-snouted, independent canines evidently toiled in the Neolithic Arctic wastes. In Stone Age Scandinavia they pulled sleds bound together by sinews, transporting pelts, amber, essential supplies and tools, running from Finland to the mid-Urals. The prehistoric inhabitants of Punuk Island and Barrow Point, Alaska, wore ingenious bone-goggles for sledding, and the dog teams were of immense cultural importance to all the primitive Arctic communities, who could scarcely have traded or survived without them.[12] Interestingly, the Eskimos themselves have a legend that all Europeans are descended from dogs, who once set sail in a shoe and were transformed on their arrival.[13]

On the edge of the world the dogs were inextricably part of life. They were fattened for the table, strangled, stuffed and served to travellers who thought they were eating pork. They drew hide boats called umiaks up river during summer, subsisting on field-mice. They provided their pelts for clothing, ate out of the Indian's own porridge bowl, and warmed the Eskimo's igloo with their fur.

A wooden club hung from a hook on the wall, for discipline. Women sat in circles, chewing the whiplashes to make them pliant, and pleating them at the handle. Siberians used their sled dogs as babysitters and pillows, breeding being mostly the responsibility of women. Elsewhere, bitches were tied out to mate with wolves, for their hardihood; the wolves themselves were generally too fractious for trouble-free sledding. If a sled-dog ran off at harnessing time, you eventually got hold of it and tied one of its legs up to prevent future excursions. When you married you toasted your beloved in the blood of a sled-dog stabbed in the chest,[14] and when you died your mortal remains went down the throat of the trusty beastie. The sled-dog slept with you, carried you here and there, hunted for you and protected you from polar bears, biting valiantly and returning later to scrape the blooded ice with his teeth.

The Samoyeds, a nomadic race, used their larger dogs for sledging and their smaller models for herding reindeer. The Russian men generally despised their sled-dogs, and travellers attempting to pat them on the head promptly saw the dog sailing through the air on the end of his master's boot.[15] Even today, for reasons best known to themselves, the Russians staunchly refuse to be associated with the Siberian husky and have done their best to dissipate the breed in its native land. The Chinese, who have heartily enjoyed eating *their* sled-labourers, used the dogs in relays, according to Marco Polo, and sat on bearskins whizzing across the winter snows.

The modern 'Eskimo dog', descended from such sledding types, is a confused animal. He does not know where he stands. He knows that he is smaller than his relative, the Alaskan Malamute, and larger than his relations, the Samoyed and Siberian husky. But his name has been changed quite a bit. In Europe he has answered to 'Esquimau', 'Eskimo', 'husky' (in the 1930s) and even 'Greenland dog'. In the US he seems to huddle under the generic umbrella 'husky', with a number of polar peers. His breed varies widely in size and handsomeness and he is not domesticated like other dogs, behaving more or less as he did when the Eskimos pounded his nose. His UK club secretary, Mrs Janet Ward, describes him as 'wilful, quarrelsome, very strong and determined, grabby about his food: a happy character who loves a good brawl – and would not have survived had he been otherwise'.

The Alaskan Malamute is a bigger, stockier dog, built for hauling sleds in winter and plodding beneath heavy loads in summer. Today's call-of-the-wild Americans take him backpacking: he likes that. The Samoyed has become the Snow White of the show ring, but is also used for sled and cart racing. The Siberian husky, *persona non grata* of the saltmines, is an amiable, athletic, free-moving racing dog, small and streamlined, who surveys you steadily with one brown eye and one blue, and then yanks you along in sled-races and wheeled carts called 'rigs' and 'gigs' (more of this in the next chapter).

Records of one very famous beast of burden came to light in 1815, when a wonderful 'Alpine Mastiff' was brought to Leasowe Castle in England and sketched by the young Landseer. The dog had come from the Hospice of Bernard de Meuthon on the Great St Bernard Pass, where others like him were apparently used to carry provisions from Banche, eighteen miles away, 'each dog bearing one cwt'.[16] Since his arrival in England this particular dog had saved a woman from drowning. This was the beginning of a tidal wave that swept over the show world. It was claimed that the breed was started in the first century AD by de Meuthon himself, though the first mentions of any dogs at the Hospice were in 1774[17] and the 1830s.[18] A picture supposed to add substance to the tale was not presented to the Hospice until 1870.[19] Whatever the truth of the matter, the Swiss suddenly found themselves the possessors of a canine saint who went out with a barrel of brandy and revived derelict snowfarers by licking them in the chops. 'Barry', who lived at the Hospice from 1810–14,[20] reputedly saved forty lives (ten a year) and was killed in an avalanche escorting the forty-first to a village called St Pierre. As the fame of these dogs grew, rescue stories waxed more incredible. Barry was not killed in an avalanche; he was shot by the delirious rescuee mistaking him for a bear. Travellers claiming to have been dragged to safety on the dogs' backs did nothing to harm the price of show dogs like Tell, very unlike the Leasowe Castle dog but owned by the Rev. McDona and valued at £10,000.[21] These saintly creatures were supposed to have double dewclaws to act as 'snowshoes'. One cynic, Hugh Dalziel, asked what happened if there were double dewclaws behind and not before: would the dog's forelegs not sink out of sight whilst his back legs continued on their way? The Swiss, warming to the controversy, responded that a 'real' St Bernard would not have a bloodhound haw, exposing that delicate membrane to the blizzards. The British show specimens were thought so magnificent, though, that a real Hospice dog exhibited among them (called 'Monk') was offered at £15 and didn't even win a card.[22]

No doubt some of the dogs did save lives, carry bandages and food and go out with the monks looking for forlorn travellers: canine life-saving is not particularly unusual. Whatever the real offices of the St Bernard, the modern Swiss army-rescue service apparently use other dogs, especially German Shepherds, for avalanche sniffing.[23]

A more easily authenticated example of life-saving in frozen wastes is the transportation of essential medical supplies to stricken communities. A Cree Indian, Albert Campbell, once drove his team 522 miles from Winnipeg to St Pauls in 118 hours and 16 seconds, carrying serum and medicine.[24] In 1925, an outbreak of diphtheria threatened to wipe out the inhabitants of Nome, Alaska. The nearest serum at Anchorage could only be railroaded as far as Nenana, 600 miles short of Nome and there were 80 m.p.h. blizzards preventing air traffic. The village was done for unless somebody could make the intervening journey over mountains and iceflows, driving 'blind' and often in darkness, fast enough to prevent the serum from freezing. Nineteen drivers and teams did the run in relays in a week, halving the previous record, and Gunnar Kasson drove into Nome on 2 February with a team on its knees, his lead husky Balto having saved his life. A statue was erected to honour the 'indomitable spirit of the sled dogs' in New York's Central Park. Ironically, the year before, 1924, the Icelandic government had banned all dogs from the city of Reykjavik for reasons of 'hygiene'. The prohibition is still in force as it is in many towns and villages in Iceland. Such is the boundless gratitude for canine services to Arctic humanity.

Small branches of a canine Transport & General Workers Union would exist outside such frigid zones, of course. The Bernese mountain dog is still used for cart-haulage in Switzerland, and so is the Leonburg, the Flanders draught dog. The Newfoundland traditionally hauled his fishing master's lobsterpots and the Meizerhund of Germany is the butcher's dog of yore, pulling the meat and guarding the takings. Until the ban of 1839, British dogs were commonly 'draughted'. From medieval times butchers' carts rattled over the London streets to Smithfield market with their Great Dane and mastiff draydogs barking sonorously, and milkcarts and even dogskin carts were drawn by dogs. Fashionable traps with four men inside were no rare sight, and the carts and carriages were only banned because they began competing with parcel-delivery firms,[25] not out of concern for the dogs. Other transport workers have included the Swiss 'ski-lift' dogs, pulling skiers up slopes individually by means of a harness with a hoop; barge dogs, acting as guards, most notably the Schipperke or Little Skipper of Holland and Belgium; and the Harlequin Great Danes and Dalmatians who trotted fore and aft of landaus and barouches for fifteen to twenty miles to signify protection against highwaymen. The Dalmatian, an indefatigable runner, lived in the stables on good terms with the horses, and was said to have been depicted centuries before, prancing ahead of charioteers.

The Union would have had a natural leader in Bob, the railway dog. Bob was the most famous of all the charity 'cadgers' who roamed about with boxes and tins on their backs, jogging the public conscience. Bob travelled thousands of miles on his own on Britain's railways, collected large sums, and returned periodically to have his box emptied by the authorities. He is not known to have requested parity, had a dispute, or gone into arbitration.

9

COME ON MY SON

There are dogs for every element: terriers for the earth, retrievers for the water, fiery dogs for war and dogs of air called gazehounds. There have been 'greyhounds' of one kind or another developed all over the world, and we cannot prove that ours are directly descended from creatures in Egyptian and Abyssinian bas-reliefs. But still, the shock of a greyhound glancing past is rather odd, like seeing the ghost of an old compulsion, the wind still whistling in its ears.

There are many theories about the greyhound. It is, after all, an important animal. Men have staked their shirts on it. Few dogs have the power to make or break as the greyhound does: punters laugh and cry like children over his performance. We think it no exaggeration when a dejected gambler tells us 'a dog let me down' and reputations are as nothing at White City on Derby night. In 1983 a dog costing £8000, called Game Ball, came nowhere at all.

Some authorities say 'greyhound' is a corruption of 'Greekhound' and that the dogs came from Greece via the Gauls. Others say the Romans found them in the Levantine deserts or Mediterranean traders touted them about ... or you might prefer this one. Greyhound was rendered in the Old English as 'gríghund' and a grig is an eel or a grasshopper. Greyhound in medieval times was spelt 'gre-hounde', 'gre' being an archaic term for 'highborn', 'fine'. Perhaps greyhound meant simply gentle dog, beautiful dog. Arrian in his lectures on coursing spoke of such a one called Impetuosity who lived in AD 90, whose 'eyes were the greyest of grey' and who was a match for any four hares. At mealtimes she would pat her master delicately with one paw and then the other and her voice had 'many tones of speech'.[1]

By AD 948 in Britain these dogs were worth six score pence, a tidy sum, and were used to pay fines. They became exclusive to the nobility. Cnute's Game Laws of 1016 ordered greyhounds of low degree to be kept away from the forests or maimed to prevent them hunting. Kings sang their praises. Edward Balliol of Scotland fastened a stag's antlers to an oak called the Hartshorn in 1333 to commemorate a royal greyhound that coursed a stag thirty miles from

Westmoreland to 'Redkirk' and thirty miles back again, falling dead behind a fence. The antlers turned up in 1731 – embedded in an oak in Westmoreland.[2] The *Book of St Albans* of 1486 includes a poem:

> The greyhound should be headed like a snake
> And necked like a drake,
> Footed like a cat, tailed like a rat,
> Ribbed like a beam, glossy like a bream;
> The first year he should learn to feed,
> The second learn to follow on a lead.[3]

Modern greyhound racing on a track with a mechanical hare is a stylized version of the agility contest of old: coursing. Ovid, the Latin poet who died when Christ was seventeen, refers to coursing the fearful hare, and even in Britain the practice goes back a long way beyond the first official meeting at Swaffham, Norfolk in 1776. Turberville gives a chapter on coursing not included in his French original. He says judges should stand on a hillside 'whither they perceive the hare will bend' to note which dog 'doeth best' and that 'some use when their greyhounds be both of a colour to bind a handkerchief about one of their necks for a difference'. This was 1575; rules for organizing public courses were drawn up by the Duke of Norfolk in Elizabeth I's reign. In 1836 an enterprising hotel-keeper promoted an eight-dog stake named after his hotel; this became the Blue Riband coursing event, the Waterloo Cup.

Hare coursing derives its tension from the hare's cornering ability versus the greyhound's speed. The hare saves herself, if she can, by jinking and turning, while the dogs (conventionally two of them) attempt to bow and snatch her ('. . . headed like a snake and necked like a drake'). Points are awarded for speed and for forcing the hare off line, but a match report usually runs something like this: 'Squiffy had one-and-a-half lengths to spare at the turn, when puss broke to Pizzle, who used her twice before pulling her down.' The dogs are often slightly sozzled. One famous Irish trainer would swill a mixture of grenadine and brandy round his mouth and spit the concoction down his dog's throat. Other restoratives include a teaspoon of sherry on the tongue. The greyhounds' lean and hungry look, frantic to get after something and with their eyes popping out of their heads, ensure their owners' entertainment. Two dogs still fastened together once got away from the Slipper and broke a hare; two others met head on and broke their necks.[4] You don't even need to give them prize-money. Nowadays, points are awarded by a judge on horseback, who signals the winner by pulling a red or white handkerchief from his coat, to match one competitor's collar. There are bloodless victories and winning is not based on the kill. Solid white greyhounds are thought conspicuous to the hare, so saplings (pups) used to be drowned, and still are for all I know. In the 1930s coursers would roll up in a charabanc with their proven longtails and let them out for a quick 'pop' behind the keeper's back if a hare were sighted.

The dogs, many of them cherished companions, are cheered on by pet names. The Great Ones of Waterloo, like Genial Nobleman, Old Kentucky Minstrel and the 'mighty' Fullerton (who stands these days in Tring Museum) melt into frenzied cries of 'Arthur!' or 'Pinky!' from a wellington-booted, rain-sodden community much vexed by hunt saboteurs. Some of the finest silversmiths in the land have been commissioned to make collars for their champions. Examples can be seen, embellished with repoussé work, in the museum at Leeds Castle. Coursers have a maxim: 'You can help a sore dog but not a tired one.' Sore dogs range from those with cramp or a broken hock to brave creatures like Hardly Ever, who ran four courses in 1975 with as bad a set of toes as even the author of *The Waterloo Cup 1922–1977* had ever seen.[5] The hare's toes are also the subject of concern if they are clogged with mud to mar her speed; and sometimes floods and 'sabs' cancel the whole proceedings.

At the end of the First World War, an American farmer, O. P. Smith, was fined for coursing a hare in his paddock in Oklahoma. He responded by opening a circular track in Oklahoma City, and by the 1920s there were over 100 such tracks dotted around the US. In England, meanwhile, on a field near the Welsh Harp in Hendon, a mechanical hare propelled by a windlass was shooting along a 400-yard grooved rail pursued by 'long dogs'. A report in *The Times* of 11 September 1876 describes such a race, a straight test of speed. The oval track arrived courtesy of the Greyhound Racing Association (GRA) and an American businessman and opened at Belle Vue, Manchester in July 1926. Coursing people didn't like the new humbug competition, but it had to happen. A real hare's unpredictable movements make coursing quite unsuccessful as a popular spectator sport where you need control, seating, lighting, punting and justice seen to be done. Sympathy for the hare, by the way, had nothing to do with it. Many modern racedogs are trained on live quarry. John Sherry, a London-based Irish trainer who coaches some of the best greyhounds in the UK at my local Walthamstow stadium, told me how new recruits are assessed.

'You show them a rabbit; they'll look at it and probably look at you, and if you encourage them: yes, go after that, they'll get a bit excited and it's a progression from there on in. You slip them to a hare and they'll show their little paces, and you'll see how they'll stride out. Some of them can't gallop, some can't extend themselves at all and they look awkward and they are awkward, and it's a big heartbreak for some people.' Initially, though, the trainer watches how the dog deports itself. 'I've got a little bitch I'm starting off at the moment. She's twelve months now and I like her attitude. She's an intelligent little one but yet she's bold. She'll accept the teaching and a little bit of discipline and she shows good sense. She grubs well, she comes out of the kennel properly, goes into the paddock properly; she'll empty on a lead, she won't foul her kennel; she's a good clean animal. Some dogs will wet their bed; they're always putting their paws on you; they're just naturally stupid. If they do something wrong and you give them a smack, they don't respond to it; they just think, "Why hit me? I'm beautiful." And you'll get a dog that runs awkwardly, acts stupid on the track, and he's probably the silly bugger at the kennels: he won't go in and out of the paddock, and he'll never learn the right thing to do.'

John Sherry's favourite dog was 'It's Stylish'. He still speaks of him with great affection. Stylish bit everyone, including a cookhouse man of thirty years' standing with never a mark on him. 'I came in one day after racing and there was blood all over the kennels, on the wall and everywhere from just a little lightning nip. But Stylish was a tremendous character and he was one that would talk to you. When he got in the back of a car, there wasn't any looking out of the window. He wasn't interested in anything except getting to this different track and having his wits about him, saving his energies. He was a competitive spirit. If a dog ran fast against him and caught him a little bit unawares, next time he would be waiting to meet that dog again, and before the traps went up he had his mind set: "It's the bugger in six I've to watch." And he would come out with the old head going up and down, the ears bopping, determined to get to that bend. He was out there absolutely doing his best.'

Racing greyhounds are smart dogs. They assess one another. 820 metres is a marathon for a modern dog, though some races in Ireland are over a nominal 1000 yards. '820 metres is about half a mile and I think it's as far as any dog really should have to go. One of the reasons I'm not in favour of the really long hard distances is because the dogs don't truly set off at a gallop and keep that gallop up over the distance. They adjust. You'll see a dog like Sandy Lane who won the 1983 BBC TV Trophy; if she gets out reasonably slowly she'll thread her way through the field, saving some of her energies for her storming finish. She allows the other dogs to make the pace. Experienced greyhounds know when they're in a marathon. A dog going over the distance for the first time will often shoot out thinking it's a four-bender and suddenly realize, "My God, it's an eight," and drop away to nothing. Eastern Highway, one of the dogs I train, shuts herself completely off. If she really put herself out early on she wouldn't be sure to stay 1000 yards, as she does.' When a dog is tired, it's looking for an excuse to get beaten. Some simply fall over their own feet.

Irish breeding is respected all over the world. John Sherry says that, whereas English breeding is often largely based on the stud book, Irishmen will go out and watch local dogs coursing or racing to spot a fiery one 'with a little bit of boldness in him'. A wellbred dog with paper qualifications may be 'nowhere keen at all'. Besides, 'The race is not always to the fastest, is it?' Irish trainers like Sherry value killer instinct. 'If you see two dogs coursing a hare they'll turn very sharply, whereas on the track they may have learned to float up around a bend. I think they've got an idea that it's just a dummy they're following, but if it were a real one and it cut to the inside, there'd be a lot of dogs who dug in after it.'

Old bruisers and tacklers like those in the Greyhound Hall of Fame in Kansas and various British museums are noticeably rougher cut, shaggier and less fairy-waisted than today's sylphs. You can't count the ribs of Mick the Miller (BMNH), whose record of nineteen consecutive wins to 1931 eluded all dogs until 1974; or of Fullerton (Tring), winner of four Waterloo Cups, 1889–92. They had to rough it in those days and grew furry and sturdy because there were no centrally heated kennels or recuperative medicines. Some of these dogs were awesome. In the States, Lucky Pilot won sixty-one of his eighty-three races, and Indy Ann won 137 in the 1950s. Master McGrath was beaten only once in his career in Britain from 1867–73, a triple Waterloo Cup champion. His owner had apparently rescued him from a farmer about to drown a worthless pup.

'Absolutely every one of them is different,' says John Sherry. 'People have a cunning and educatedness about them, but dogs tend to be true to their character.' There are extroverts, wide runners, dogs that check on bends and dogs like Adamstown Miller that never stop barking. The trainers, owners and high rollers know who they are. The form line in your race programme gives you the date of the dog's last outing, distance, going, trap, position on each bend, finish, nearest rival, distance between them, time, weight and starting price. There is a column called 'remarks' with abbreviations for bumped, bunched, baulked, cramp, forced wide, hampered, knocked over, slow away and so forth. 'Brit' denotes British bred (Irish being the norm) and 'S' in the breeding line denotes the seasonal date for bitches. Races are over in a flash but there is a lengthy check-in beforehand to prevent easy-money shenanigans. The dogs are trained to urinate in a bowl for chromotography testing and their ears are tattooed with an identity number to prevent last-minute swops ('ringing'). Nobbling with titbits is deterred by muzzles and tight security and the dogs are weighed in like boxers and scrutinized by a vet. Weren't they a little thin? I asked. 'No,' said vet Mike Findlay of the British Small Animals Veterinary Association (BSAVA). 'If a dog is starved it won't race.'

The big money comes from the tote, the tick-tack and the betting rather than prize-money, though the *Daily Mirror* Derby offers £25,000. The dogs do it for nothing and from their viewpoint it can be dangerous. Spills, pile-ups and dogs lamed at 35 m.p.h. are not uncommon. 'And that,' said a commentator's voice over a three-dog crash on screen before one of the TV Trophy heats, 'is an example of the sort of thrills one can expect to see in greyhound racing!'

For dogs that provide no thrills, there is abandonment, especially from the unlicensed amateur flapper tracks up and down the country. Every animal-rescue centre I visited had greyhounds a-plenty, skeletons covered in sores who had come fifth or sixth instead of first or second. There are emaciated creatures like 'Bambi', re-christened by kennel girls of the NCDL, whose PR officer Clarissa Baldwin told me, 'Ten per cent of the dogs brought to us are greyhounds: they are our very biggest problem.' They haven't been housetrained and the staff have to put jumpers on them in the winter to stop their bones from rattling and waking up the other waifs. An RSPCA treasurer, Philip Hale, described a batch they had in from Brighton. 'Failed racers. We had a lot of trouble re-homing them and most had to be put down.' And Battersea manager, Major Eric Stones, told me, 'I get in about twenty greyhounds a month.' (He says they make dear pets, if you're interested.)

The greyhound, with its well-sprung ribs and muscular physique, hauling its hind paws in front of its extended fore paws like a hare, is the archetypal race-dog. There are others. The American Sighthound Field Association organizes lure field trials for gazehounds: greyhounds, salukis, borzois, whippets, Scottish deerhounds, Irish wolfhounds and Afghans. Three dogs are brought to the starting line and released to the cry of 'Tally Ho!' after a mechanical lure doing 35–50 m.p.h. The borzoi was the coursing hound of the Tsars and was used against wolves. Callow dogs were torn down in their quarry's fury, considered an elegant spectacle. The borzoi has (or had) great strength and speed, but needed a ten-acre field to turn in. He was known as the 'fantailed greyhound' then. Other cousins, like the deerhound or buckhound, coursed stags. The elkhound and Irish wolfhound provided terrific 'sport', and the 'gre-hounde' himself was often wirehaired and very like them. The saluki, or his lookalike ancestor, was admitted to the tents of Sheikhs and Bedouin warriors. He coursed the gazelle, blinded by hawks, and outstripped the wild ass of the desert. When the saluki saw game afoot, his legs and toes went so rigid that it was impossible to move them until he took flight. An Arab poet of AD 800 (Abu Nawass) said of the elfin creature, 'He peels the skin of the earth with his four feet.' The Afghanistan version was also used for coursing, though Afghans of old were small and short-coated. (The first pair Britain ever set eyes on are in Tring Museum.) They race today in the UK, as do most gazehounds, information available courtesy of the breed clubs.

Or how about British whippet racing 'to the rag' as Northern 'butties' used to say? Whippets have out-cross terrier blood in their veins. They do not take kindly to being beaten, or even to winning, and set about their fellow competitors over the smallest point. Hence the name 'snap dogs'. Muzzled, they do a ferocious 30-odd m.p.h. Their old sport was to course rabbits on enclosed ground, the rabbits being netted and bundled in sacks for the purpose.[6] Lures, mechanically drawn or flapped at the finishing line are more convenient.

Whippets racing to stuffed rabbitskins, rags, streamers and onion bags were popular long before greyhound tracks, especially in colliery towns. On Sunday mornings miners are still at it, boasting and wagering in the pub beforehand. They don't have 'throwers' any more to hurl the dogs on their way[7] though a good thrower was worth 5 yards on the cinder tracks. They are now held neck and crotch and handslipped, or put in staggered traps. Whippets are even thinner than greyhounds, because in their races there's a handicapping system. Owners are forever weighing them in canvass trusses from hooks, as a pound in weight equals a yard handicap, which means a 30lbs dog having to catch up 10 yards (in 165) on a dog of 20lbs. The whippet gobbles his meals with the speed of an advertisement. They cry frenziedly in the traps and go snarling mad when they find they have been deceived in the matter of the lure. Miners who love them keep them as house pets. They are fiercely affectionate and though thin are not as frail as the miniatures they resemble. (Italian greyhounds of old could be seen through if you held them up to the sun, and broken if handled roughly.)

Not all racing dogs are emaciated whisps, or course. You may not see Yorkshire terriers coursing rats these days, but you can watch other terriers such as Jack Russells exploding like bats out of hell after a rabbitskin and fighting afterwards over technicalities. The South East Jack Russell Club organizes races for fun at Farncombe in Surrey, and there are other clubs and venues. You should see them go.

Perhaps you don't just want to watch, though. Sled-racing with coonhounds, Malamutes (USA), Irish setters, retrievers, elkhounds, Dalmatians, Akitas, GSDs, Samoyeds and *especially* huskies, is a growth sport in North America and Europe. You don't have to have snow. Wheeled carts (called rigs in Europe and gigs in the States) glide just as thrillingly behind a loping team, and as one American racer puts it: 'It is a silent ride and takes the driver back to nature and the elements.'[8] The Siberian Husky Club of GB organizes both snow and wheel rallies in the UK at venues like Glen Esk, Perth (snow), Aviemore in the Highlands (snow) and Thetford, Norfolk (wheels). They've only just started but hope to make the sled rally an annual event. Huskies are excellent team dogs, though Sammies (Samoyeds) pull with them amicably, for example in Leeds and Manchester. European events are controlled by the European Sled Dog Racing Association (ESDRA) and American and international races by the International Sled Dog Racing Association (ISDRA). There are even weight-pulling contests in the US; a dog must drag a sled or 'gig' with 200lbs on board for 20 feet in ninety seconds in order to qualify. Races are either sprint or long-distance (150–250 miles), though the most famous one of all, the Iditarod, is 1049 miles between Anchorage and Nome, Alaska, over rugged terrain in blizzards. The prize is $250,000. Cries of Moosh, Mush and Ka-ka-ka echo down the Bering Sea coast, with banners posted along the way saying 'Nome or bust!' Many bust. The trail began as a diversion for bored gold-panners in winter months, and now provides an agony for the world's best mushers and their dogs. Few teams finish with their full complement in harness, and a lot don't finish at all. The rules are pretty simple. 'Hike' means 'go', 'Whoa' means 'stop', 'Gee' means 'right turn', 'Haw' means 'left turn' and 'Aagh!' means 'help!'

THE EARTH DOG

Do not go gentle into that good night.
Rage, rage against the dying of the light.
Dylan Thomas

When animals are sawn-off little runts, it is usual to trivialize their passions. The lower and nearer to earth an animal is, the more man looks down on its rage and fear as having comical significance, or no significance at all. It is very well for man's conscience that this is so, or his imagination might make the nightmare journey into a creature cowering in the ground, or a creature sent into the blackness to look for it.

Terriers derive their name from the latin *terra*, earth. Elizabethan Dr Caius, though, alludes both to the earth and the terror.

> Another sort there is which hunteth the fox and badger or grey only – whom we call Terrars because they creep into the ground and by that means make afraid, nip and bite the fox and badger in such sort, that either they tear them in pieces with their teeth, baying in the bosom of the earth, or else nail and pull them perforce out of their lurking angles, dark dungeons and close caves.

The courage necessary to perform this service for man, challenging an animal perhaps larger than itself, desperate and in its own den, can scarcely be guessed at. The badger, mink and otter (seeking refuge in a holt) are *mustelidae*, ferocious dragons to a little dog. Yet terriers have been shoved into holes and crevices for centuries to kill or bolt whatever lurked there. Many have never come out again, or reappeared triumphant only to be broken by hounds mistaking the terrier for their quarry. The earth dog is purpose-built for his calling. Short-legged, small and compact for boring down tunnels, flexible-backed for wriggling in labyrinths, strong-pawed and clawed for scuttling, stern-jawed and scissor-biting, harsh-coated against the elements, indomitable and heedless of pain or death, and with a frenzied high-pitched yapping bark to signal the quarry's position to heroes standing above ground with spades. Many old-fashioned terriers had folded ears to keep the dirt out, though this was the least of their worries. Practically all of the fighting pit-dogs had terrier blood, because unlike most other hunting assistants the earth dog is not just an accomplice. He is a pugnacious killer in his own right.

Most dog people, be they never so snobbish or pedigree-conscious, salute the terrier, though his origins are humble and obscure. The varieties we have now owe their distinction to shows, beginning in 1859. Before that, terriers were local boys with no time for primping or prettifying. They were lucky if they fell in the river and got a bath.

Many of the old names are forgotten, the dogs going to ground or marauding about the countryside killing anything remotely verminous. There is a lot of tiresome romancing among nineteenth-century breeders concerning dogs rescued from shipwrecks, and other myths of origin, to account for their particular breeds. All we can say with certainty is that most were British (isolated Boston, Tibetan and Schnauzery types are not of The Family). Many were grizzle, or black-and-tan, and variations of this rough type occurred in different areas by crossing with hounds or other dogs, according to the work in hand.

Peering through the mists of time, some authorities believe they see terriers in Egyptian bas-reliefs and imagine they were used to protect grain stores. I've never seen any myself. There's a skeleton about the size of a foxterrier at Windmill Hill, dated to 1750 BC[1] and the second-century Greek writer Oppian could well have been referring to terriers when he says,

> But there is a certain strong breed of hunting dogs, small, but worthy of a sublime song, which the wild tribes of Britain maintain. . . . Their size is indeed equal to that of the pampered domestic table dogs – crooked, slight, shaggy, dull-eyed, but their feet armed with formidable nails, and furnished with numerous envenomed teeth.

One of Oppian's translators calls the dogs *Agassoei*, 'beagles'.[2] 'Beagle' came from the Celtic word *beag* meaning 'little 'un' like the Welsh *bach*. The English corruption, 'brach', appears in Tom's list of dogs in *King Lear*. A book about rural sport of 1486 lists various 'houndes' of England including 'Teroures' (terrors?).[3] And to cap it all, Turberville in his *Noble Art of Venerie or Hunting* (1575) describes how 'terryers' should go to earth, translating from a French original by du Fouilloux who says the dog is called a 'basset'.[4] Commentators say 'basset' here is just a generic term for little 'un, like beagle, because nobody can picture either hound going to earth. The reader is left to ponder the matter. Turberville, who knew a bit about British dogs, is quite clear that a 'terryer' is the dog for the job. That popular excavator of gardens, the Jack-of-all-trades Russell, has often been used for rabbiting, alone or with ferrets, and in the nineteenth century there was a rickety relation of his whose legs splayed out to prevent him from flushing too quickly for the muzzle-loaded gun.[5] The Jack Russell is still used in 'bobbery' packs hunting rabbits (Sealyhams were once used the same way) and, of course, he goes to earth too, like a true 'terryer'. One called Micky recently burrowed down and dug up his canine friend Percy, presumed dead and buried in the garden.

Terriers are much older than organized foxhunting. They were the traditional rodenting and rabbiting dogs of farmworkers, tinkers and gipsies. When the king and his court hunted the stag and boar, they had little use for the curs of yokels and crofters rabbiting and ratting in the back spinney. Shepherds had little time for them either and called all terriers 'rabbit dogs'.[6] The gentry, limited to smaller quarry than their lords and masters, took more interest and may have called upon a local 'varmint' to bolt the odd fox for them if their hounds weren't up to it (or rather down to it). There were plenty of foxes then; you scarcely needed to worry the ones that found sanctuary and ferrets were on hand for emergencies. Gradually though, the big game ran out and the king and court competed with the gentry for smaller fry – there were less to go round. Foxes no longer had their holes in which to lay their heads; these were stopped with earth or flushed with the yokel's varmint. In time, M F Hs began breeding earth dogs of their own, perfecting an elegant, often predominantly white terrier so that idiots would not yell 'Gone away!' when it poked its head out of the ground. Some are long-legged and run with hounds; others are hauled along in bags and baskets, bumping rudely against a huntsman's saddle, or are summoned, with the 'terrier man' who also stops the earths, by a blast of the horn.

The Rev. W. B. Daniel in 1801, describing badger digging and baiting, says there were then two kinds of terrier: one long-backed, short-legged and rough, either black or cream coloured; the other short-bodied, smooth and beautifully formed, either red-brown or black-and-tan.[7] Many of these dogs were killed in the badger's set or burrow because, whereas a fox will usually stand at bay unless driven to desperation, a badger will charge and can inflict terrible wounds by clenching the dog's chest and throat. A sporting magazine of 1834 seems to confirm the terrier 'types' of the period. 'There are two kinds of terriers – the rough-haired Scotch and the smooth English.'[8] The Scottish were apparently sand, black, white or pied, harsh-coated and of a general cairn-cum-Scottie-cum-Westie aspect. The English were said to be smooth black-and-tan, though there was also an English white, now extinct.

Apart from earthworks, there was another little job. Farm labourers have traditionally made whoopee at harvest time – ratting. A few lanterns or torches, a few terriers, and a ferret released into a hayrick have provided many an evening's entertainment. The terrier usually dispatches a rat by the viverrid kill: a neck snap accompanied by shaking. In towns the rat-catcher, with his bundle of implements in a kerchief and a long cane with a brass concussion knob on the end, would bring his crop-eared terriers round at your request and bear the corpses away afterwards. He sometimes carried a set of ferrets in a cage for flushing tight corners, wore clodhoppers, and his trousers securely fastened below the knee with gaiters.

When the animal-loving British public were cruelly deprived, by prohibition, of bull baiting and dog-fights, they were sorely pressed to find something to do. Zoos were all right, but none of the inhabitants got killed and you couldn't bet on the chimps' tea-party. So the dog pits were adapted slightly and became the rat pits. It gave the ex-champion gladiators a new start in life. Large pockets were hung on the side posts for the dead, and ingenious wooden blocks were nailed into each corner of the high-sided pits to prevent the rats forming a pyramid and climbing into the crowd. Sacks full of rats (ratbags) were brought in and wagers struck on the first dog to kill one, the dog to kill most, and the dog to break the killing record, held by a bullterrier bitch, Jenny Lind, with 500 in one-and-a-half hours. Billy the black-and-tan hung his head in shame, with only 100 rats in one hour forty minutes.

None of those do-gooding animal-welfare people could have any objection to this pastime: why, it was a service to humanity. The smooth-haired black-and-tan terrier from Manchester was a star, as was that tough miners' terrier, the Yorkshire, the grim reaper of rodents. What the miners would have said to the modern show Yorkie with his hair in paper bangers, decency forbids speculating. The Australian terrier, a nephew of the ratting Yorkshire, is still used for work Down Under. The dogs' ears and tails were often cropped to offer less tiny teethholds. Terriers are employed ratting in the UK and US today, but anyone about to put his dogs down a manhole should consider carefully: ratting can be extremely dangerous for them. Not only will they sometimes kill one another in their hunting frenzy, but they may be seriously injured by their quarry. Rats carry a form of Leptospirosis known as L. Icterohaemorrhagiae. The disease will probably kill an uninoculated dog and can be transmitted to humans. You may imagine what happened before modern medicine when the town and country rat-disposer went to work in plague years.

Some Earthy Characters

Since the first great terrier show, 1886, most of the dogs have become stylish, or stylized, depending whether you like shows or not. Those that work hardest have changed least; some have divided into show and working varieties; a few are unrecognizable. Despite their vocation, terriers seem to bear mankind no illwill, and with few exceptions make staunch and devoted friends. Here's a Who's Who of a few:

Airedale   The largest, formerly Waterside or Bingley terrier, bred in the Aire Valley, Yorkshire. Quiet (for a terrier), responsible, trusted with war and police work. Used to be even larger.

Bedlington   From the Northumberland nailers' village. Once a fighter, poacher, hunter and courser. Now lamblike, fleecy but fast.

Border   Can run with hounds all day over Northumberland and Border heather. Outstandingly brave, squirms into tiny crevices after the fox. 'Many of the Border Terriers go to ground every season, never to reappear.'[9]

Cairn   For dislodging quarry from cairns and caverns. Many have been wedged fast pursuing the fox, wildcat and otter. A 9lbs mite received a working certificate from the master of North Warwick Hounds for bolting a fox and a big badger on one outing. Cornerstone of the Scottish stock.

Dandie Dinmont   Once the hard, mustard-and-pepper hunter of gipsies and Border farmers, like Walter Scott's in *Guy Mannering*, published 1815. A judge at the 1867 Birmingham show said they were all mongrels, but the modern Dandie is very natty, with a fetching bouffant hairstyle.

Jack Russell   The Vicar of Swimbridge's terrier, larger than today's and valued for pluck and good sense. 'Tip' would go off alone and wait outside the earth for the homecoming fox. 'Not meant to murder,' Russell said, but to bay and bolt the quarry.

Lakeland   Surefooted local terriers like the Patterdale have both run with hounds and followed the Fell packs on foot; they still do. They work on rough terrain; Lakelands have died of exposure and been buried alive in the rocks where they kill and bolt the formidable Fell fox.

Manchester   The old-fashioned black-and-tan. Called the English terrier but 'Manchester' to distinguish him from the extinct English white. Champion ratter.

Norfolk and **Norwich**   Cousins. Both game and conscientious roughcoats. The hairy-chested Norfolk was originally the Drop-Eared Norwich.

Sealyham   Bred by Captain John Edwardes of Sealyham House, Pembroke in the 1850s as a fox, badger and otter dog. Tested by Edwardes for bravery, using polecats. Show variety very posh.

Skye   Shaggy Scots burrower used to drive badger, fox and marten. Defended Scottish flocks from wildcats and other predators in 1700. Now a *chien de luxe*.

Smooth and Wirehaired Fox Terriers   Very popular chaps at the turn of the century. Show variety with so-called 'punishing jaw' very different from the worker. The wirehaired was common in Durham, Derby and Wales.

Staffordshire and **Bullterrier**   Fighting dogs from the Black Country and working districts (see chapter on Gladiators).

Yorkshire   Tiny now; once a fiery miners' ratter.

Welsh   A sterling black-and-tan worker; very brave and once often torn to pieces by hounds mistaking his colouring for their fox. Probably ancient and not just a 'miniature Airedale'.

Scottish Descended from the old cairn, Highland and Aberdeen ('Scottie') types. Rough and bonnie wee hunters. The West Highland White was made famous by Colonel E. D. Malcolm of Poltalloch, Argyll. In two years (1901–2) his dogs killed 193 foxes with their own teeth. Before this, white pups were generally drowned as 'weaklings'.

Irish terriers Fierce and fiery. The Irish proper or 'Red Devil', and the Blue Irish or Kerry Blue, were traditionally bred to kill. The Glen of Imaal and Soft-Coated Wheaten champions are still required to undergo trials for courage and gameness using badgers, rabbits, rats, foxes and water-tests.

II

SNIFFERS AND TRACKERS

Eager 'Glen', a small black labrador, comes into the vast training hanger at RAF Newton with his tongue hanging out of his head, tail wagging furiously. A piece of cannabis resin, about the size of your little fingernail, inside a polythene bag, inside a plastic carton, has been hidden somewhere in the hanger, amongst furniture, training equipment, coaches, cars and GSDs, as big as donkeys, barking in temporary kennels.

'There's no hokey-pokey laid on for the press,' says Warrant Officer George Clapperton, pointing out car interiors torn to bits by the drug and FX (firearms and explosives) search dogs. 'They go in everywhere.' Glen, aged two, prancing and dancing, is keen to get on with it. His harness is put on and he runs in a 'free search', his handler watching carefully. 'When the dog gets near the object, you'll see that extra fizz. That's what we call body language,' says Flight Sergeant Trevor Figgins. 'The drug sniffer has complete freedom; the FX dog always works 40 yards in front of you – you don't go anywhere the dog hasn't been. We put distractions in their way during training, like other animals, a bitch in season, and the dog must walk round them. You imagine the country roads in unfriendly territory, all those Jack Russells coming out and having a go. The concentration comes from the reward at the end. The dog thinks: "I've got to get that reward! It's mine! My plaything!"' Warrant Officer Clapperton: 'He's got to be fit, a bit of a hooligan, jumping onto obstacles, and robust so that he can bash into things without hurting himself. Note the slippery lino too: a dog can be super and yet pack up on polished linoleum.'

Glen rushes up to the hot spot, his feet scuttling and sliding, his whole body suddenly a-quiver. He's got it. A couple of minutes, a whole hanger, a little dog.

'We encourage possession,' says Flt Sgt Figgins, 'and we ask for the thing. It's not an order. Which is why we never use check chains.' Glen is now involved in a tremendous game of 'Wassiss!' with the empty carton, leaping and fetching. They show me the cannabis, unlicked. Don't the dogs get

94

addicted? 'No, they never come into contact with the substance. Only the scent. It's like you smelling perfume or aftershave.' The RAF Police Dog School trains an elite (as we shall see) with a 3 per cent selection rate on the search side, for the Royal Air Force, HM Customs and Excise, the US Air Force, the Royal Navy and the US Navy, and they are constantly consulted by authorities around the world. How do their dogs do it? Who knows? Over at the Royal Army Veterinary Corps Training Centre in Melton Mowbray I asked the same question.

'In Northern Ireland we've had a dog indicate on a brick wall, and found a rifle that had been cemented up for twenty-five years. What scent is that?' says Captain Tony Rossell. 'We're probably just scratching the surface of the animal's ability. If I could talk to a dog for five minutes in my life, that would be better than winning the pools. Take our mine-detection dogs, for instance. We assume the dog is using scent, but what if it isn't? What if it's detecting density differences in the ground, or sending out radio waves, or detecting thermal differences? We don't know. In the early fifties a veterinary surgeon came here and removed the scenting membranes of certain dogs, yet they could still work. Of course, that doesn't prove anything. Taste and scent are inextricably linked; perhaps they were using taste.' (More on military sniffing in the chapter on War and Patrol.)

What about the civilian Police Force? Police sniffers and trackers are, for the most part, general-duty dogs, though they do have specialists for FX, drugs and bodies, rather misleadingly called 'dual purpose'. The Dog in Blue, whether searching an area for property or persons, or following a 'track' or ground scent, is keying on that most sensitive of targets, humanity. Because he is dealing with the public he must always mind his 'p's and 'q's. When he finds an article bearing human scent, he brings it back to 'dad' who decides if it's the murder weapon or a cigarette packet. That decision is not the dog's job. He is a 'Good lad!' whatever he fetches. When he finds a fugitive, that person may not be a criminal. It may be a child or a mental patient. That decision is not the dog's job either. An RAF patrol dog who 'windscents' you on an Air Force installation will aggressively attack you because you have no right to be there. A police dog, once he reaches his quarry, must use the softly softly approach. He must guard it, scrutinize it, bark at it to tell 'dad', but he must not bite, unless instructed to do so. The police are full of admiration for the canine proboscis. How do they do it? I asked Inspector Simon Edwards of Kent Constabulary's dog section at Maidstone? 'Nobody knows.' (See The Dog in Blue.) Consider the past.

During the tyrannical rule of the dinosaurs in the Mezozoic our poor little shrew-like mammal ancestors ran and hid in the forests away from those clumping feet. It was very dark and they developed a brain modification called the neopallium, a sort of inner space for interpreting the murky world outside through scenting, whiskering and listening. Eventually man's line, the primates, diverged and began climbing up trees into the light. They developed colour vision and forward-facing eyes. Their noses fell into disrepair.

The dog's ancestors (*Canidae*) remained in the dark. Dogs still see in wooded shades of green, grey and brown, but their noses are magic. The dog has a wonderful array of nasal epithelia and blood vessels, and glands at the base of his tail and between his toes for leaving complex messages and markings we humbly call 'scents'.[1] They are chemically extremely complex and contain information on mood, sex, dominance, time and space. The dog's urine and faeces are imbued with highly specific traces and he has a pair of small apertures, called Jacobson's organs, in the roof of his mouth, for 'tasting' the air and decoding all the information. He grins and licks, and licks and grins; we call this *Flehmen*, but we don't really know what he's smiling about. Nor can we say how a dog 'vets' our acquaintances for us: scent is evidently more sophisticated than language. It enables dogs to travel vast distances over unfamiliar country in search of their owners. One dog, during the First World War, went all the way from Hammersmith to Armentières to find his master in the trenches,[2] and there are other reliably authenticated stories of bizarre dog journeys. We talk vaguely about 'homing instinct', though the direction is often not homewards at all. Perhaps the dog is keying on what Russian parapsychologists call bioenergy, the aura of whiskery traces given off by animals and inanimate objects that psychics claim to be able to see. The traces have been photographed by a process known as Kirlian photography (I had my hands done once) and marine biologists are now suggesting this energy source is the trigger for shark attacks. Could this be how little Glen finds his cannabis?

Since the RAF began recruiting dogs in 1941, well over 10,000 have been trained. Nine have won the Dickin medal, the animals' VC. Worldwide, the Air Force have around 800 dogs operational, on patrol at military installations, and detecting drugs, firearms and explosives. (They have sniffed for 'black boxes' or flight recorders too.) All their dogs are unconditional gifts from the public. (Their shop window, the demonstration team, travel over the country in coaches, to jump through hoops of fire, etc.)

The RAF look for GSDs for patrol and, principally, gundogs for sniffing, although the first three sniffers were GSDs. The individual is more important than the breed and they've had success with labradors, springer spaniels, a flat-coated retriever called Wallace, a Münsterlander, the Irish water spaniel, GSDs, Weimaraners, German shorthaired pointers and nose-orientated Border collies. (Bloodhounds? 'No thanks: their eyes are dust traps.') They need a dog with hunting determination, retrieving talent, mobility and robustness, that won't get sick in a van. They don't like 'nervous aggression' but would consider other breeds, crosses and personalities with the right qualifications. If you have such a one to give, under three years, write to the Officer Commanding, RAF Police School, RAF Newton, Notts NG13 8HL, and their experts will travel out, anywhere, to have a look at it. (If it's under ten months, plan ahead.) It's hard work, nosing over big ships and jumbos, but the dogs are considered precious jewels and have grand careers. They are not regimental tools and the emphasis is on a rapport between the handler and his dog, whose welfare comes before domestic problems.

The sniffer is a dog of initiative. No one must interfere with his scent patterns. 'If we make a mistake with a trainee handler, we whittle him out. He'll never touch one of our search dogs again. A handler can ruin a dog on a scent pattern in five minutes; less than that. You saw Glen running round there; if that handler had raised his voice and given Glen a good shouting at just as he was getting near the article – that dog is trained to have possessional rights – a lot of time would have to be spent recovering the dog. That man would be out. Finished.' When a sniffer does hear a harsh word, it generally means 'danger'.

The RAF basically loan the trained dog out to one of their user agencies with his or her trained handler. The dog is checked every six weeks by inspectors 'and they'll take the dog away if it's not being properly treated or falling down on training'. Demand for RAF dogs worldwide is enormous and growing, though they are the most expensive in the business. This is because, for every 100 dogs offered for search work, on average three will pass out of their rigorous fifteen-week course. Most don't get on it. 'We're so exacting on search, especially FX,' says Warrant Officer Clapperton, 'where we've got to be minutely correct. It's not just the handler's life that's at stake; it's all the people coming behind him when the area's been cleared'.

Not everyone under investigation likes the sniffer dogs. They get the odd crafty kick from 'searchees', but this is in contrast to their five-star treatment at the RAF. Newton has a specially designed complex for them where the recruits are inspected monthly by a vet. 'If a month is missed, somebody gets his head in his hands to play with.' Each dog has his own file, called a 4629, recording his personal details. These make amazing reading. Take, for example, Brandy, a ten-year-old yellow labrador cross, with an NCDL Certificate for Services to Humanity. Brandy has made over 160 finds, itemized in his file, amounting to 4040 kilos of drugs worth £4 million. Discoveries range from seeds and particles to 230lbs of herbal cannabis hidden in seventy-seven oil paintings, sealed and crated, worth £115,000 and four arrests; 25 kilos of compressed herbal hidden in a consignment of New Testaments, and 97¾lbs of herbal locked behind steel doors below deck on a ship. From 30 yards off, Brandy's nose was infallible. Drugs hidden in bath salts, chilli powder, a hollow elephant, cold-drink cans, toilet rolls, film cannisters; 4 tons of Colombian 'grass', stacked in an Essex shed; 400 grammes of herbal wrapped in four plastic bags, bound with sellotape, and submerged in a tank of coolant fluid. All fell to the deadly nostrils of Brandy.

A black labrador, Brumby, another decorated sniffer (Pro-Dog's Gold Medal) was a failed guide dog. Seconded to HM Customs and Excise, Brumby made 210 drug finds, also totalling £4 million-odd, concealed in everything from cars to antiseptic cream. One whiff was enough. The drug industry is rich and sophisticated, as the RAF search museum at Newton demonstrates. The tide of stuff hidden in sports gear, furniture, car engines, piping and hollow screwdrivers may also be treated with pungent smells, mothballs, perfume, dog odours and suchlike to trick the dog's nose. ('When there's a strong disguising scent you suspect something anyway.') One ruse is to stash the contraband in a petrol tank, with a couple of pints of petrol, to squeak through Customs. But no matter what the human imagination can devise, the dog goes straight to the merchandise. Dogs are not logical; wit is wasted on them. Of course they can get bored. 'A dog at Heathrow is going to burn out quicker than a dog at an easier collection.' The RAF emphasize variety, keeping doggy happy.

Just how 'happy' are they? The drug-detection ones are trained for cannabis (all types and derivatives), cocaine and heroin rather than hallucinogens that can be absorbed through the skin. 'The drugs are hidden in retrievable aids. In the field the dog can never get to it anyway. He will simply indicate, say, the bulkhead of a ship, and we'll reward the dog with something of our own that has the scent on it. Good dog. Then we get our screwdrivers out.' They have to have absolute confidence in the dog's judgement. If we start taking a person's car to bit, we have to justify our actions.'

Any accidents? 'We've had a dog in training that's ingested a small piece of cannabis – a simple case of making the dog vomit – but in all the years we've been using the dogs, we've never had a drug accident.' In the US narcotics' dogs go on busts and are given regular blood and urine checks to test for absorption. They don't seem to be addicted either. They sniff the substances out to please man and, if possible, have a game, or a peppermint. 'We only train on the real thing here,' said Trevor Figgins. 'Real drugs, real explosives. We re-pack the drug every time because the only thing you want constant in every single search is the sample. All accompanying scents must be different, even the packer.' The aids are sterilized. 'There are four things that go to make up a scent picture: the drug, the scent of the aid, the human scent, and the disturbance. You change the other three all the time.' Gluts create more addicts; the pushers love that. Heroin is going for a song at the moment, and arrives in kilos like packets of sugar: £60 a gramme at 30 per cent purity, £180 a gramme at 90 per cent. Without the dogs we should be swamped.

How was the first drug-dog chosen? 'The search side came about as an experiment,' said George Clapperton. 'We were asked if we could train a dog to detect drugs, and we weren't too sure. A GSD called Rex, with a very bad hip deformity, was about to be put down, so we tried him out and he was so successful that we progressed from there. I'd like to convince you that Glen's not just a one-off. Every dog passing out of here is as good as Glen.'

George Clapperton's dream is to return to the early days of their illustrious founder, Colonel James Baldin, by breeding their own dogs. He personally feels it's a 'tremendous lottery' at the moment, competing for publicly rejected GSDs with the Army, Police and security firms. 'I'm hoping like billio to get to Sweden, where they've got a fantastic government breeding complex, and a computer *at the kennels*, mind you, to eradicate hip dysplasia and other serious canine defects.' For scenting, the US like beagles, but the RAF don't think they're quite up to scratch. They take a pride in their own methods, though they get to see everyone else's. The Germans use dual-purpose dogs for drugs and tracking. One centre George Clapperton visited trained dogs on bits of bodies from a mortuary, buried in the soil.

The best RAF sniffers are assigned to bomb-detection. It's more demanding. 'We get feedback from various agencies,' says Trevor Figgins. 'If they're using new methods or new explosives, we have to conquer it.' Forensic laboratories have broken down all FX materials into scent patterns, of sulphur, nitroglycerin, etc., and a lot of research has been carried out in the States since the Federal government began sponsoring a bomb-detection programme in the 1970s. A dog can find a gun muzzle in a scrap-metal yard fairly easily; a scrap-metal yard hasn't got cordite or gun oil in it. But the real secrets remain locked away behind the peculiar *Flehmen* grin of a scenting dog. One found a rocket-launcher hidden in bales of straw. He was out exercising.

The technology ranged against FX dogs is macabre: detonators and trigger mechanisms hidden in cigarette packets, sex books, light bulbs; bombs designed to go off as a car goes uphill, like Airey Neave's; contacts made with ball-bearings, pins, crystals, barley. The dogs only have to indicate to be called away: they don't go sticking their noses into it. 'It wouldn't be worth spending five months training them if they got blown up,' said Trevor Figgins. 'I'm not saying they never do, but we're working as a team, dog and handler. We haven't lost a dog yet, and that's through control. When the dog indicates he's into the scent, he's called off. We clear the way for the Army. Goodbye, we're going.' (For RAF patrol dogs, see the chapter on War and Patrol.)

Hounds that hunt by scent, as distinct from gazehounds, have given man a new lease on whatever is lost or hidden. A scent-hound may be trained to find just about anything sniffy in return for praise. He doesn't mind if he can't eat it. He relinquished that right long ago, when man began using his canines as cutlery. There are accounts of dogs locating all sorts of fascinating things: fish, for instance, like salmon, trout, carp, even minnows. Dogs were popularly used on the coast of Normandy, until quite recently, to take the conger eel. An old woman with a pick-axe and her dog 'Trompette' (a white Spitz) are described 'eeling' in Jesse's famous canine history. The dog scratches and whines to 'indicate' and the old girl, brandishing her pick, tears at the sand until an eel falls out. Braining it on the beach she drops it into her basket and the two trot quietly on their way.[3]

The bloodhound hunts bigger fish: any sort of fugitive, slave or criminal – it's all the same to him. Although he is now a mild fellow, his footfall once struck terror in the fugitive's heart. How he acquired his Baskervillian reputation is interesting. Our huge black-and-tan friend with the baggy eyes is descended from the hound of St Hubert at his monastery in the Ardennes (the white version or Talbot was an equally famous packhound). Whether William the Conqueror brought him to Britain or found him here already, the bloodhound soon became very adept at owning the line of cattle-thieves and raiders, called moss troopers, along the Scottish border. A tax was levied by the Crown to pay for 'the dogges' policing the swamps. The Bishop of Ross in 1578 wrote that 'these are endowed with great sagacity and fierceness, that they pursue thieves in a direct course without any deviation, and this with such ferocity of nature that they tear them to pieces, even by chance lying down in company with many others'.[4]

Another authority in 1777 refers to 'slough-dogs' pursuing moss troopers. 'The dogs were commonly called blood-hounds . . . the Scots used the term "red-hand" to this pursuit method,'[5] hence 'caught red-handed'. Sounds rather messy.

Columbus used the hounds against the Indians. And 100 bloodhounds from Havana were sent to quell a Maroon uprising in Jamaica in 1795.[6] A demonstration was ordered at Seven Rivers to quieten the African insurgents. Forty thousand fusiliers discharged their guns and the dogs were sufficiently upset to drag their Spanish chasseurs along, in spite of all endeavours, and seize some of the hardware. They were with difficulty restrained from setting about a lofty general, who got back very smartly into his chaise, and the negroes, having capitulated, were sent to Halifax, North America, to cool their heels. Advertisements appeared in Britain for bloodhounds guaranteed game for slaves, as a deterrent to escapees, and bloodcurdling stories abounded of dogs fed on slave-flesh.

Modern bloodhound-lovers are quick to defend the dogs from such character-assassination, saying it was all a ploy to frighten the natives. Peter Boddy runs the famous Reddyfield pack who 'hunt the clean boot'. The quarry is given an hour's start or so, 'depending on how good a runner he is', and the hounds are set on. 'You can read all sorts of things in books,' says Mr Boddy, 'but there never has been a vicious strain of bloodhounds. Our hounds don't attack the quarry. If they know him they'll lick him, and if they don't they'll fade away 10 or 15 yards from him, which is why the police don't use them.' (A couple of policemen, one from Durham with bloodhound experience, confirmed this observation.) Mr Boddy's bloodhounds are of the old type. 'To breed anything with such a big ugly head as they do now is sheer cruelty. They can't see where they're going.'

Major Harding Cox judged a clean-boot hunt at Welwyn some sixty years ago. His acquaintance, Lord Wolverton, had hounds who were indeed surly and went after a postman in earnest. Lt-Col. Richardson of *British War Dogs* fame was a bloodhound trainer in the war years, and admitted that, while most were benign, there were odd exceptions. His dogs' nosework secured the first modern conviction on bloodhound evidence at Northampton Assizes – on a twenty-hour-old scent.

Police authorities in the past have enthused about the old-fashioned bloodhounds' services. One Chief Constable, Capt. A. S. Williams, of West Sussex, thought that they had reduced serious crime by 50 per cent.[7]

The UK Bloodhound Club holds spring and autumn tracking trials: novice lines are ten minutes old; senior ones an hour. But today the US dog is the working detective. The most famous escapee of modern times was Martin Luther King's convicted killer, James Earl Ray, who fled into the hills of East Tennessee in 1977. Bloodhounds nosed him out.

Another sniffer who has sadly lost his job in Britain, is the truffle dog. Before the 1796 dog tax weighed on the village trufflers of Hampshire and adjoining counties, you could always see truffling in the autumn mists around old oak, beech and lime boles and under dripping branches. The truffles they found were red and knobbly. The dogs, descended from poodles and the Spanish ancestors of certain 'toy' spaniels, were small, spitzy, prick-eared and usually curly-coated, and could target accurately from 20 yards. They scuffed at the loamy soil with their claws and retrieved the fungus in exchange for a piece of bread. The truffler himself rarely ate the fruits of his labour: they fetched too good a price as an epicurean delicacy. An old magazine, *Once a Week*, gives an account of a dog called Nelly finding five truffles in ten minutes – a good rate. Her owner was asked if Nell would eat them, given the chance. 'Oh dear, yes, dogs likes 'em beyond anything else; it's their food, only we don't let them have any.'[8]

He said the pigs trained to truffle in France 'were such fools that immediately they found them, they eat 'em'. The town of Alba near Turin stages a truffle fair annually in honour of the white fungus of Alba and the province of Cuneo. The white *tuber magnatum* fetches £200–250 a pound. The nearby town of Roddi has a truffle-sniffing college for dogs, though the pig was used originally because pigs hunt them on their own account. Dogs can be muzzled or simply disciplined. A professional truffler can find as many as 300–400lbs in a week; that's a lot of dog biscuits. The French have the black truffle, Périgueux; Alba the white. But where, these days, is the Hampshire red? An Oxfordshire man recently digging under an oak in his Finstock garden found some 'funny little round things', which were bought by a restaurateur. I mention it only in passing . . .

12

WAR AND PATROL

Before gunpowder, dogs were used in combat. Gigantic jowly battle-dogs, starved and goaded to make them savage, were suited up in chainmail, plate, spiked collars, leather-mounted knives and even headpieces with flaming torches on top, and trained to attack in formation. They got amongst infantry, cavalry and elephant-mounted archers. Some of them doubled in peacetime as mountain-pass guards defending livestock. Everyone used them, from the Persians and Celts to Alexander the Great and Attila the Hun. The Greek Molossian, a sort of furiously active mastiff, was greatly feared. So were the nightmarish battle-dogs of Albania and the black baying hound of the Middle Ages, variously Allan, Alaunt and Allande. The Roman war-dog fought as an auxiliary against the Samarantes, the Gauls, the Teutons, the Britons; and the enemies of Rome fought back with monstrous breeds of their own. To many a soldier, the prospect of falling down amid this canine maelstrom was worse than death by weapons, and the dogs posed a psychological threat as well as a physical one. 'Cry "havoc!" and let slip the dogs of war,'[1] had real meaning for classical armies.

The advent of firepower should have made the dogs redundant. It didn't. The Tudors prized them; Henry VIII sent 400 iron-collared battle-beasts to Charles V of Poland, 'vast, huge, ugly and stubborn', as Elizabethan Dr Caius called the type. Armies are romantic organizations dealing with death and fear. They do not abandon a psychological weapon simply for the sake of logistics. There is an amusing illustration of Prince Rupert's poodle, Boy, confronting the Roundheads (Boy was killed at Marston Moor in 1643).[2]

Guerrillas and terrorists have used dogs to deal more than a blow to morale. The Riffs of Morocco would send dogs out at night to draw the Spaniards' fire so they could pick off the guns. The Algerians used similar tactics against the French. In Northern Ireland civilian canines exhibit a peculiar fondness for hounding the British military; a recently retired member of the First Battalion, Welsh Guards, has had his memoirs published under the title *Rats*[3] – recalling the perils of dog soldiery.

Frederick the Great's dog, a Great Dane called Gengesk, was made a POW at the Battle of the Soor. This was upsetting, because Frederick had come to like dogs better than people. Napoleon, who drafted in local curs to picket ramparts as watchdogs, was so moved by the sight of a little Barbet dog guarding his dead master that he called a halt to the slaughter of the Austrians at the Battle of Castiglione, saying that the dog had looked at him 'with all the poignancy of bitterness'. Canine sentries and pets stood over fallen men in the American Civil War, and the Russians had canine sentries in the Crimea and established a war-dog school before 1914. The Israelis, who traditionally despise dogs, deployed Spitz 'Canaans' as sentries and pathfinders in 1948 against the Arabs.[4]

The dog's instincts make him a first-rate recruit. He is a superior guard or sentry, tireless, incorruptible and able to 'pick up' much more quickly than a man; an unswerving messenger when lines are down, capable of great speed over unfamiliar terrain even at night and presenting a small target during heavy bombardment; a useful draught-animal for pulling cannon or machine-guns: an average-size dog is mobile under 45lbs, 750 rounds of rifle ammunition or two shells for an 18-pounder field gun.[5] He is utterly reliable for locating parachutists or guarding military property, positions and prisoners, to release men for the front; for scouting with reconnaissance parties, laying telegraphic lines, searching for the wounded, carrying first-aid, detecting mines, dropping from planes and digging in rubble for human casualties. In twentieth-century warfare the dog has two paradoxical virtues: he is invaluable yet he is expendable. His life is 'cheap as beast's'. A letter to *The Times* of September 1917 refers to the untrained dogs of Northern France and Flanders, sent like lambs to the slaughter of the First World War:

> It is the dogs who enlist men's sympathy more than anything else. Like frightened children they joined the ranks, nestling down by the side of the men for warmth and protection. Their piteous eyes seem to ask, What does it all mean? What has happened to the world?

Around 1900 several nations had begun experimenting with army dogs: Russia, Belgium, Holland, France, Sweden and especially the Jäger regiments of Germany. Colonel Edward Richardson, an Airedale breeder and service-dog trainer, warned the British Government of the German work he'd seen. No response. At the outbreak of the First World War the French unofficially had dogs with several regiments, at least for draught and rescue and personal protection; so had the Italians who had used such dogs in Tripoli. The Germans, though, were organized and their dogs meticulously trained for war, and cared for at a *Hunde Lazarett* (dog's hospital) behind the Front Lines.

Many nations used rescue and Red Cross dogs. Ambulance service had originated in Germany in 1893, though the British had made trials in the Boer war of 1899–1902 and the French had a depot in Fontainebleau in 1910. The dogs were supposed to detect the unconscious and wounded among the dead, quartering the ground ahead of stretcher bearers and returning with a cap. But in trench warfare this work became so hazardous and the Red Cross dogs so vulnerable under fire, that the French soon discontinued the service.[6]

Canine combatants in the First World War, by one estimate, totalled over 75,000: sentries, draught dogs, mine-dogs, wire-layers and messengers. Of these, 30,000 were German,[7] many of them GSDs thanks to founding breeder Capt. Max von Stephanitz. The British opened hostilities with the magnificent sum of one dog, an Airedale trained by Col. Richardson as a sentry. He was posted to France and died by shellfire on the Aisne. Richardson offered his trained dogs to guard British military installations in order to release manpower. No takers. A defiant sort of chap, he persisted with his training methods and eventually requests began to trickle in from the Front, especially for messenger dogs. Two 'pilot' messengers, Airedales Wolf and Prince, proved such stars that the War Office sucked their whiskers and ordered Richardson to open a war-dog school at Shoeburyness in 1916. Dogs' homes were combed for 'volunteers' and an appeal to the public started them flooding in, many of them mongrels 'with wise faces and willing hearts' as Richardson recalls. For the poor conscientious objectors there was the 'excellent lethal chamber at Battersea'.

A batch of messengers was posted as follows: collies 74; lurchers 70; Airedales 66; sheepdogs 36; retrievers 33; Irish terriers 18; and a few others totalling 340. Many mongrels and crossbreeds were evidently called purebred for classification purposes. The messengers with their cannister collars saved many lives, not only of human runners but of units whose urgent information they carried. A large proportion was drafted into the American Expeditionary Force in France.[8] The messenger dog was a Roman invention, except that the Romans made the dog swallow the message; the cur was slit open on arrival.[9]

The British dogs were trained with kindness ('The man whose only idea of control is by coercion and fear is quite useless') to return to a handler three or four miles away through shell-holes, mud, smoke, gas, barbed wire, darkness and incredible bombardment. Situations of anxiety, says Richardson, were transformed by these brave dogs appearing out of the chaos with their vital messages. Training at Shoeburyness had innured them to gunfire, thunderflash bombs, 18-pounder artillery guns and 12-inch 'heavies'. There was also a 'Liaison Dog' that made the hazardous double journey from the Front and back between two handlers, a system involving 'greater wastage of life', and there were pigeon-carriers with baskets of birds on their backs to save the return journey. Other dogs served as 'sentries' and 'guards'. The 'guard' defended an area, an outpost or a munitions dump. The 'sentry' patrolled with a handler, scenting attacks.

The men on all sides loved the dogs. Even a humble mascot, of which there were many, could keep socks and pecker up, and head glued together. Handlers logged reports of their dogs' work, saying how quick, efficient or brave they were. Keeper Rea wrote in, 'It is a hard job to keep the lads from making a fuss of [the messengers]; it seems as though man and dog were made to go together.' Many were shelled, wounded, blinded and burned with mustard gas. Keeper Osborne complained, 'When gas is about, I have to see to the putting of Jimmy's head in a man's P.H. smoke helmet, and I should be greatly pleased if you could inform me where to secure a mask for his proper protection.' A dog, like Christmas, was a reminder of higher things.

A French Canadian vet, Lieutenant Paul George, found a wounded German Shepherd in a trench, bandaged it up and called a ceasefire by yelling '1826 Karl!'[10] at the top of his voice from No Man's Land. The dog's German handler called another ceasefire a week later, parading the restored Karl up and down to storms of whistles and applause from all trenches, before they got on with the serious business of killing one another. A US regiment found a GSD in a ruined German headquarters. He died on them as they were examining his message, 'Hill No. – surrounded; send reinforcements at once!' The hill had fallen but a trail of blood testified to the dog's painful journey through heavy fire to the abandoned HQ to deliver his message. The tough Americans, all in tears, buried the dog beneath a wooden cross with an inscription in indelible ink: 'The most loyal subject the Kaiser had.'[11]

Despite the work of the British dogs and the concern of their handlers, it was left to the RSPCA to bring them back from Europe in 1918. The great fear of a rabies outbreak was well founded. The dogs were quarantined for six months in a Battersea annexe, the Soldiers' Quarantine Kennels at Hackbridge, Surrey, where most succumbed to distemper.[12] The bravery of dogs in war (and in peacetime) has elicited many awards and citations for services to humanity and the saving of life. Col. Richardson's book *British War Dogs*[13] is dedicated to 'the brave dogs of Britain . . . faithful unto death', and Ernest Baynes's *Animal Heroes of the Great War* (1925) is a similar salute. The Germans struck bronze medals for their honoured trench dogs, and British and American charities, though they had no VCs to give, made up awards of their own, among them the Royal Humane Society, the American Humane Association (Stillman Award), the People's Dispensary for Sick Animals (Animals' Roll of Honour and Dickin Medal), the RSPCA (Medallion for Valour), the National Canine Defence League (Certificate for

Services to Humanity) and, in post-war years, the Pro-Dog's Gold Medal and the American Dog Hero of the Year Award, presented by the Quaker Oats Company for heroism. Quaker's Doug Burson wrote to me, 'I receive as many as 20 different stories each week about heroic acts performed by dogs.'

Some of the heroes of the First and Second World Wars were celebrated in a recent exhibition at the Imperial War Museum in London. In the Second World War six of the sixteen canine Dickin medallists were mongrels and crossbreeds, like Rob and Brian, paratroopers dropped behind enemy lines with recce parties. There were mine-detection dogs like Rickie, wounded in the face but continuing with his duties, and Scamp, the Dalmatian, blown up clearing shu-mines; ARP dogs, detecting air-raid victims in the Blitz, like Star of Whitehaven medallist Jet, Irma the GSD and Beauty, the foxterrier, whose feet got so bad she had to wear boots. The ARP dogs were trained at the Ministry of Aircraft Production Dog School by Mrs M. B. Griffin, who logged all their work. When the Second World War began, the Germans had 50,000 dogs trained and waiting.[14] The Americans were ready with their volunteer K-9 corps, 25,000 strong, drawn up from a 'Dogs for Defense' appeal and delivered for service in North Africa, Italy, France and the Pacific. A similar idea in Britain, called the Volunteer Trained Dog Reserve, was eventually pushed through by Col. James Baldwin DSO.

> As a result of this suggestion, the committee of the Kennel Club invited representatives of the Royal Navy, Army and Air Force and the Association of Chief Police Officers in England and Wales to meet at the Kennel Club with a view to forming a register of owners of trained dogs who would be prepared to offer their dogs to the services at short notice in the event of a national emergency.[15]

Col. Baldwin, one of the original importers of the British Alsatian (GSD) was busy writing articles asking why the devil the British government declined to use Alsatians in the war. 'Why do we go on muddling through?' he pleaded in 1940 (Dog World, 3 May), pointing out how useful dogs were to the Germans and Canadians. The Government was standoffish. Dogs were outdated. Colonel Baldwin was being silly. He went to the War Office and banged on the table, arguing with 'sundry big shots' in London. Warrant Officer George Clapperton of the RAF School (now at Newton): 'He could have wiped himself and his Picardy kennels off the map. He was pitching at a high level.'

In 1941 Baldwin was asked by the Ministry of Aircraft Production, amid much chortling, to form a school, and the first trained team turned out in January 1942. General Eisenhower showed interest, and sent along some colonels to have a look. The following year the dogs began guarding POW camps. *No one* escaped. The school began training dogs and handlers for the US Forces, notably the Air Force, and in 1944 the first ARP dogs went into training, to work in the London Blitz. All these animals were either loaned or donated by the public through the efforts of the RSPCA. I am grateful to the Society's Executive Officer, W. J. Pimm, for an official record of their work during the Second World War. The book, called *Animals were There*,[16] contains Montgomery's letter of appreciation to the RSPCA for alleviating the suffering of 'animals who have helped us to win the War', and explains that the policy of recruiting war-dogs was seen as protecting the nation's animals from invasion. Of 10,000 pets offered 3500 were accepted for training. *Animals were There* is an account of the RSPCA's rescue services during the Second World War, and is a tribute to serving animals, British or otherwise. These included Russian mine-detecting dogs who discovered 529,000 mines in 1943 and over a million during the whole war, and a German propaganda mongrel christened 'Rocket Dispatch' by the Americans, who went back and forth carrying rude and demoralizing messages in the Siegfried region.

RAF Patrol

The RAF patrol dogs now are 'police' rather than war-dogs, but fearsome all the same. At the end of the Second World War, Airedales, terriers, collies and even beardies were used; now they are all publicly donated GSDs. (See Sniffers and Trackers chapter for donation procedure for GSDs.) They guard installations, aerodromes and other property of the RAF and user agencies around the world. They are taught to wind scent ('pick up') the presence of an intruder and indicate to a handler who 'runs in' with the dog. On command it will then attack the trespasser until called to heel, and lie couchant until the intruder has been searched.

The dogs' training begins with obedience and agility work. They live in five-star kennels on an elaborate complex with clinic and x-ray facilities to detect the *degree* of hip dysplasia. Patrol work is strenuous, much of it on hard surfaces, and the RAF do not want any dog working in pain. 'The breeders went for the shell,' says Warrant Officer Clapperton sadly, 'like a car.' The key to the patrol dog's job is controlled aggression. Practical Training Assistants pad up in felt and hessian suits which they make themselves, and bait the dogs to encourage aerial attacks rather than just ankle biting. Bitches are often a bit dubious. 'We want the dogs to get involved in the game of attack,' says Flight Sergeant Al Murray cheerily. 'They have a well-developed protective instinct for the man at the other end of the lead.' The sight of Al's gigantic GSDs hurling themselves at the fencing, showing you their dental arrangements, does nothing to harm their image as guardians.

The ones that fail his rigorous course can occasionally be recycled, but never as family pets. 'There's one on top of a patio roof in Bingham that gives voice. As a patrol dog he was terrible.'

They showed me a recently used saliva-covered baiting suit, rent with teethmarks through two layers of hessian and several thicknesses of felt. The PTAs wear grid-iron helmets like American football players; the vizors keep their faces on. Initially the dog is fed (if you'll pardon the expression) an arm covered with hessian, and works up from there. 'We like a dog to go in high up,' says Clapperton poetically. Don't ever break into an RAF installation. I noticed a metal pail on the floor, punctured and mangled up like a paper plane. The dogs had remodelled it for something to do.

'It's a lot to ask of a lad of eighteen or nineteen – dog-handling,' says George Clapperton. 'But as soon as they get the job and find the dog leaping up to greet them – "Hello Dad!" – it's heartbreaking if they get taken off. I could sit four of my hardest men down here and tell them they're off the job and I guarantee you'd see all four weeping with disappointment. When you're walking out for six hours with a dog, there's a terribly strong attachment formed. You tell it all your worries. At 4 a.m. you'll turn to the dog and say "Bloody nuisance tonight," and it's even worse when the dog turns back and says "Yes I know." 4 a.m. when all is quiet, when not even the bunny rabbits are stirring, and the only ones walking about are you and the dog, you start counting the stars or the rivets in a V-bomber.'

Space will not permit me to quote all the stories and citations describing the acts of heroism of service dogs, but the following could not be omitted. A PDSA silver medal for gallantry was awarded posthumously to 6073 Airdog Prince, with this citation:

> On the night of 20th November 1964, Prince and his handler challenged 3 armed men on the RAF base at El Adem, Libya. In spite of his severe injuries from which he later died, Prince persisted in his attacks on the intruders, loyally defending his handler who had been rendered unconscious, displaying outstanding devotion and courage as a result of which his handler's life was saved.

Army Dogs

Over to the Royal Army Veterinary Corps Training Centre at Melton Mowbray, Leicester, where Capt. Tony Rossell is showing me live mines from the Falklands.

'That's a rubbery one there; these are plastic; that's all metal except for the explosives inside it. They vary in size from this one [banging it] which contains about 20lbs of explosives, down to that, which is only a few ounces, the size of a shoe-polish tin. That one is designed to be thrown from helicopters or the backs of vehicles, and you can hit it like this [bang bang] and it won't go off: it needs progressive pressure. That one is the Argentinians' own anti-personnel mine. These will go off at a very low pressure but those need a vehicle to drive over them. The Argentinian FMKI fits *inside* their anti-tank mine and detonates it with human pressure. That's a shoebox mine: it can be set to an ounce. Those small ones will take your leg off. That's an Israeli mine, though the Russians have an identical one. This is an MI, an American, date of production 1944 (these weapons tend to change hands a lot). The modern mines like that you can find with conventional mine detectors from two or three feet away; absolutely no danger of missing that, it's so big. But these are all plastic. This is why we've had to go back to the mine-detection dogs.'

What do the dogs key on? 'We don't know. Nobody's ever been a dog. We *believe* it's a combination of scents: the casing, the explosive, the earth disturbance and human scent when somebody plants it, crushed insects, crushed vegetation. It's a combination of these that the dog is looking for. We believe. But nobody will ever know and the scientists can go and rip their hair out as much as they want; they'll never convince me they even know what scent is.'

A golden retriever, very proud in his breast harness, demonstrates a free search, working 'loose', forward of his handler. The dog finds a mine and sits down – behind it, not on it. 'Now operationally, if you're walking across what you believe to be a cleared area like this and the dog sits, you would call it back to you, remember the point, and then change over to this type – the fine-search dog. This minefield is six weeks old; we've got others several months old for training purposes. Again the breast harness, but this time we've got a very short lead, for control, because we want to cover every inch of the ground.' A white tape is laid, the dog walking on the minefield side of it and the handler, in flak jacket and Cromwell helmet, on the safe side. After each narrow strip is cleared the tape is moved one foot forward and the dog doubles back, turning outwards, his nose following a prodder along the ground. The dog sits. His handler taps the mine gently with the prodder to confirm – they're only just below the surface – and a mine marker cone goes on. The mine-detection dog is the only Army dog actually *trained* with a titbit. 'This is the begging syndrome. He finds the mine and begs at it. He has a rest about every hour and we'd get about four hours' work out of him in a day.'

The Army had metal-detectors and explosives-detectors in the Falklands, but nothing was 100 per cent accurate. Even the latest anomaly detectors, keying on density, can be fooled by a sheep's hoofprint. Dogs have often been preferred to machinery for speedy pathfinding in war, called 'breaching'. 'If they'd taken dogs initially to the Falklands when they attacked, they'd have been used to breach the minefields for transport. Instead of that they had poor old sappers lying down on their bellies, prodding. And that's why there are a lot of people today with no legs.' Was this because of a lack of confidence in the dogs? 'We had none at that stage. Mine-detection dogs were considered old-fashioned, like messenger dogs. Well I can think of circumstances where the messenger dog might be useful even now.' During radio silences, for instance. Or after the Bomb drops, to measure radiation – send for the Dogsbody. Why are the mine-detection dogs still here? 'Because the minimum requirement is for a 98 per cent success rate. The highest we got was 94.4. There's no equivalent machinery but if you're missing mines, that's lives being lost. Even a dog that's 99.9 per cent is still missing one in 1000. There are 15,000 mines in the Falklands; that could mean fifteen men with no legs.'

The Army has 1400 dogs in service around the world with British Forces, MOD Police and Naval bases in places like Hong Kong, Cyprus, British Army of the Rhine (BAOR), Belgium and Northern Ireland. An inspectorate keeps an eye on them, and they are all trained at Melton Mowbray by RAVC professionals before being married up with handlers, instructed as a unit and posted. 'We say we can train a dog better with a professional dog trainer,' say the Army when you mention the RAF one-man-and-his-dog policy. The 300 acres here include a mock-up village in which the search dogs do their stuff, sniffing for firearms, ammunition, explosives and bomb-making materials. The 'students' are at various stages: a beginner retrieves a weapons' magazine wrapped in hessian; another search-dog watches keenly as his trainer pretends to hide a pistol in various places; a third 'indicates' on a firearm in a doorway. Objects hidden for several months will have to be recovered, before the dog is considered trained. 'The reward is to be allowed to fetch a pistol. Now, operationally, the IRA aren't going to leave things lying around for the dogs to find: they'd be booby-trapped and it's very important that the handler leaving here at the end of his three months with that dog can read him very accurately and see when he's picked up before he goes into it. Then he can immediately stop the dog, withdraw and leave it to an engineer search-team to lift the item. It's only during the dog's training that he's allowed to touch the weapon. For forensic purposes they don't want the dog slobbering over it anyway.'

The Army's other specialist dogs include drug-detectors (Do they come in contact with the substance? 'Yes.' Do they get hooked? 'No.'), tracking dogs, casualty-detection dogs, liaison dogs, infantry-patrol dogs (to pick up on ambushes in the jungle) and sweep dogs, used in Hong Kong to detect 3500 illegal immigrants in eighteen months. But the Army's 'bread and butter', as Capt. Rossell puts it, are protection dogs, of which there are four kinds, all jobs for the GSD. They have others breeds enlisted, Labradors, Rottweilers,

Belgian Shepherds, Groenendahls, etc., for various duties. Bloodhounds? 'We've had stacks, but an Army dog has got to have basic obedience and some have turned vicious. Besides, it's no good trying to get into the front of a helicopter with a bloodhound that's going to lick the pilot's face and jump all over him. He'll never get there to track. And in jungle like Borneo, where I was, a dog that gets its head down would lead you straight into an ambush. We need a dog that will pick up on air scents.' So they go in helicopters; how about parachute drops? 'The last one I think was called Tudor. But we still abseil them. We used to do that in Malaya and Borneo because you couldn't land the helicopters in the jungle. The old dog just thinks the helicopter is a three-tonner gone crazy. The harnesses vary. You can get two ordinary tracking harnesses and put one on the right way round and the other upside down, and join them up. We still board and disembark from big ships abseiling the dogs like that for search work.'

The protection dog is the Army's pride and joy. The first type is called the guard. He patrols with a handler, picks up, locates and, if the intruder tries to escape, arrests by biting, 'high up', to disable him. The second type is the security dog, much the same, except that his arrest procedure is more polite, circling and 'hindering'. He's used where there might be innocent people about. The third kind is called security arm true, taught to attack the arm of a gunman. ('At one time we called this one right arm true, but the Army abbreviates everything.') The fourth is the police dog, similar to the civilian kind, taught to stand off, give voice, circle, track, property search, etc. No dog gets into the Army if it's gun-shy but a 'gun green' recruit can be polished up, if it's simply not used to the bang.

The guard dog begins with obedience, then he's teased up with a stick and a sack. 'Once we've got him attacking on command, we move to something solid – a sleeve. The next stage is the suit.' A training assistant steps up to show me his padded baiting suit and caged head protector. The jacket is very heavy; the GSD hanging from it weighs 73–82lbs ('He varies,' says Corporal O'Flynn). The final stage is the muzzle attack on an unprotected man, to ensure that the dog isn't 'padding happy' on the hessian. 'Boxers are very prone to that.'

These dogs have an average working life of eight years, though fit ones can last much longer. Then they are put down. It would be like selling weapons to the public to re-home them. (This is also the case with RAF baited dogs.) Large numbers of de-mobbed GSDs, barking savagely, are chained at intervals around an enclosure and used for course work. Most of the hundreds of publicly rejected GSDs now serving with the Forces, were under stay of execution to begin with; these at least have had a decent working life. How about casualties? 'All the way through the troubles in Northern Ireland, we've lost one dog, and that was an RAF recruit attached to us at the time. A dog in the Army has a better life than a civilian, or my three at home. What other dog gets a batman?'

The Army are 'into recruiting in a big way'. They need 300–350 dogs a year, 'and we may have to look at 500 or even 600 to find those'. The usual policy for anyone with a bold, steady dog to offer (not a bitch), aged one to three, is to take it along to the Army for them to have a look. If it's suitable they will pay up to £70 for it. (Write to The Commandant, RAVC Training Centre, Welby Lane, Melton Mowbray, Leicester LE13 0SL. Tel. 0664 63281, Ex. 52.) 'We're looking for "purebred" dogs, but if it *looks* like an Alsatian that's good enough for us.' They've tried breeding their own, as have the US Army in Singapore, but prefer to go to the public or to dealers. 'The individual dog is more important than the pedigree. Let's face it, if the old Alsatians – I call them Alsatians – had a dip into the mongrels, they wouldn't have all this hip dysplasia. We x-ray every dog.' Isn't £70 a bit steep for the Army to fork out for its recruits? 'It's peanuts when you consider how cost-effective a dog is, giving the same level of security as seven or eight men. And on the search side, if one dog finds one detonator, how many lives have been saved? What price can you put on that detonator?' What price the dogs of war?

13

THE DOG IN BLUE

Most of the service dogs we've looked at so far, whether hunting, hauling, nosing or gnashing, have been specialists called in for a particular purpose. The civilian police do indeed have specialist search dogs for drugs, firearms and explosives, and I was shown a very good game of Hunt-the-Cannabis by a labrador on the staff of the Staffordshire police, who turned over a lot of files and furniture in the Commander's office in his determination to go to pot. But the British police GSD is a general-duty dog, a Jack of all Trades who must track and search for persons and property, patrol, stand off, climb up, lie down, apprehend, control crowds, control himself, seek, 'speak', shut up and be always on his best behaviour. Everyone who claims to like dogs should really put his hand in his pocket and make a little donation to the country's dogs in blue, because praise is insufficient for what they do for us. Many of them are cast-offs from the public. Some forces breed their own; for a big outfit like the Metropolitan with some 370 trained dogs, this is financially practicable. But the police who use public rejects seem to like them all the better on that account. They say the backyard castaway has the best character. He'll do anything for 'dad'.

At the twenty-fifth National Champion Police Dog Trials in Yorkshire, I sat a couple of benches along from a canine spectator who'd already had his turn and was watching the competition with his handler. A dog from Kent, struggling to get over the agility A-frame, set him whining; he couldn't take his eyes off the long jump worth 10 marks, barked loudly at the crowd control worth 60 and when it came to the 'chase and attack' of a fleeing criminal, worth 100, he nearly had to go and interfere with the proceedings. The Trials give the country's eight regions something to aim at; they also give an idea of police priorities. General obedience, agility and control carry 200 marks. Criminal or 'manwork', by which is meant conduct of the dog in crowds and dealing with an 'incident', chase and attack of the criminal, chase and stand off and tests of courage against the stick and the gun, are collectively worth 300. The most marks of all, though, 500, go to 'nosework': a two-hour track, a hard surface track, an investigation, searching an area for articles, indicating a non-retrievable object by barking and, last, quartering and searching for a hidden person.

'Operationally, for every 100 tracks, a dog might be called to chase after five people, and I wouldn't even put it as high as that,' says Inspector Simon Edwards, in charge of the day-to-day running of Kent Constabulary's renowned dog section at Maidstone. 'It's a very emotive issue, police dogs and people. Our major work is tracking and searching, deterrent patrols in shopping precincts, that sort of thing. But the dogs have to be trained for the manwork side, in case it's required. The average criminal has a healthy respect for dogs. Even one that is only mediocre at manwork, if it's biting a bare arm, can make a hard man wince a little and if he's wearing a sweater and he's got 80 or 90lbs of Alsatian hanging on his arm, he's not going to swing it far.' Do the dogs get killed? 'My connection with the dog section goes back ten years and in that time in Kent we have not had one dog that's suffered a serious attack. Odd dogs get kicked, legs and pads get lacerated scaling walls and so on, but the last serious injury I can think of was about sixteen years ago when a dog was stabbed by a chap outside a cinema in Rochester.' (A Metropolitan dog was fatally wounded in the recent Harrods bomb blast.)

In the armed forces and certain police forces up and down the country, there's a strong feeling that bitch GSDs are no good at manwork; some don't take them at all. Well, for all you canine chauvinists, here's mud in your eye. Police-dog heroes get a special commendation called the Action of the Year Award, presented jointly in 1982 to two handlers and their dogs. One was Constable Kirwood of North Wales, with Joss, for a track six hours old; the other was Constable Ray Cooper of the Met with his soon-to-retire seven-year-old bitch Myra. I asked PC Cooper what happened. 'I was on duty with other dog-handlers in the Piccadilly Circus area; we had information that there was going to be a big confrontation between Leeds and Chelsea football supporters. I ended up by myself with Myra on the westbound Piccadilly Line platform amid a fight involving approximately 300 football fans. The dog split them up and forced a way between the two groups. Most of the Chelsea lot ran off. The remaining 153 Leeds supporters were trapped down the end of the platform, with their only escape route along the tunnel and onto the lines. So I confronted them with the dog and detained them. They made several charges but the dog forced them back and kept them there for ten or twenty minutes until assistance arrived and everyone was arrested. Myra's a very small bitch and not alarming to look at, but I disagree strongly about bitches not being good at manwork: what Myra lacks in size, she makes up for in aggression and without a doubt there were a few bitten that day.' (This means that brave Myra wouldn't win any trials.)

A police dog is required to tackle a gunman 'resolutely', according to the schedule, 'without undue viciousness or apprehension'. Inspector Edwards: 'If somebody's holed up at the end of a field with a shotgun I'd consider the matter very carefully before sending a dog in. If it's a last resort – fine. I'm not saying a dog should be elevated above a human life, but there are situations where it would be wasting a dog just for the sake of it. With a handgun it's slightly different. But we do train them on shotguns and handguns.' The training begins with 'the old sausage', a long hessian bag stuffed with rags to get the dog biting and tugging, which changes up by degrees to a real arm, slightly padded. 'The dog has to go in and take the arm that has the gun or the stick. If he went for the other arm, while he's biting the gunman thinking, "Aren't I doing well, dad?", the gunman could be shooting him.' Some US police dogs (not all) are trained to dislodge a weapon by an aerial attack on the gunman's shoulder, knocking him down. The British police dog grabs the arm and hangs on. 'You should never overprotect the criminal. Obviously you've got to protect him sufficiently, but if you place too much emphasis on that, you put the dog right off.' They're inured to gunfire by degrees.

Why don't the police use baiting suits like the armed forces? Chief Inspector Bryn Phillips, Commander of Staffordshire Dog School: 'We don't want anyone mauled. We're out in the streets, not on military property. Their dogs can go in anywhere. Ours only go for the arm. We don't send a dog out to search for an armed criminal tonight and then send a different dog along to the infants' school tomorrow doing a PR exercise. The same dog goes along. Many years ago when I was a dog-handler myself, stationed in Tenby, a man came out of a dance hall one night, stroked my dog's head and said, "What a useless police dog!" I could see what he meant but I said, "Have you done anything wrong?" "No." "Well there you are then."'

Chief Inspector Phillips is a Welsh ex-boxer. He's been on BBC's 'It's a Dog's Life' and he has been with dogs for twenty-two years. His school has trained recruits for twenty-three different countries, including Australia, Jordan, Sweden and Nigeria, plus dogs for the Army before they had their own school, the Prison Service, the island of Jersey, British Transport Police and the Central Electricity Generating Board. He says, 'I wouldn't describe myself as an expert,' but everyone in the Force on dog-handling knows who he is. 'In a million dogs you'll never get two the same, but I think "intelligence" is the worst word anyone could use in referring to dogs. Their instincts are far superior to ours but they have no intellect. They can't "understand". They're relying all the time on memory and association, and they become what we make them. I think the relationship between dog and handler is terribly important. A dog can't reason and I'm sure it looks upon the handler as a pack leader.' Its attention span is rather like a child's. 'It gets bored very quickly so the training has got to be kept like a game, and you must always finish on a happy note, something the dog's good at.'

Something the dogs clearly enjoy on the nosework side is searching for a hidden person, such as a trainer concealed above the door of the gents in a disused Staffordshire factory. 'Searching' differs from tracking in that the dog is using airborne scent to 'wind' where to look in a large area. He doesn't follow a trail but gives the place the once-over for human smells. A warning is given that the handler is sending in his dog, who gets excited at being told 'Seek him! Where is he?' The dog goes round the place on his own, his whole body alert, his black eyes big as tinderboxes, puffing and panting into every room. It takes him about ten seconds – he doesn't need to examine the nooks and crannies. There's a momentary pause as he pushes into the loo – fee, fi, fo, fum – followed by a sudden deafening racket of GSD barking. 'It would be no good finding the fugitive and keeping quiet,' says Chief Inspector Phillips, 'or the handler's got to go in and look for the man and the dog as well.' To the dog it's all a game; the quarry can stroke him with impunity once he's been apprehended by 'dad'.

How do they teach the dog to 'speak' in these circumstances? Kent's Inspector Edwards: 'Some dogs are natural barkers. I've got one on duty today that barks and barks and barks – how the handler puts up with it I do not know. Most dogs will bark if encouraged. You get the dog's best cuddly toy and you tie the dog to a railing, and say "Speak!" And as soon as he speaks, lots of praise and you give him the article. If that doesn't work you do it with food. You sit there in the kennels with a giant tin of meat and about five cups full of biscuit all mixed in, and you hold it up in the air. Sometimes you've got a dog that's really difficult and you've had a shattering day and you hold up the big food bowl and say "Speak! Speak!" and he sits there looking at you thinking, Well I'm not going to speak, and he's going to give me that because his arm's starting to flag.' The dog's voice is very important in a building search: the dog is alone and might get trapped between swing doors, and 'speaking' is the only way he can communicate with the handler.

Meanwhile, back at the Staffordshire factory, beginners are casting about in the grass outside for small articles thrown by their handlers. 'If you can, you always send your dog into the wind,' says Chief Inspector Phillips, 'because the scent's being blown towards him. That's wrong now, he's having a wee. In a trial he'd be docked marks for contaminating the area.' Another trainee dog 'winds' an article after he's gone past it. Wind scents blow about rather like smoke. They may be a long way from the original ground scent and alter course in the lee of obstacles and buildings. A stiff breeze livens them up and gives the dogs more latitude.

Searching an area, whether for persons or property, the dog is keying on human scent. Chief Inspector Phillips: 'You might get a call one morning, saying there's been a stabbing here and they haven't found the knife. So you send out your dog and suddenly he picks up something and brings it back to you. An empty cigarette packet. You don't chastise the dog. You say good boy! because he doesn't know. He's brought you something with human scent on it. You send him out again. Eventually he'll come up with the knife if it's there.' It might not be a murder weapon. It might be stolen property, a ring. 'The first dog I ever had was a bitch called Abbey. At night I'd stand at the front door and throw a nickel threepenny bit as far as I could, and she'd vanish over the far wall. Two or three minutes later she'd be back with that threepenny bit, without fail.'

'Tracking' is following a human scent on the ground. The line itself, as a steward at the Trials had explained to me, is a bit like water dribbling from a can. Both evaporate, and the rate of evaporation depends on the surface and conditions. One test was about half a mile long and two hours old, for a leash-held dog, with four small articles dropped en route by the tracklayer. The test I saw was on a field outside Catterick in Yorkshire. One of the judges, Chief Inspector Ray Wood of Nottinghamshire: 'All humans have a nose for is to fill a hole in their face. The dog's scenting powers are magnificent. You see the area with four posts? The dog must find the start and follow the track faithfully to its conclusion. Each pattern is different – our tracklayers are experts, plotting and studying the land. As a judge I need to know how each particular dog will indicate when he finds an article and the handler must declare it to me. There's no cheating: I'm watching him.' They have to rely on the dogs. Judge Inspector Gummery of South Wales: 'When they start trying to think for the dog, they're in trouble.' Inspector Gummery's school in South Wales trains for Wales and the South West. Chief Inspector Wood's Nottinghamshire school trains for Eastern England. 'Anything which dissipates the scent makes it more difficult. It won't disappear but it will have less density. We each of us have a different scent, and when we walk on a surface like a field there is also crushed vegetation and disturbed earth.' Anything can happen to a track in two hours, but a good dog will ignore cross-tracks and animal smells. The finer hard-surface track tests the dog's precision. If he loses his trace the handler may 'recast' him as an angler does with rod and line, or the huntsman with hounds.

How are police dogs trained to track? The dog's favourite plaything is deposited on a lush surface like grass; the handler walks back to the dog, puts on his tracking harness, and encourages the dog to hunt. Most dogs twig very quickly that a clue to the article's whereabouts is the scent leading up to it and, once this breakthrough is made, you start making the track longer, with arcs, and then right angles. This is called a 'pattern track'. It's important that you know every inch of the line you have laid, to correct the dog when he deviates from it. Simon Edwards: 'You get to the stage where your dog's done, say, 150 tracks, and you'll go out on the 151st and do the first couple of legs and suddenly he'll take you off for a walk through the countryside. You don't know what's going on in the dog's mind. And when that happens it's like chopping nine inches off the bottom of the handler's legs because until that moment, wherever his dog's gone, he's followed.' What can you do about such a crisis of confidence? Not a lot. Even dogs have days when they can't be bothered. You have to be patient, know the track you've laid like the back of your hand, and learn to read the dog's indications. Good boy! you say gently when he owns the line. 'And the sooner you can do without verbal commands the better,' says Chief Inspector Phillips.

What happens when there's a break-in, or break-out, and you want the dog to track a fugitive? The main problem the police face is scent contamination, from other people arriving on the scene and having a look round. The local bobby is always requested to avoid interfering with the scent picture if he can, and if he can't to tell the handler *exactly* where he's been. 'You're not necessarily following the last scent because the burglar is not necessarily the last man,' says Chief Inspector Phillips. 'It's a team effort, handler and dog, and it's up to the handler to use his own powers of observation, asking questions. Otherwise they could be following the postman for half an hour.'

Whether tracking or searching, the fugitive must not be savaged; he might be perfectly innocent, an old chap who's run away from a home. Simon Edwards: 'Say you're working a line through some woodland and you're directing your dog to search. The old dog'll go off and you might hear him barking and you go leaping in there to find a bloke with his binoculars raised on the Dartford Warbler. If he suddenly finds an Alsatian breathing hot air up his parka, all sorts of difficulties arise.' So the handler 'challenges the area' and warns whoever is in it to come out, and the GSD must find whoever remains in hiding – find, guard and scrutinize, but not attack.

Not all police dogs are GSDs of course. In the past, many Airedales and bloodhounds have been used (see chapter on Sniffers and Trackers), and different countries have different tastes. The United States still recruit bloodhounds and use them advisedly, alongside GSDs and Dobermanns, of which the FBI have been fond. The Dobermann Pinscher was produced originally as the 'ideal' police and security dog by Ludwig Dobermann of Apolda in the 1890s and European forces who use it crop its ears and dock its tail to make it look more forbidding. The bullmastiff, Rottweiler, Bouvier and Briard are variously employed on the Continent; the 'Picardy Shepherd' is preferred in France. The Paris police used to use Newfoundlands[1] as rescue dogs on the Seine, throwing amusingly dressed stuffed sacks into the water for the dogs to practise on. Even the resolute Giant Schnauzer, cropped and docked, patrols in some parts of Europe.

But the pioneers in the field of police-dog research, the Germans, began experimenting after the Franco-Prussian War, and the GSD is the result of their endeavours. The dogs were called Alsatians when they were imported into Britain after the First World War, to make believe they came from Alsace-Lorraine rather than from Germany. The Nazis loved them because of their Teutonic lupine appearance. Both Hitler's best friends were GSDs (not surprisingly when his East Prussian HQ was called 'Wolf's Lair' and his U-boat fleets 'Wolfpacks'), and the SS found them wonderfully frightening for guarding POW and other camps, and placed great emphasis on loyalty among dogs and handlers. Unfortunately for anyone keen on the wolfy aspect, crossing the GSD with wolf blood generally makes him more nervous, since wolves have a congenital terror of mankind.[2]

In Britain at the time of writing, police dogs are as follows: GSDs – 1768; labradors – 99; Dobermanns – 2; Border collies – 3; Rottweilers – 4; Reisenschnazer – 1; Weimaraners – 4; golden retrievers – 3; Bouvier – 1; pointers – 2; springers – 2; Total – 1889.

The labradors are either specialists or royal-protection dogs; Her Majesty's Corgis and GSDs apparently don't see eye to eye. But the reliance on GSDs for everything else is obvious. Dog and handler are married up according to personality: give a slow handler a sharp dog and the animal would be 'looking to have him over'. The dog is kept in a purpose-built kennel in the handler's back garden: they're not pets but need to be family-orientated. The handler works seven hours a day and spends another hour on duty for his dog, grooming, feeding and exercising. Handler and dog train together, live together and work together, usually for about seven or eight years. Most handlers keep the dog when it retires though some prefer not to. Seeing 'Dad' putting on his blues and taken a new sidekick to work can be even sadder for the dog than going to a new home.

The police are always on the look-out for gifts of bold, unwanted GSDs from the public, with 'a bit of spirit', as Inspector Edwards puts it, though they don't want vicious dogs or child-biters thank you, and some forces don't take bitches either. Sorry Myra. The ideal age for them to come into the Force is twelve to fourteen months, but if you have a young GSD that's outgrown its welcome, give them a ring.

If they like the sound of a dog, they'll pay you a visit and take him away to see how he gets on in a van, in kennels, under the x-ray, etc. Then you sign an indemnity form and he goes into training to be one of the best dogs in the world.

14

THE BIG TIME

The Marquis de Gaillerdain and Madame de Poncette danced the minuet, their little legs working furiously beneath their satin finery, their ears wiggling in time to the music. Queen Anne applauded and the whole troupe, all the way from Belgium, caused a stir in polite society. Their impresario called the act 'The Ball of the Little Dogs.[1] Performing poodle mania seized London. Elsewhere spaniels, mongrels and terriers somersaulted and jigged to music, sometimes with bears, all hopping and straining in crinolines, plumed hats and military uniforms, in the heat of the dusty summer streets of Europe. Their art was as old as begging itself; a really good performance meant they wouldn't be starved or whacked. Dr Johnson sniffed his snuff and opined on women preachers: 'Sir, a woman preaching is like a dog walking on his hind legs. It is not done well, but you are surprised to find it done at all.'

Another troupe, eighty-strong and mostly miniature poodles, performed an extravaganza sitting at a banqueting table and being served by canine menials who also walked on their hind legs on tightropes, and raced with monkeys on their backs. In truth they were very scared, as the training was what you might call rigorous. A woman purchased a small white poodle from a trainer in Barcelona, supposedly coached by professionals. For two years the dog behaved normally, but hearing Spanish spoken one day it suddenly sprang up in a frenzy and started turning somersaults and trying to stand on its head.[2]

Hundreds of circuses and Punch and Judy knockabouts, with terriers in ruffs, played to children, who formed the impression animals were sent to make us laugh. Sir Walter Scott, who loved dogs, commented, 'The *garçon perruquier* and his barebottomed, red-eyed poodle, though they are both amusing animals and play ten thousand tricks which are diverting enough; yet there is more of human and dog-like sympathy in the wag of old Trusty's tail than if his rival Toutou had stood on head for a twelvemonth.'

The RSPCA deplores exhibitions or presentations of animals in circuses, travelling menageries and theatres, and the Council of the RSPCA calls for television companies to avoid coverage of circus acts involving animals. This is not to say that *all* performing animals are miserable, or all training methods cruel; far from it. Many dogs are lovingly taught and enjoy pleasing people and showing off their ingenuity. A well-known poodle-breeder I consulted (Shirley Walne) told me, 'Poodles are highly intelligent and they love something to do. We knew Phyllis Allan of Bertram Mills Circus well, and we gave her two little dogs. She was very kind and they loved her. They learned the usual things, running through hoops, two holding a skipping rope and a third jumping, that sort of thing. I don't train dogs to do tricks myself; to tell the truth I don't particularly like all that rather regimental obedience training one sees nowadays either; I find it rather sad. Miss Allan never dressed the poodles up, but there again you do get the occasional one that actually revels in it. I once took one of mine to a fancy-dress party as the Sugar Plum fairy, but then she was very small and sweet and she loved all the attention.' Meanwhile, though, in Leicester Square most evenings, two dirty little dogs with hats on, looking exceedingly miserable in a caged trolly between turns, hurl themselves about collecting money for a raucous showman. I confess I lacked the composure to interview him.

Dogs have made the big time now, in television, theatre and films, but they have always popped up in the Arts. Homer, Plutarch, Shakespeare, Herrick, Pope, Swift, Crabbe, Cowper, Byron, Southey, Wordsworth, Matthew Arnold, the Brownings, Sir Walter Scott, and a great many more have waxed poetical on the dog. Albert Payson Terhune (with Lad the collie), Fred Gipson (with *Old Yeller*), Jack London (with Buck and *The Call of the Wild*), Mark Twain (with 'A Dog's Tail'), James Thurber (with Muggs, *The Dog That Bit People*) and Richard Adams (with *The Plague Dogs*) have all made individual dogs and dog stories famous. Painters, from Renoir, Gauguin, and Brueghel to Sir Edwin Landseer, Francis Bacon and Janet Ledger have drawn dogs to the life; there is even an annual exhibition of dogs in art at the Cadogan Gallery in London (information on 01 235 4526), though perhaps the most celebrated dog painting of all was by the little-known Francis Barraud in 1899, of Nipper the Fox Terrier cocking his ear at an old gramophone. The picture became the trademark of the Gramophone Company Limited, and later HMV (His Master's Voice). Cartoonists from Jack Fish (with Bill) and Charles Schultz (with Snoopy) to Disney himself with his *Pluto, Lady and the Tramp* and *101 Dalmatians* have found dogs a useful medium of humour. Musicians have fallen for their charms. Elgar worked his spaniels into the *Enigma Variations* and mutts with good singing voices have been assembled in choirs and had signature tunes composed for them. Even sculptors have got in on the act. The most ghastly object I have ever clapped eyes on was 'Dog' by Alberto Giacometti, in New York's Museum of Modern Art.

Mrs Worthingtons have been putting their dogs on the stage (and screen) for quite a while. Roman Emperor Vespasian (AD 9–79) records how impressed he was, in the theatre of Marcellus, with the acting skills of a particular dog who, being presented with a piece of 'poisoned' bread, ate it and fell down 'dead' on the stage. He doesn't tell us whether the same dog appeared in subsequent performances.[3]

Stage and movie animals are not indispensable. Several collies actually played 'Lassie', and one of them, Pal, only landed the part because he looked convincingly done in at the end of a flood-swimming stunt: too weak even to shake the water off his fur. In a multi-million dollar industry with cameras rolling, who cares if an animal is acting or not? Trip wires for horses, once banned, are back in business, and this is merely the tip of the iceberg. Clint Eastwood, whose own films have grossed over $500 million at the box office, doesn't think his money should be made at the expense of his animal co-stars.

> I feel nothing but scathing contempt for those thoughtless, unfeeling directors who are willing to kill or maim animals in a misguided attempt at realism, when they can just as easily portray the same illusion by using camera tricks. A good director can have an animal appear to be under terrible stress, can have it do some terrific stunts, but they don't have to be real – and they don't have to involve cruelty.[4]

The RSPCA in Britain has long been concerned about pressures on performing animals in films and television. 'In the past,' says Executive Officer Pimm, 'many animals have been ill-treated and a number have died, like the horses in *The Charge of the Light Brigade*, starring Errol Flynn. We work closely with the American Humane Association who have an entrée to Hollywood and we have a code of practice for producers.' This includes the following suggestions: 'Tranquillizers and sedatives should not be used on animals solely for the purpose of filming, nor should animals be anaesthetized to produce an effect.' 'Quarter-load ammunition and minimal explosive loads for firing on or near stock should be the rule,' and 'Scheduling should be such that the animal is not exposed for long periods to hot lights.' The RSPCA got a conviction against one film company contravening the Cinematographic Films (Animals) Act 1937, which states that:

> No person shall exhibit to the public ... any cinematograph film (whether produced in Great Britain or elsewhere) if in connection with the production of the film any scene represented in the film was organised and directed in such a way as to involve the cruel infliction of pain or terror on any animal or the cruel goading of an animal to fury.

Not all screen horrors are what they seem. In *Equus* the horses weren't really blinded; in *Blue Remembered Hills* the squirrel wasn't really stoned, and 'Lassie's' stunts were generally produced by off-camera hand signals from trainer Rudd Weatherwax, standing by with a rag or a biscuit. But there are exceptions. Dorothy Steves has been training dogs to act for many years; she coached Radar, the chief police dog in 'Softly Softly', and has 120 canines on her books, eight of them working on a BBC comedy series called 'Wuffer'.

She says, 'There have been cases in this country where whole crews have walked off the set over the treatment of animal actors. There's nothing to protect them in TV studios in the UK, and some unenlightened directors think you can leave a dog waiting about all day and then expect it to walk on and act without proper training. I think animals in the cast should be treated with the same consideration as children. I sometimes have literally three days to prepare a dog for some fantastic stunt, but I refuse to do anything that has to be faked with tranquillizers. A dog can so easily be taught to act these things; they have a very great sense of occasion, and when a trainer has a direct line to their minds, there's nothing they can't do, usually cued by hand signals.' Dorothy Steves thinks there's a trend away from pedigree screen actors towards mongrels. 'It isn't just a question of temperament; physically in many ways pedigrees are contrary to nature.' But she loves GSDs ('they have such a great intelligence') and the enormous Irish wolfhound she happens to be working with at the moment. She doesn't train dogs for commercials. 'That really is cruelty; all day long doing stupid tiny little shots. What I do has to involve a dog's intelligence. I train them to act in specific dog "parts".' Watch out for a GSD protegé currently learning to operate a computer.

Animal talent agencies expect a lot from canine hopefuls. In America a director of one agency hiring and firing for films, ads and publicity, says 'gorgeous highly trained animals are a dime a dozen'.[5] Most lack the necessary obedience to sit under hot lights all day doing indescribably boring advertising re-takes. Pedigrees are generally preferred to mongrels for marketing products; they have a certain snob value. In the UK Barbara Woodhouse trained all the Old English Sheepdogs for Dulux, from Digby to a seven-week-old pup on a paint pot who did all his tricks like a prodigy. She says it's hard to make dogs look asleep when the script requires, as their tongues hang out under the lights. Bobtails like Digby are marvellous to train, but their mouths go a dirty brown and if it rains they have to go to the toilet in boots and waterproofs to keep them ticky boo. Retakes kill spontaneity: the first take is usually the best. I asked Mrs Woodhouse, trainer of so many canine Thespians, if the dogs know what they are doing.

'It entirely depends on the training of a dog as to whether it reacts with pleasure when acting. The praise it gets when it does right matters so much.

Anubis, the Egyptian jackal-headed god

A Roman lamp in bronze

The wolf – believed by most scientists to be the dogfather

A fox torn alive. Painting by Henry Alken

French staghounds waiting for offal

Left : Mary Queen of Scots with her last and best friend

Below : King Edward VII and little Caesar

...ove : The shadow of a smile. No monarch ever ...ed dogs more than Queen Victoria

...ght : Princess Elizabeth with Dookie

A dog-powered roasting spit.
The animal is shut in a treadmill on the wall

An Eskimo driver with wolfish team

An Antwerp milkcart *c.* 1888

Above : A terrier ratting

Right : Hampshire's lost art of truffling

French war dogs with *Poilus*, 1939

Two Stockholm police cairns on the beat.
One recently cornered a burglar

Keen to get on with it. Police dog airlifted to manhunt by army helicopter

Above : Kent dogs in blue. Harmless to the law-abiding.

Left : A drug-detection dog with suspicious package

Left : This bulldog visage has little to do with bull-baiting and much to do with fashion

Below : Korea's favourite sport, and increasingly popular in Britain and America

Dogs very much sense an important occasion which of course acting is. If kindly trained I believe dogs look forward to this type of work. Mongrels react in exactly the same way as purebred dogs. Overseas I train 99 per cent mongrels in my TV work, from the animal shelters, always hoping they will get homes after seeing how well they work.'

The late Charles Hawtrey, actor-manager, tells an amusing story (in his memoirs, *The Truth at Last*) of a canine stage actor in the very first play he ever produced. It was a foxterrier belonging to his brother Edward, called 'Bob'. Night after night Bob was required to come out on cue from under a sofa and growl at one of the actors and for several weeks performed without mishap. Then one night he was stolen and a substitute had to be rehearsed, an old spaniel belonging to the theatre fireman. The understudy, no canine Brando he, had to be stirred up at the psychological moment by means of a broom from behind the scenes. The affair ended sensationally. In his debut performance the spaniel shot out from under the sofa and was attacked by another dog jumping on stage, trailing a length of rope from his collar. It was Bob.

A modern *chien celebré* of the stage is Dougal, belonging to actor David King. Dougal (the real dog not the floor mop) has done Shakespeare, Chekhov, *Toad of Toad Hall*, and suitable television work. Being a mongrel he gets a very fine write-up in Jilly Cooper's *Intelligent and Loyal*, where we learn he was a cast-off with a tendency to rip people's homes up. (The young Edmund Kean's guardian used to put a dog's collar on *him* inscribed, 'Bring this boy to Miss Tidswell,' when the lad ran wild backstage.) Dougal's Moonshine in *Midsummer Night's Dream* really slayed 'em. He got rave reviews, a Chocolate Bar Award and three Shin Bone Nominations. No such glittering prizes for poor Rocky, a six-year-old bull terrier who played opposite Jimmy Edwards, Roy Hudd, and about twenty children at the Birmingham Hippodrome, as Bill Sykes's 'Bullseye' in the musical *Oliver!* One day while out walking in the city centre Rocky was roused from his stage reflections by a toddler suddenly falling on top of him, and bit the child on the nose. The girl's mother called for Rocky to be put down immediately, acting talent or no. He got the sack and, for all anyone can discover, the chop.

Dog screen actors have been legion. One of the earliest movie stars was 'Teddy', of Mack Sennett's comedies. Teddy took it all very seriously and never wagged his tail on the set. Then there was Rin-Tin-Tin, the GSD who at young Rusty's warcry, 'Yo, Rinny!' would leap on villains from cliff or car. Another magnificent American GSD, Max, the US television 'Bionic dog' goes one better and unclamps bear-traps with his teeth. Any dog can act tough, perhaps, but a real performer gives the human co-star something to act against, like Dolores, the Battersea mongrel with Rod Steiger in *Across the Bridge*, or Toto the cairn who shares Judy Garland's wonderment in *The*

Wizard of Oz. These are no mere stage props; the dogs are required to reflect back attitude and emotion. You can play opposite *such* a dog without losing face, despite what theatre aphorisms might say.

But the greatest of them all was Lassie, a collie collective rather than an individual dog, based on the canine character in a 1938 short story, who gets lost and tries to find her master. The story was expanded into a bestseller, became a movie in 1943, and spawned five sequels and a television series. What was it about *Lassie Come Home*, a tear-jerker, in many ways contrived and cloyingly sloppy, that made it such a blockbuster?

The first time William Shatner ever 'acted' was in a children's camp play at the age of six. He was cast as a Jewish child having to leave home because of the Nazis, and saying goodbye to his dog, played by another little boy.

> And whether it was because I had always wanted a dog and never had been able to have one. . . . I did have dogs as I got older but never for any length of time and not the *kind* of dog and the way I wanted a dog in some inchoate way. . . . There I was talking to this camper that I now imagined to be the dog I had always wanted. And the audience were seeing a Jewish child being pulled away from his home. So that the environment was right from the audience's point of view, the situation with a dog and a child was right from my point of view, so that in some manner or in *that* manner in which an actor touches an audience, I touched that audience. . . . I cried on stage – and the people in the audience cried.[6]

There are few better ways of signifying on screen that 'inchoate' yearning, which the Germans call *Sehnsucht* but which we don't really have a word for, than by showing an exchange between a child and his dog, and few better ways than this of reminding an audience of loving and longing in the terrible bottomless way we all did as children. This is the lynchpin of Eric Knight's original Lassie story, with the boy's collie missing, presumed dead, and the child looking forlornly across the schoolyard where Lassie used to wait, and suddenly spotting

> . . . a dog. Not a dog, this one, that lifted glad ears above a proud slim head with its black-and-gold mask, but a dog that lay weakly, trying to lift a head that would no longer lift, trying to wag a tail that was torn and blotched and matted with dirt and burs, and managing to do nothing much except to whine in a weak, happy, crying way as a boy on his knees threw arms about it, and hands touched it that had not touched it for many a day.[7]

15

IN DEATH AND DARKNESS

The real worth of the dog is rather like inspiration, not vouchsafed for everyone to know, and often only revealed in dire emergencies, when love and loyalty become more than just words. Dogs really have rescued large numbers of people from great suffering, visible danger and invisible prisons of blindness, deafness and loneliness where no human hand could reach to help them. This chapter is devoted to dogs who have saved people's bacon.

In 1919 a steamer with ninety-two men, women and children aboard foundered in terrific gales on the jagged coast of Newfoundland. Conditions were too bad for the lifeboats. All else having failed, a light line was tied to the collar of a Newfoundland dog belonging to one of the crew and he was put to sea, his old head bobbing between the rocks, his great body smacked about like a float and disappearing from view. What was a dog's life, after all, in this mess? On shore, rescuers watched the wreck stave in, but waited about in case there were one or two survivors. Out of the water bobbed a dark shape that looked at first like a seal. It shook itself and came waddling up with a rolling sailor's gait, to show them its collar and line. The cord brought in a rope, a block and tackle were rigged, and every one of the ninety-two souls aboard, including an eighteen-month-old baby in a mailbag, were brought across in a breeches buoy.[1]

Newfoundlands are old seadogs, once used in their namesake country as fishermen's mates for rescue and retrieving nets, catching their own grub (usually cod) and being sold to curious foreigners. Later they worked aboard trading vessels and even sloops as line-haulers and lifeguards. Napoleon was reputedly saved by a 'Newf' and in France they still work with spotters on dangerous beaches. Many modern Newf clubs offer lifesaving certificates to dogs that can retrieve, rescue, tow a boat and deliver line, and records of children hauled out of canals and rivers, as well as sea-rescues, are numerous because the dogs were regular crew members. (Two pups taken off a wrecked English brig near the coast of Maryland helped found the Chesapeake Bay retrievers.) Bob, a Victorian black-and-white Newfoundland, twice set sail for America with his master. The first time the boat sank and Bob was able to save his owner by swimming two miles in a rough sea. The second time he failed to save his owner, and found his way back to London where, as a stray, he began compulsively fishing people out of the Thames. He was decorated and adopted by the Royal Humane Society, who found out his history, and when he died in 1874 he was credited with saving twenty-three persons. Edwin Landseer painted him as 'A Member of the Humane Society'. Another RHS Newfoundland 'member' collected for the lifeboat fund. He would turn up at resorts, offer his paw and shake himself to rattle his tin. By a lake in Travancore, near Quilion, there is a monument to a Newfoundland who interposed himself between his bathing master and a crocodile. 'Greater love hath no man than this' it says; the dog was killed. Among the sad stories there are also some funny ones. Pre-war dog historian Edward Ash says nobody ever wanted to be rescued by a Newfoundland twice: one man, swimming happily, was so roughly hauled ashore that he had to be taken to hospital in a hansom cab.[2] A lifesaving demonstration in Maidstone, featuring the famous 'Nero' who would reputedly leap from a liner, was a fiasco. A straw dummy was tossed in the river and all the dogs sat on a wall, barking. One brindle-and-white fell in, but otherwise there was not a lot to see.

Other strong swimming breeds have saved humans from a watery end. The Portuguese water-dog used to carry messages from boat to boat, retrieve nets and lifeguard, and labradors were, of course, fishermen's dogs: note the characteristic 'otter' tail. A retriever of some sort leapt into a drain in Hull in 1921 and came out with a child. The dog was found to have a silver medal for lifesaving already. A collie called Lassie, of the Pilot Boat Inn, stood by Scots sailor John Cowan, taken off the wreck of the *Formidable* on the south coast in 1915, and given up for dead. Lassie became so agitated that a doctor returned to have one more go at reviving him. Cowan recovered. One lifesaving story from the RSPCA archives concerns a spaniel whose master, a drunk, fell in a pond. 'Wallack' seized him by the collar but couldn't keep his face out of the water and finally hit on the idea of buoying the man's head up with his own little head until help arrived. The whole scene was watched by a lame man from a balcony. The dipsomaniac dried out; the dog drowned.

There are many awards and citations for canine valour. In Britain these include the PDSA Roll of Honour, the Dickin Medal and the NCDL Certificate for Services to Humanity. In America the Humane Association, founded in 1877, offers the prestigious Stillman Award. One winner was Gretchen, a Weimaraner, who defended her one-legged master from wild animals for a week in the Mojave desert after his car ran out of petrol, despite being in great pain from her wounds. Several dogs have hauled children by their clothing from the path of oncoming vehicles, like Jane the golden retriever, Bob the sheepdog, and a collie who was killed in 1923 pushing a little girl from under a bus. A retriever out shooting with his master in a turnip field found something alive and refused to budge. It was a starving boy, missing from home for three days.

In 1919 an attempt to derail the Paris–Bordeaux express was foiled by a dog barking and fetching the stationmaster to have a look at two sleepers laid across the track. On a smaller scale, a whippet, Lucky Prince, rushed for help when his master fell in quicksand. Rescuers arrived with ropes but the man couldn't get hold of any of them. The dog waded out with one in his teeth. And then there was Tripper the collie, who ran for help when his epileptic master had a fit on a deserted beach, Three Cliffs Bay near Swansea. When the RAF helicopter airlifted his owner away, Tripper thrashed about in the sea, desperate. He was eventually reunited with Jim Rigg who had bought him for 50p from a dogs' home.

In the US, every year since 1954, an American Dog Hero of the Year has been feted by the Quaker Oats Company, who name their award after their Ken-L Ration petfood. One of their staff, Doug Burson, tells me he receives twenty different stories a week of dog heroism, ranging 'anywhere from lifesaving deeds such as pulling an owner or neighbor from water, to dogs alerting their owners to fire'. The Hero is chosen from dozens of bronze medallists whose stories have been chosen and authenticated. One was Zorro, a GSD who went backpacking with his master in the Sierra Nevada in 1975, and saw him slip 85 feet into a creek. Zorro dragged poor Mark Cooper out of the water but he kept sliding back down the steep bank, so Zorro gave the matter some thought and then sat on his legs to anchor him. Like little Tripper, Zorro was distraught to see his owner being airlifted by the rescue helicopter, leaving him behind. He was discovered next day by volunteers, still guarding his master's backpack.

Even if a dog cannot save you, it will not leave you. In September 1967 a Welsh mountain-rescue team found the body of a missing climber. Standing over him in the wind and sleet was his starving brown-and-white spaniel. Another dog, a collie called Tip, kept watch over the body of an eighty-six-year-old shepherd through fifteen weeks of a moorland winter, and there are a number of authenticated accounts of dogs dying on their masters' and mistresses' graves.

Chico the Chihuahua woke up a family of four in St Paul, Minnesota, barking and carrying on. She could smell smoke. When the firemen arrived, they estimated that the family had got out with five minutes to spare.[3] Terence, an Irish terrier, saved a young child in a burning house in Devon. Firemen broke in to find the dog, soaking wet from jumping in the cistern, lying on top of the toddler who was unharmed. Many dogs have raised the alarm, like two Peke Stillman Award winners, Sen Su and Penny Sing Lee.

Sen Su's cousin had performed a similar service years before for his mistress, but died of his burns. And then there was Fritz, a GSD belonging to the Müller family, at the top of a burning apartment block in Chicago. Frau Müller had managed to get all the children out, bar the youngest, when the stairs became unsafe. Firemen were driven back by the flames but Fritz was told, 'Go and fetch baby!' Ten minutes later the dog reappeared carrying the child, slightly burned on its hands and face but otherwise OK. Fritz was unrecognizable. His coat was burned away, along with most of his skin, and he was in agony from his injuries and had lost the sight of an eye.[4]

Hearing Dogs for the Deaf

Some emergencies are not shortlived, like shipwrecks or fires. Some last a lifetime. There are 14 million people in America who are hard of hearing, and deafness, partial or total, strikes one in five people in the UK. For the rest of their lives, sufferers enter a silent prison, suspicious, dependent on other people and increasingly lonely. Many turn in on themselves. There are amplifiers for their telephones but, if they can't hear them ringing, they don't get a lot of calls. Visitors ring the doorbell and go away, and very often they don't come back. Since 1976 in the States, over 500 dogs, mostly ex-strays, have been trained as 'hearing aids', living in the deaf persons' homes, and rushing to fetch them to the source of a sound, like the kettle whistling, or the doorbell, or baby crying. In 1982 the Royal National Institute for the Deaf, which had maintained close links with its US counterparts, sent ex-police-dog handler Tony Blunt to America to study the training.

At one of the largest veterinary congresses ever held in this country, attended by 1500 vets and world authorities on companion animals, I was privileged to meet Chum, who is black, shiny, sixteen months old and a pioneer British Hearing Dog for the Deaf. He listened to my questions carefully but declined to discuss his training methods, so I asked Tony Blunt, who said: 'Chum is halfway through the four-month course. What I do first of all is to go to the deaf person's house and make recordings of particular sounds they'd like to be alerted to – I think a dog can learn five or six before getting into problems – then I put myself in all the situations that I think the deaf person might be in, like washing up at the kitchen sink, and when the dog hears the recording he must come and touch me on the leg and take me to the source of the sound. He must make contact: you ignore him till he does.' A hearing dog must be curious, friendly, willing to please, and with a keen nose for noises: the sort of dog who goes to investigate anyway, and can be trained to make a diversion to nudge a deaf friend. American vet and author Bruce Fogle: 'Generally the best dogs are the smaller, more alert ones that are shot out of a cannon when they hear a sound. Chum happens to be a cross-labrador but the pilot scheme dog, Favour, was a stray from the NCDL and there's no way you can figure out what breed he is. Purebred labradors are generally too laid back. They hear the doorbell and think "Hmm. Doorbell rang."'

All the dogs that have been trained so far are mongrels or crossbreeds. 'There are 50,000 strays in this country; mongrels are good, intelligent dogs. There's no reason why they shouldn't have a purpose in life like everybody ·else,' says Tony Blunt.

At the moment it costs £2500 to produce each trained dog because the scale is so small; the newly opened training centre is at Chinnor, Oxfordshire and the scheme relies entirely on sponsorship and donations. The dogs are provided free to deaf people who could best benefit from them; for example, those at home all day alone or those who, like James and Isabella Chapman, have a special case. James and Isabella, both profoundly deaf themselves, run a rehabilitation centre for deaf boys trying to cope with their disability. Chum will be the Chapmans' 'ears'. Said Isabella: 'He will give us that bit more confidence to cope,' and James explained, 'Chum will be a really big help to us. Deafness sets people apart.'

The hearing dog gives deaf owners a new lease on life, a companion, a clue to what's going on in the world, a friend to jump on them in the mornings when the alarm goes off. Dean Leo Bustad, Professor of Veterinary Medicine at Washington State University, has been with the American scheme from its inception. 'I was involved in the placement of the first hearing dog, in Northwestern US, with a Mrs Christianson. The dog's name was Ranger, and I taught it to rouse her when the smoke alarm went off. When she took me to the door she said, "Important as it was for me to have a hearing dog, it was even more important that I have a companion." It was a very moving event for me because two years ago I came home one day from work and my wife could no longer hear me. We now have a hearing dog ourselves, so I have great empathy with people who are hard of hearing. Two years ago though, if I'd told Jim and Isabella Chapman, "I have something for you that will bring laughter into your lives, give you unconditional love, security, forgiveness, a reason for living, and in addition to all that, *hear* for you, and its name is Chum," I'm sure they'd have questioned my sanity.'

While the scheme here is in its infancy, might I suggest one breed with a special interest in ringing telephones? There are a number of Jack Russells in Britain already leaping into the air to knock receivers off the hook, even from wall phones, and all of their own accord. One of them belonging to seventy-four-year-old Mrs Helen Rowbotham of Scunthorpe, also howls down the mouthpiece, though Mrs Rowbotham can hear perfectly well and has never asked for this service. His last long-distance call was from a French mayor, ringing up about exchange visits. He asked M. le Maire for a woo-woo-woo to be considered for a ro-ro in the Humberside area.

Hearing Dogs for the Deaf, RNID, 105 Gower Street, London WC1E 6AH. Tel. 01 387 8033; Training Centre, 2 Chinnor Hill, Chinnor, Oxon OX9 4BA. Tel. Kingston Blount 53898.

Guide Dogs for the Blind

A wall painting from Herculaneum, dated to the time of Christ, shows a blind beggar with a dog on a lead; there are many medieval woodcuts of the subject. In Paris in the late eighteenth century, blind patients from the hospital Quinze-Vingt were led through the streets by dogs, and in the 1780s a blind Viennese, Joseph Reisinger, hearing of the hospital's work, had a Spitz specially trained for him to negotiate staircases and traffic. When it died Reisinger trained replacements using a stick to feel his way and thwack the dog when it made an error. An instruction manual appeared in 1819 in Vienna, and another handbook by a blind Swiss, Jakob Birrer, in 1847, shows how he used a stick to train his own Spitz to pull slightly ahead, avoiding obstacles on a set route. Nothing, though, was organized until the Germans went to work. When their soldiers came back blinded from the First World War, the Austrian Police and War Dog Institute set up a German Association for Serving Dogs, to arrange GSD guides for their veterans. They had a school at Potsdam, which captured the imagination of two visiting American dog-trainers, Dorothy Harrison Eustis and her husband. So moved were they at the sight of blinded Germans walking proudly about with their shepherds, that Dorothy and husband determined to set up a school themselves – which they did, in Switzerland in 1928. It was called L'Oeil Qui Voit (The Seeing Eye, from Proverbs XX, xii). Through their work and articles in the press, guide-dog training began to spread. Schools were opened in Wallasey, Cheshire in 1931 and in New Jersey, US, in 1932.

The British school began with seven GSDs and five blind students. Four pairs emerged successful. At first only GSDs were used but, as these became scarce in the war effort, collies, sheepdogs, keeshonds, retrievers, boxers and crossbreeds were trained. Bitches were found to be less bossy and cock-a-leaky than males. Using public cast-offs the failure rate was high (70 per cent) but when a breeding and puppy-walking scheme began in the 1950s the success rate rose rapidly. About half of modern British guide dogs are labradors (another one third are cross-labrador/golden retrievers), though in Germany and the US, GSDs are preferred, along with Dobermanns. The Guide Dogs for the Blind Association now has 150 brood bitches and 35 studs 'on tap' as it were.

Pups born at the breeding centre at Tollgate House, near Warwick, are housetrained and urbanized in private homes from about six weeks until ten to twelve months. They learn standardized commands (like 'busy' for toiletry), walking straight and sitting neatly. Then they are returned, reassessed and allocated to one of six training centres (Exeter, Leamington Spa, Wokingham, Bolton, Middlesbrough and Forfar). The few failures usually become house-pets – although some have made useful police or customs dogs. The rest are neutered and given a comprehensive seven to nine months' training programme. Training consists of three months' rudimentary work followed by advanced coaching with a different instructor. Gradually they learn what is expected of them: no puppy habits, frisking, sniffing or meandering while in harness (though the dogs can romp about while off-duty), straight ahead through mock-up streets and then on to the real thing.

When dealing with traffic a moving car is the signal to stop, overriding the forward command from the handler. This is called trained disobedience and, surprisingly, doesn't cause the dogs to become confused – they simply learn that the forward 'signal' (it is not, strictly speaking, a command) should be disregarded when certain external conditions prevail, e.g. the close proximity of a moving car.

Finally, blind students are carefully matched with suitable dogs and take a month's course together, the new partners sharing rooms in a residential block. The students learn every aspect of dog ownership whilst at the centre and gradually acquire new skills which develop confidence in themselves and their dogs. They get used to the new language transmitted through the animal's body harness and handle. The dogs have been taught to be obedient, to stop at kerbs and guide their owners safely in crowds; lifts, shops, heights, widths. They ignore distractions and avoid obstacles that would impede their blind 'other half', thinking of the blind person as part of themselves. But, highly trained though they are, the dogs will in the long run only be as good as their owners. The ability of the blind owner to get the best out of his guide is crucial to the success of the team.

There are over 3000 guide dogs in Britain and nearly 600 more are trained every year, many replacing old dogs retired as house-pets. A guide dog gives mobility, healthy exercise, independence, companionship and security based on trust – quite a lot for 50p which is all the blind person is required to pay for the dog. It costs well over £4000 to train each animal and the scheme runs entirely on public generosity.

The Guide Dogs for the Blind Association, Alexandra House, 9–11 Park Street, Windsor, Berkshire SL4 1JR. Tel. Windsor 55711.

Bill Harman's Lady

What difference does a guide dog make to someone who is blind? Bill Harman from East Ham finally lost his sight in 1954 ('I regain it every night – I dream'). He's eighty-four, says he could still chase me round the table, and travels with his jet-black GSD Lady all over London, giving talks at schools and hospitals and raising money for the GDBA. This is Bill, talking about his Lady:

When we go out, we take each other. I tell her where to go and she follows my directions. A guide dog only obeys orders. It walks along the pavement till it gets to a kerb, then it awaits instructions. It stops at every step down, even if it's a kerb an inch deep. If I want to cross a road I say 'Forward!' and then she waits till it's clear and she judges it's safe. If I don't say 'Forward!' she just sits there. She only obeys my orders – forward, right, left, etc. – but once I give that command, my life is in her judgement. Once she starts to move, I'm not in charge of my dog; she is in sole charge of me, until she stops and waits for the next instruction. I wasn't worried the first time a guide dog took me across the road, because I'm a confident person and I have confidence in the dog. You have to have, for it to work. A lot of guide-dog owners haven't really the authority with the dogs that they ought to have, so they're not so successful. When I give my dog an order, I speak firmly and clearly. It's not unkind. In the Army they don't say 'Attention please'. If my dog does anything wrong, she's brought back on the instant, and I shake the harness, growl at her in a gruff voice, and make her do it correctly, because they're like children, they do take advantage given the chance. On the other hand, you don't hold the handle: it rests in the crooks of your fingers, or you stifle all the feelings transmitted to you, like the handle going slightly up when you're about to go up.

Lady and I travel all over on the railway, sometimes changing trains four times. I know all the London tube stops and when the door opens I give the handle a tiny jerk and she's up like a shot, and I say 'Out you go darling' and out she goes. On some stations where there's a choice of trains, I have to ask, because Lady can do a lot of things but she can't read the indicators yet. I don't like travelling on buses because you can never tell when you're at a stop with all the pausing and starting, and conductors have been known to leave us sitting there, sailing past our destination.

When we're walking along the pavement, sometimes she'll slow up, and it may be because she's having a sly sniff or a look at another dog, rather than for any good reason. So I say 'Come on Lady, get a move on.' I'm told women have turned round and glared at me. Once we were in a shop and I said, 'Come on Lady, get your behind out of the way!' and the shopkeeper said I'd offended one of his customers. The dogs are named as pups; it's not my fault. Actually Lady is my third guide dog. When I had my first one I went to Exeter and I was five years older than what they call the 'exceptional age' for a blind man student –

fifty-five. The *recommended* age is fifty. I was sixty. I was the oldest man, by five years, ever to be trained with a first guide dog. I was old enough to be two of the other students' grandfather. My first dog was called Cora, but the GDBA nicknamed her the Galloping Guide Dog. GSDs are live, fast-moving dogs and normally, though you can slow them down or speed them up, you need to keep pace with the dog's natural walking speed, or it's under restraint all the time. Cora's normal walking speed was fast, like mine. After a while, you become part of the dog. The perfect unit is when you and the dog are one. I go everywhere with Lady, and even at nursery schools with three-year-olds pulling her about and kissing her, I never have to worry. There's no dog in the world to beat the GSD for gentleness, faithfulness and sheer intelligence. If I just pat my leg, wherever she is, she's here! I know some blind people don't want a guide dog: they're a little extra work in the house, you have to vac the floor a lot, and get their food. But what they do for you *far* outweighs anything you do for them.

16

THE PROTECTION RACKET

A man walking down the street with his new *Schutzhund*, or personal-protection dog, is a stirring sight, like a lad in his first pair of long trousers. All gnawing doubts about his own masculinity suddenly vanquished, he feels he can now take us to the cleaners. Indeed, the sizeable responsibility for guarding his person, property and ego is an important and time-honoured job for dogs. The bigger and more ferocious they are, the better our self-aggrandized little wimp likes them. After seeing all the sterling work of those Army, RAF patrol and police dogs, we'd better have a brief look at the watchdog, bandog, guard-dog, attack dog, security dog or whatever you like to call the unfortunate beast who once stared out from mosaics in Roman entrance lobbies inscribed *Cave canem* (beware of the dog) – or our *Schutzhund* owner will never forgive us.

Guarding comes naturally to dogs. They are territorial animals, proud to be associated with humans (for some reason) and, if the worst comes to the worst, will lay down their lives in defence of persons and property. Older male wolves will act as watchdogs outside the den during cubbing; their job is clearly defined and they do not bring food to the nursery like other pack members.[1] A dog who has only ever owned a bone learns what human property is by association. Ethologist Konrad Lorenz points out that, although a dog finds it a trial when you leave his side, he can be easily trained to lie down and stay if you put one or two personal possessions by him. 'Should a stranger attempt to purloin something, the dog will become half-frenzied with anger, not because he has a real sense of his duty to protect his master's belongings, but because these objects infused with his master's smell symbolize for him the home which in some way they represent, and give him the guarantee that his master will sooner or later return to the place.'[2]

The dog has other qualifications for the job. George Nash, the Lancashire cricketer, once kept a hotel at Over Darwen with numbered room bells hanging from the kitchen ceiling. One of them, indistinguishable from the general jangle, was for the front door and, if it so much as trembled, George's pom, Floss, would be catapulted into the foyer, barking. Pavlov, the Russian vivisector, would call a group of laboratory 'tools' to dinner by sounding True C with a pitchfork. The dogs were then starved and found to salivate at True C, not C flat or sharp. Consultant in animal behaviour Dr Roger Mugford, the only 'pet psychiatrist' in the UK, told me he recently had to deal with a dog whose New York mistress clicked the lock of her front door once to go down to the basement and twice to go out. The dog only tore the place apart when the lock clicked twice.

Not that *all* dogs bestir themselves after burglars three doors away, or even in the house! Frankly, some don't care to own a video recorder. But for centuries, hundreds of thousands of canines *have* guarded man's belongings, even when all he had was a cave with a couple of goats in it. The Athenians, Corinthians, Romans, Persians, Egyptians and Orientals all had notable watchdogs and in the mythologies of several races, dogs guard everything from the Seven Sleepers' Den to the Creation itself, as well as the gates of important little places, like Hell. Dogs have been entrusted with minding Joseph's Tomb, geisha girls and the League of Nations secretariat buildings during the Sacco-Vanzetti riots of 1927.[3] The Rottweiler, GSD, Briard and Groenendael have all distinguished themselves as guardians; some breeds have been purpose-built. The Rhodesian Ridgeback used to patrol the boundaries of plantations in colonial Africa looking for robbers. His hackles are ready raised. The good old mastiff, who these days will very likely sit on the burglar rather than eat him, has always been used as a guard and was once inordinately savage. Bloodhounds prowled medieval premises, Dalmatians deterred highwaymen from coaches, and keeshonds and Shipperkes looked after barges in Holland and Belgium in case anyone came barging in. All the big breeds do their bit: the Pyrenean patrols French estates; the Bouvier and Maremma look after the silverware as well as livestock.

Traditionally, the watchdog has been hideously treated. The Tibetan mastiff, chained up for most of his life, grows fierce as a tiger, and in Britain as late as the 1930s Major Harding Cox of the Kennel Club was calling for a change in the law to protect shackled watchdogs he had seen 'which were never let loose or even occasionally exercised. Such grew so savage that none dared approach them; consequently they were left in a state of indescribable filth and squalor, having their foetid water and foul offal thrust within their reach with a long pole.'[4] Bandogs, as these were called, were kept chained to a barrel or post and, in some cases, were let loose at night to frighten wayfarers. A Long Island vet, Dr John B. Swinford, has recently crossed pit bullterriers with Neopolitan and English mastiffs to produce the Swinford Bandog, a new version,[5] reviving the old 'manacled maniac' idea. Guards don't need to like folk. 'A Mr Mattison made a business in the 1950s of training dogs for guard work on parcels and goods vans. . . . Mr Mattison's methods of training were quaint, but they evidently produced the required results. His assertion was that dogs had to hate their handler first, and then grow to like him.'[6] Public anxiety over the death of a child in Glasgow, mauled by guard dogs, led to the Guard Dogs Act 1975. The act 'requires that a much closer control be kept over guard dogs and that guard dog businesses shall be licensed by the local authority', says a government report.[7]

The most famous (or infamous) modern purpose-built guard-dog is the Dobermann, called Doberman Pinscher in America and used by the US police and Marines. The dog was devised by a German, Louis Dobermann of Apolda, who brewed him up from several breeds in his dog pound to make the perfect police/protection animal. Well, almost perfect. Unfortunately when any dog is bred like mad for the sake of a market, some of the progeny behave accordingly – like mad. The Dobermann has had his reputation sullied by the protection racket. One British trainer I spoke to explained, 'Dobermanns and security are dirty words at the moment. Dobermanns are fast-thinking, fast-acting guard-dogs but they are essentially *personal* guards. Too many dogs have been bred and a lot of people who cannot cope with them have got rid of them to be teased up and used for security work – and those dogs are maniacs.'

It isn't the dog's fault if he is exploited by unscrupulous outfits. The Dobermann is a loyal, passionate beast, deeply proud of his owner and his home (if he has one) and highly territorial. If invited to do so he is well equipped to cut up rough: fleet afoot, brainy, muscular as a horse and with steel jaws. Responsible UK breeders have worked very hard to eradicate all viciousness from the English strains and in the right hands the dogs are now pillars of society. The same cannot be said for certain German and American crop-eared contenders who look rather like bats out of hell, poor devils. The Dobermann is volatile and proud, and any breed can be goaded to nastiness, even a Yorkie. It is the Dobermann's misfortune that, when he bites, he does more damage than most angry dogs.

To clear the Dobermann's name caring British clubs hold working trials for him which are rigorous tests of control as well as courage, to show how an obedient, safe dog can be used to defend a handler from assault. They point out that manwork is best left to the experts; a biting dog can be a legal liability. Before the Dobermann was phased out of police service in this country in favour of the superb GSD, he was obedient and heroic in performance of his duties, good at nosework, and won several trials.[8] One brave police Dober, Pablo, had to be put down after being blinded with acid as he was making an arrest in Macclesfield. The dogs lost ground to the GSD chiefly because they got bored and cold; other police forces around the world still use them extensively as Herr Dobermann intended.

Dogs teased up and chained in scrapyards, or left to maraud over premises without a handler at night, quickly lose their respect for humanity. Responsible security firms both here and in the States, using mostly GSDs, are at pains to avoid indiscriminate savagery and select and breed their dogs carefully. They provide static guards and patrol dogs for hospitals, schools and parks where control is essential, as well as business and industrial premises. The dogs are trained to bark on command, 'rag' with a piece of cloth, then attack a protective hessian sleeve. Their job is to defend the handler, not take over the place. They work usually six nights a week, returning in the morning to be fed, kennelled and allowed to rest all day. When they retire, often after as little as four years of total alertness, they become 'semi-pets', such as pub dogs. In the States there are now organized *Schutzhund* training schemes designed to produce non-demonic guards who will only hurt an aggressor. The training originated in Germany where the *Schutzhund* (SchH) qualification is also recognized.

Unfortunately there are unscrupulous outfits in America and elsewhere offering 'attack dogs' even by mail order, and these eventually bite most people, including the purchaser. Some cities and states have begun licensing both protection dogs and their trainers to avoid abuse.[9] A recent well-publicized case was of a Seattle mugger who trained his dog as an offensive weapon. 'Rocky', the pit bullterrier, ended up on death row, and was only reprieved by animal-lovers' protests. It would indeed be a pity if the guard-dog became the bandog once again, or if the 'macho' male were allowed to aim its muzzle at his rivals.

17

BRUTES OF SCIENCE

Of all the jobs dogs do for us, and they are prepared to do practically anything, the one they like least is working in laboratories. Dogs cannot speak but they can scream, and many 'research workers' have to be de-barked. For readers who prefer to turn the page, I'll give a warning in the text when we come to awful bits. Unfortunately the subjects cannot turn the page.

Researchers who experiment on animals have it both ways. Animals are like us but, there again, animals are not like us. They tell you they are like us when you ask how animals' responses can possibly be relevant to the study of mankind, and they tell you they are not like us when you inquire about the distress of creatures in their experiments. Animals are like us *a bit* but, since they cannot reason, we needn't trouble about their feelings. A baby or a human vegetable cannot reason either, but they are protected from the scientists' itchy fingers. Concentration-camp inmates, Burke & Hare supplies, human embryos and Eastern Bloc athletes have all felt the spider's touch, and animals, being dumb and defenceless, feel it constantly.

Statistics issued by the Home Office and provided by the scientists themselves (there is no independent audit) show that, exclusive of certain categories from 1977 to 1982, 28,447,000 experiments were carried out on living animals in the UK, 23,093,000 without anaesthetic. The total from 1952 was approximately 135 million, the majority carried out by commercial concerns for profit. In 1982, of 4,221,801 experiments 'calculated to cause pain', 13,146 were performed on dogs, 7774 of them without anaesthetic. From 1977 to 1982 78,100 dogs were used, a proportion acquired from casual dealers and some of them stolen pets. Vivisection runners have been using vans like those of local authorities[1] and the British Union for the Abolition of Vivisection (BUAV) offers £5000 for information leading to a conviction.

No RSPCA inspector is ever allowed into the laboratories, and though licensees performing experiments need neither animal-handling skills nor biological qualifications, there have been no convictions for abuse in this country since the enabling Cruelty to Animals Act was framed in 1876. The law contains six humane safeguards, but four can be overruled by certificates. Most experiments are certified. In any case the experimenters are left to judge the degree of pain they inflict and its duration, because the millions of experiments in 1982 were supervised by just fifteen Home Office inspectors. A recent Government White Paper, promising to 'help the plight of laboratory animals', contains recommendations that actually make matters worse;[2] no wonder animal-rights' groups are growing large and restive.

Unfortunately, though animals are like us a bit, medically speaking they are unreliable analogues. Drugs like Thalidomide, Eraldin, Opren, Flosint, Tanderil and Butazoldin all reached the market through vivisection. They were found safe on animals. Had penicillin been screened using guinea-pigs, it would probably not be available now: one species' cure is another species' poison. The National Anti-Vivisection Society's (NAVS) scientific research officer, Dr Robert Sharpe, wishes we could stop testing drugs on the wrong subjects. 'Concentrating more on human beings rather than "animal models" makes good sense when it is realized that, *at best*, animal tests correctly predict only one in four side-effects.'[3]

Brave physicians once tested new substances on themselves; why not brave researchers? Or perhaps the human muggers and murderers idling in our prisons at the taxpayer's expense would care to repay their debt to society? What a deterrent to knocking a pensioner's brains in!

Dogs are cheap and relatively cheerful research 'tools'. Beagles and greyhounds are forgiving and gentle. In Britain in 1972, 71 per cent of dogs used were beagles and 9 per cent greyhounds. In the US, of over 70 million experiments per year, an estimated 500,000 are performed on dogs,[4] mostly beagles. Many have died testing radioactive substances and pesticides such as methoxychlor (by force-feeding), and great numbers succumb to 'intentional induction of neoplasia' – cancer implants. RSPCA Chief Animal Experimentation Research Officer, Dr Judith Hampson: 'In the USA the collective paranoia about cancer has led to a presidential mandate to the National Cancer Institute to spend as much as it possibly can from an unlimited budget on research. This has not resulted in a "cure" for cancer, but in a vast wastage of animal life, with much of the data not even being collected because many of the experiments were ill thought-out and badly designed in the first place.'[5]

A cure for cancer may well emerge, not from giving the disease to terrified laboratory animals, but from *in vitro* (tissue and cell culture) techniques which deal with first principles. In Britain some portion of the cancer charities' collective assets of £44 million, and yearly expenditure of over £13 million, has been spent on these non-animal-based methods; a great deal is spent on neoplasia induction and dogs are among the victims.

Objectors to vivisection, from Richard Wagner to Spike Milligan, have tended to side with the brutes undergoing procedures rather than with those conducting them. One of the earliest objectors was a dog working for experimental psychologist, Professor Liddell, who in 1936 was studying the problem of driving dogs insane by forcing them to distinguish between two identical circles. This dog, whenever it saw Professor Liddell coming, would deliberately attack him or wee on his trouser leg. Another early objector was Alexander Pope. A friend commended the famous Dr Stephen Hales to Pope as a very good and worthy man. 'Yes,' said Pope, 'he is a very good man; only I am sorry he has his hands so much imbued with blood.'

'What, he cuts up rats?'

'Ay, and dogs too! Indeed he commits most of these barbarities with the thought of being of use to man; but how do we know that we have a right to kill creatures that we are so little above as dogs, for our curiosity, or even for some use to us?'[6] Jeremy Bentham thought the decision to exploit a living creature should depend not on whether it can reason or talk, but on whether it can suffer. Modern objectors question the motives of vivisection scientists. After all, competing pharmaceutical firms, worth billions, conduct endless duplicate tests in secret, behind barbed wire, to produce countless cosmetics, household products and 'me-too' drugs (as the variants are called) which differ only in brand names and vie for a share of the market. Yet if the drug trade were for the public good, the companies would not compete but would pool their research. Indeed, they would be nationalized. The drug firms, say sceptics, have a vested interest, not in eradicating illness but in alleviating it with expensive pills and potions. Infectious diseases yielded not so much to drugs as to improved hygiene, and modern preventable diseases of the environment are the result of our own affluence and folly. We have a few thousand drugs too many as it is.

The addresses of anti-vivisection charities, should you wish to get in touch with any of them, are given at the end of the section. The following passages contain details of experiments on dogs which some readers may find upsetting. Many of them are taken from ex-animal researcher Richard Ryder's outstanding *Victims of Science*,[7] where primary sources in the scientific literature are quoted. Sometimes, when details of an experiment are leaked to the public beforehand, an outcry forestalls the research. This has happened several times in America. In 1973, when the press discovered 600 beagles were about to test poison gases, the House of Representatives Armed Services Committee reportedly received more mail than on any subject since Truman fired General MacArthur.[8] Another storm followed the revelation in 1983 that trainee army surgeons were about to ply their skills on the *shot* hindquarters of live dogs suspended in net slings on a soundproof firing range at the Bethesda Medical School. Nevertheless, de-barked beagles were being exposed to mustard and nerve gases at Edgewood Arsenal, Maryland, in 1973, and war gases have elsewhere been applied to the skin of dogs causing blistering, gangrene and death. In the US and Britain (at Porton, Harwell and Aldermaston) dogs have been used to test radiation, chemical, biological, ultrasonic, photic, explosive and ballistic weapons, and the US Air Force thought it necessary to de-bark 200 beagles before they inhaled aviation fumes.

Human curiosity about pain kills many dogs. Soviet scientists at Lugansk, studying lavatorial functions, subjected ten dogs to stimulation of the sciatic nerve and spinal nerve roots for three or four weeks to see if they evacuated from the pain. South American researchers 'evoked the "pain" response' by injecting brandykinin peptides into the splenic artery, and by mechanical and thermal abrasion of the nipple, prepuce and footpad. The dogs showed they were being hurt by 'repeated vocalization, struggling and biting behaviour'. US researchers boast, 'We have found that ischemic sensitization of mechanical, electrical and chemical stimulation of the "pain" receptors in the spleen of the dog can be readily demonstrated by clamping the splenic artery.' At US universities, including Arkansas, Harvard and Pennsylvania, dogs shocked with electric collars are observed 'often rolling on their backs and howling' and also 'yelping and shrieking'. Some are restrained in hammocks; others 'freeze' when sizzled.

Dogs' teeth are quite unlike our own, yet dogs are increasingly used in dental research. At the Turner Dental School, Manchester, researchers drilled holes in the teeth of thirteen beagles and then daubed them with a chemical irritant. The pulps of sixty-eight teeth were exposed and allowed to erupt. (Dentists do not want for human subjects. Many of us go willingly to teaching hospitals.) Elsewhere in the UK, dogs with induced malignant tumours wear Elizabethan collars to prevent them from licking their wounds; dogs are subjected to heart puncture without anaesthetic, and daily 'infusion' or force-feeding by means of a tube down the gullet. Force-feeding in Britain and the US is common; ingestible products are routinely submitted for toxicity testing by this procedure. The validity of our notorious LD50 Test (the Lethal Dose at which half the force-fed animals die) has been queried by some toxicity researchers,[9] and criticized by the European Commission's Expert Committee on drug testing, who recommended that it be dropped.

Some dogs have been force-fed alcohol to damage their livers. The animals have consumed vast quantities of anti-freeze, weedkillers and handcream, vomiting, bleeding from the mouth, and being left to suffer convulsions and death without anaesthetic.

But the most pitiless tests are not for 'medical' purposes. Canadian psychologist Dr Alan Bowd, Associate Professor of the University of Victoria, writes, 'Animals are blinded, crippled, isolated from their own species, shocked, encouraged to attack one another, burned and beaten in psychological laboratories.'[10] Behavioural research owes much to Ivan P. Pavlov (1849–1936), a Russian who started off studying indigestion and ended up studying 'conditioning'. One of his dogs got into such a condition that it threw itself in the river. Another, Pavlov reports, 'became quite crazy, unceasingly and violently working all parts of its body, howling, barking and squealing intolerably'.[11] Pavlov reasoned that, with so much cruelty to animals and people in the world, 'how can we object to the sacrifice of a few animals on the altar of the supreme aspiration of man for knowledge . . .?[12] He got the Nobel Prize and his work continues, especially in America. One dog there became rigid with distress, and 'allowed passive moulding of limbs into bizarre poses' (which sounds as if researchers amused themselves). Another dog made neurotic was tortured with explosions, injections and electric shocks to the genitals for twelve years. The induced disorders persisted in some cases until death intervened. A Leningrad scientist found dogs that were driven mad also recovered less quickly from lacerations, burns and radiation sickness – if they recovered at all.

US psychologists subjected pups to sensory deprivation in separate little boxes, preventing any contact, even with their own bodies, for nine months. There seems no limit to the scientific imagination. Photos of Soviet scientists bottle-feeding the head of a pup grafted onto a living adult dog's chest make one wonder what they will think of next. What 'altar of the supreme aspiration of man' might dogs be sacrificed on in the future? They have already been shot into space to pave the way for human astronauts. In November 1957 little 'Laika', her reactions monitored by TV cameras and with wires all over her body, sailed into orbit in a Soviet satellite. It was a permanent trip: she was destroyed by remote control in her lonely coffin. (Later, dogs were brought back alive.) On earth, in the laboratories, 'tools' that do not die of unnatural causes are disposed of to save feeding expense: shot, decompressed, electrocuted, poisoned with cyanide, barbiturates or magnesium sulphate, or gassed. Some of the deaths are neither quick nor pretty, but then scientists have strong stomachs.

The case that upset the British public most, though, was that of the smoking beagles. Dogs have never done ICI any harm; the 'Dulux dogs' boosted their profits somewhat. In 1975 ICI's laboratories were penetrated by a *Sunday People* reporter posing as a technician. Here are some extracts from Mary Beith's diary,[13] on the forty-eight beagles forced to inhale tobacco substitutes during the 1970s.

Day One: The dogs' heads are restrained by locking two boards in place . . .
rather like medieval stocks . . . and masks, valves and tubes put into place.
During the session the dogs smoke continuously. Some are continually trying

to shake themselves free from muzzles. Today at least two dogs heaved as though they were going to vomit. Others twitched nervously, one tried to bite my hand as I put the muzzle on.
Day Three: Some of the dogs have actually got what must be a smoker's cough.
Day Four: The dog Buster worse ... continually pulling himself free of his mask. When he is smoking, he takes a lot more puffs because someone is pushing the air valve to hurry him up.

Over 300,000 people petitioned I C I to reprieve the dogs; I C I refused. When the experiments were finally completed, the forty-eight beagles were officially destroyed, but two were, in fact, rescued. One, called Bonzo, was recently visited by N A V S General Secretary Brian Gunn. He says, 'I found my visit to this dog, which had previously been used in a most disgusting and cruel experiment, in some ways more distressing than many of the laboratory scenes which I have witnessed, and the memory of his fear is with me still.'[14]

After eight years, Bonzo remains petrified of strangers, clicking noises, and anything that sounds like compressed air. His ears bear his I C I tattoos and, when he was first examined by a vet, he could not walk properly because he had always been suspended in a hammock on the machine, pushing his leg joints out. His new owners love him very much.

National Anti-Vivisection Society, 51 Harley Street, London W1N 1DD. Tel. 01 580 4034.

British Union for the Abolition of Vivisection (new address), 16A Crane Grove, Islington, London N7 8LB. Tel. 01 607 1545/607 1892

Animal Aid, 7 Castle Street, Tonbridge, Kent, TN9 1BH. Tel. 0732 364546.

Doggie Doolittle

And now, to cheer you up, something completely different. You may have heard of Batir, the talking elephant in Kazakhstan Zoo, U S S R, and chimps using sign language to communicate with scientists in America. But did you know there are talking dogs? Not trick ones, canine mimics growling 'sausages' and 'Raymond' on B B C television, but real ones, chattering away?

Sir Walter Scott said of his bulldog terrier Camp, 'I taught him to understand a great many words, insomuch that I am positive the communication between the canine species and ourselves might be greatly enlarged.' Now it has been. This century over 100 cases have been recorded of counting and tapping animals, knocking or barking out an agreed morse code. They include horses, cats, Dobermanns, G S Ds, a King Charles and a

Scottie. Several dogs have had a recognition vocabulary of 200 words and up (the average is nearer sixteen to twenty-six key words plus sequences). Dogs are great communicators, chemically, perceptually and by body language; they observe us to a 'telepathic' degree. William J. Long's classic, *How Animals Talk* (Harper), attempted to get to the bottom of inter-dog talk or 'chumfo' as he calls it, by meticulous observation of a setter, Don, and his canine acquaintances. Long follows that 'trail of silence' and 'this language ... made up of whines, growls, howls, and all the scale of barks. For a *tête-à-tête* conversation they have a whole series of signs, attitudes and signals.' He thinks animals have too long been regarded as 'dumb'.

In the *Annales des Sciences Psychiques* of October 1913 there appeared a report concerning a stray Airedale, Rolf, adopted by the wife of a Mannheim solicitor, Frau Paula Moekel. Having demonstrated he could count better than her children, Rolf clearly deserved lessons on the alphabet, and soon he was tapping out a morse for his mistress and for visiting experts and professors. He disliked the trials and tests very much and often tried to hide. A number of scientists documented 'conversations'. A Professor Ziegler took Rolf a rat in a box. Asked what it was Rolf tapped, 'Lol doesn't wish to say anything.' Young Louise Moekel insisted he answer. 'I can't, on account of that nasty little rat.' He added, 'Too hot to work,' and then, 'Stupid Ziegler.' Ziegler brought a solicitor to authenticate his tests. A Monsieur Morandetti travelled up specially from Berlin to get Rolf to do square roots. Rolf spelled out, 'Tell him to do them himself.' It all sounds rather preposterous, but soon more talking dogs emerged.

In 1916 another Airedale, called Lola, belonging to Frau Dr Henny Kindermann, began tapping out curious conversations with her mistress (Henny: What do dogs feel when they see the eyes and sorrows of men? Lola: No. Henny: Tell me! Lola: Love). Lola, and another Kindermann dog, Ulse, were visited by many European scientists, some cynical, some genuinely impressed. Dr Kindermann published *Lola* in 1916 and *Can Animals Think?* in 1954, and did some fifty years' research on talking animals. Her work attracted many admirers, Hermann Goering among them. Both her phonetically morsing dogs were descendants of Rolf of Mannheim: Germans all.

More recently, two new cases have come to light, in Hitler's Berchtesgaden. Maurice Rowdon's *The Talking Dogs* [Macmillan, 1978] covers 500 lessons with a white poodle bitch, Elke II, and a tall, shy, boney saluki called Belam. They were trained by Dorothy Meyer. Both dogs have learned the standard tapping position, putting either paw in their trainer's hand, and tapping codes for each letter of the alphabet. Elke is the more proficient, but Rowdon observes that they are both definite, excited and expressive. (Belam's mate Keesha was also taught, but tapped a lot of nonsense.) When

Rowdon arrived, veteran of eleven books on other things, he was sceptical, but slowly became convinced that he was watching something remarkable. What finally convinced him was an ugly scene. One day, Belam badly mauled a miniature poodle, called Peggy, in the garden. When the vet had gone, Belam was ordered to tap. 'Are you sorry you did it?' 'No,' said the dog. 'If she died you'd be a murderer! How can Mami love a murderer?' asks Frau Hilde Heilmaier, the dog's owner.

She pulled him straight when he started to lurch away from the tapping position, trying to lie down. His eyes were heavy, his jowl drooped. His neck arched, pathetically. 'Why did you do it?' she asked him. The answer came with remarkable steadiness. Not until the end of the long sentence were there errors. These were the letters I took down:

SOOFROTURONSCLUSLGEUBERESCHIMPFNLGE

The first three letters SOO on enquiry turned out to be irrelevant. But the rest broke up clearly into:

'Froh Tür ohne Schlüssel geübere schimpfen Lge.'
'Do you mean by the last word LGE, Elke?'
'Yes.'
'Glad door without key scold Elke (Geübere was not clear).'

His owner had forgotten to lock the door onto the garden terrace, and Elke could open it by smacking her paw on the handle. Belam thought Elke responsible: Elke had opened the door.

'Do you know what pain you've caused . . . what would you have done if Peggy had died? Tell me that.' This time he tapped with a certain eagerness ROI for 'reue', regret. He gazed up at Dorothy with clear, trusting eyes, very close to her, making little kisses in the air.

'And what do you think Peggy's master and mistress would want to do to you if she died?'

'SCHINPN' (Schimpfen – scold).

'They wouldn't only scold you. They might want to kill you! What would you say if they killed you?'

RUF MAN AOS SCHLAGDHAUS BELAM HOLEN (Call man from slaughterhouse to take Belam.)

'Why did you bite the poodle?'

'NIGT ANDERS KAN' (Cannot do otherwise.)

There are more things in heaven and earth than are dreamt of in a scientist's philosophy.

18

DOGS FOR SHOW

If there is any justice in heaven, men will be paraded up and down before a panel of dog and women judges and awarded marks for beauty; if they don't possess any the judges will quietly press a button marked 'Basement – trapdoor'. Men have escaped for far too long from the tyranny of conforming to 'beauty-contestant' standards of appearance by valuing themselves for themselves. My big, bluebottle-eating, non-show, Yorkshire terrier and beautiful mongrel are both highly discerning dogs and can't wait to get their paws on the buzzer.

Show fever, and breed battiness, were invented in the 1850s for dogs and mad Englishmen. Competition by blood in the fighting pits had been prohibited and a new competition by 'superior blood' was needed to soothe piqued pride. A leading pit-man helped organize a 'Fancy Dog Show'. Elsewhere sportsmen were pitting their dogs' wits in field trials and the two sets, working and showing, began to dislike each other. The first gate show (paying to get in) was probably a setter-and-pointer exhibition at Newcastle upon Tyne in 1859, followed by the inaugural Birmingham event.

A London affair, the Cremorne Show, disorganized by E. T. Smith and involving 1200 alleged mongrels, was an utter shambles. Parched, unwatered dogs stared fixedly at a great fountain in the hall; they had arrived en masse, having stood in crates on the station and lost their labels. Entrants were fastened together willy-nilly and set about one another and passersby. Late exhibitors let their specimens run free; some were trampled; others seized spectators hopping to the chemist with recent bites. Entries were judged in the wrong order and decisions reversed. One catalogue-listed 'Wolf from the Crimea' turned out to be two dachshunds. Dogs with fashionable 'strangle tongues', 'dish faces', shambling coats and paint-blackened noses got out and roamed the streets. Some were returned by rail to their owners, completely cowed.

A much-needed governing body, the Kennel Club, was formed in 1873, holding its own show at Crystal Palace the following year (Jack Russell judged the foxterriers). In 1878 an Englishman called Charles Cruft who, as a youngster, had worked in James Spratt's dog-biscuit bakery, helped stage the great Paris Exhibition Dog Show. It offered entry to many categories including 'Poodles and Woolly Retrievers', 'Bassett Hounds of All Kinds', 'Various Pet Dogs and Drawingroom Dogs', 'Dogs used for Human Food', 'Dogs Untamed by Man' (like the dhole, dingo and the onomatopoeic Himalayan Wahh) and 'Dogs which Become Wild' (such as the American chestnut-coloured dog). The early shows were very broadminded about breeds. In 1877, when America contracted show fever, the first 'Westminster Kennel Club Dog Show' in New York featured a dog with no forelimbs whatsoever and an enormous hippo-eared harlequin Great Dane-mastiff cross called a Siberian bloodhound. No off-the-peg dogs in those days; all bespoke canines. Meanwhile Charles Cruft's London shows gained prestige when Queen Victoria began sending some of her beloved menagerie and 'Cruft's dog affairs flourished in Islington. In 1948, under Kennel Club management, the show moved to Olympia. The 1984 canine show had 10,272 entries.

Being a judge in the old days wasn't easy. Many an early show, like the first bulldog and St Bernard ones, ended in acrimony and litigation. A lot of money was at stake. Rival *mafiosi* followed the judges about, muttering insults. A new-style white bullterrier champion was poisoned at the Hull Show by jealous exhibitors.[1] Judges looked to the wrong end of the leash and there were other malpractices.[2] Even the incorruptible Major Harding Cox of the Kennel Club had his decisions queried, like this 'third':

> 'I beg your pardon Major, but what is the matter with my dog?'
> 'Why, is he ill?'
> 'I meant why did he not take the first prize? Mr "R" gave him the Challenge prize at Barkwell last week.'
> 'I venture to think that if those who were first and second had been at Barkwell, my good friend Mr "R" would have placed yours third, instead of first – get me?'
> 'Then I suppose it is no good my showing my Pingo of Putfield if Napper of Nunbury and Gog of Gumwick are entered at the same show.'
> 'Oh I won't go as far as that, Madam. Different judges have different opinions. . . .'[3]

Anyone who thinks showing isn't a 'job' for dogs has never been to a show. The animals are shaved, showered, shampooed, transported for miles, groomed, barbered, bandaged, tweaked, handled by strangers, hustled round rings; and berthed on benches, waiting their turn – bored, barking and bamboozled by it all. 'Prestige' and 'Champion' are not dog words. They do it for their owners and some are sold, resold, and live their lives in kennels. But many exhibitors build their lives around the dogs and would never part with them. I peeked at a tiny Peke in a hot tent at the 1983 Windsor Show, 8649, Pendenrah Angela. 'Her pet name is Poppy,' said her owner Mrs G. Glenister. 'I've only got three at the moment and they live in the house. Sometimes, with litters, I've had eight or nine running around. I like to keep them with me, not shut up in kennels as they usually are, for convenience. I was involved with Pekingese fourteen years ago and I've just started again: I bought this small one from another breeder. Years ago, when I left school, I became a kennel maid for one of the large breeding concerns and that's where I got my love. You get "bitten" by a breed and once you've had them you always want to keep them: others don't seem to compare. They're characters, Pekingese. I had a little miniature who lived till he was sixteen-and-a-half and there's never been one like him. They're rather like people and when they live with you in the house you can see what they're thinking before they do it. This is Poppy's first show – she's seven months. I keep walking her round because she's a little bit flat with her tail at the moment and Pekingese must carry their tails over their backs. Even if Poppy never becomes a champion, I would never sell her. I'm in it as a hobby, not to make money. I just enjoy being with Pekingese.'

Mrs P. M. Petch, herself an international-show judge, breeds flat-coated 'Rase' retrievers. Three joyous-looking black beauties watched their breeder being interviewed. They all had the longish 'Rase' head which is their hallmark but they are not just pretty faces. They work. Mrs Petch said, 'Flat-coats were the original shooting dog, earlier than the golden or the lab. I breed dual-purpose dogs. In a lot of gundog breeds there are differences between show and working strains, because the work's been bred out of them over several generations. If you don't use something, it goes. We're very lucky in flat-coats: we work and show the same dogs.' Mrs Petch didn't start out with pedigree dogs. She found 'a stray springer spaniel cross, and I had to find a car to put him in', and then 'a curly-coated collie called Buster' followed by 'a sort of cross collie-labrador that everybody said looked like a flat-coat', which she eventually replaced with the real Macoy. She worked them all in obedience in Nottingham, but found the dogs got a bit bored. 'Rase Lysander', 'Lapwing' and 'Kittiwake' were getting bored as we spoke. 'Sit, everybody', said Mrs Petch. Kelly, Sally and Kitty squatted in a neat arc.

Mrs Petch, like the Dog Breeders Association, recommends anyone buying a pedigree dog to go to a breeder, not to a shop or a puppy-farm. Less than 38 per cent of British pedigrees come from licensed breeders. 'People who have these backstreet litters can't get rid of them and they are all too often mated with other poor specimens. I have a waiting list for puppies because I only breed two, or at most three, litters a year. My dogs live in the house; they're on the bed and part of the family. They're a damn nuisance at times, but we wouldn't be without them for the world. I wouldn't sell my prizewinners: I've been asked to name my own price on one or two occasions, but my dogs are my dogs. I'll sell puppies at eight, ten or even twelve weeks if they're going abroad, but I don't like to because, by then, they're becoming part of our family. Some people will: to some breeders money is all-important. But I think you'll find most are like me.'

If all the dogs were like little Poppy or the Rase retrievers, it would be difficult to see how anyone could criticize shows or show people. Unfortunately, this is not the case. Major Harding Cox refers in his book to a 'chump-headed, bandy-legged, flat-footed and three-cornered monstrosity' which, as a judge he awarded 'the order of the boot' but which came back into the ring with a different handler – 'the same vile animal'.[4] To someone like myself, incapable of understanding what ugliness might mean in a dog, calling one 'a monstrosity' is positively offensive, and it is an attitude which is actively encouraged by shows. A dog is not a daub in a gallery but a living individual capable of love, instinctive skills and loyalty beyond human comprehension, and if he is bandy-legged, or flat-footed, or has some worse congenital deformity known to dogs, ninety-nine times out of 100 it is because a human being put it there. Nature militates against mistakes.

Nobel-Prizewinning ethologist Konrad Lorenz, himself a breeder, condemned competition as a bad influence on conformation and character, and attacked the show obsession with beauty:

> It is a sad but undeniable fact that breeding to a strict standard of physical points is incompatible with breeding for mental qualities. . . . In dog and pigeon-breeding this compromise between two breeding ideals has been circumvented by separating 'show' and 'working' strains from each other. . . . Dog shows in themselves involve certain dangers, since competition between pedigree dogs at shows must automatically lead to an exaggeration of all those points which characterise the breed.[5]

This is how so-called 'fancy points'[6] become insidiously established; by degrees these mar a breed for its vocation, whether or not that job still exists. Sometimes all that is left of a working breed is the ghost of a dog, with bizarre reference to his former qualities. The bulldog's gasping flat face 'to breathe while attached to the bull'; the Victorian St Bernard's double dew-claws 'to bear him up in the snow'; the foxterrier's punishing jaw to seize the fox, supposing the huntsman wanted him to, and so on. Since 1959 gundog show champions have needed no trial certificates and show judges differ with sportsmen over eyes, backs and tails. The show spaniel is actually docked much shorter than the working spaniel.

Breed fashions undoubtedly excite people to buy dogs they do not want. RAF Civilian Dog Advisor Terry McHaffie: 'The average chap spends more time choosing a tie than he does choosing a puppy, and then after twelve months he gets rid of it for no good reason.' The thousands of discarded GSDs and other pedigrees that end up in pounds and rescue societies, or with the police or armed services, must mean *something* is wrong. Battersea Manager Major Eric Stones: 'I personally think that the root of the trouble is indiscriminate breeding. It should be stopped at source. Breeders as a whole I have a pretty low opinion of: they certainly exploit an animal for financial gain and in certain parts of the country there are "puppy-farms" that produce a so-called breed dog whose chances of survival are minimal. The owner is forever putting his hand in his pocket taking it to the local vet. People who sell dogs should themselves be vetted. They should come under Ministry of Agriculture regulations and they should pay a hefty licence fee.' Some people training working dogs haven't a civil word to say about breeders. Chief Inspector Ray Wood of Nottinghamshire Police, one of the nation's leading police-dog trainers: 'They're just in it for the money. They're not interested in working qualities – they don't know anything about them. They just want dogs that look beautiful.' He has to contend, he says, with 'GSDs like camels'. No wonder the public give them away.

Animal-behaviour consultant Dr Roger Mugford spends his days trying to help reasonable dog-owners who find they have bought canine nutcases. Most of his patients are pedigree dogs; many have been to training classes, yet still bite the vet, bury pups alive and defecate on the carpet. 'This is why the whole area of dog production has to be greatly professionalized; why we should see geneticists more involved, why the Kennel Club should be disbanded in its present form and run by professionals using computers. Dog breeders and show judges would like to suggest that, when a breed evolves, all the changes are in positive directions because of their skill and high morals. And when there are negative changes, it's because of "irresponsible ownership". Actually genetic selection for behaviour is not that difficult.' President of the BSAVA, Des Thompson: 'I don't think I would accept that neurosis is on the increase in dogs; obviously one of the major problems as far as this aspect is concerned is very close breeding and this is liable to build up problems as well as good qualities. The majority of sensible breeders will breed for temperament, along with the other factors. Any breeder who accepts a perfect-looking animal with a terrible temperament is an idiot.' A PDSA official wall poster on 'Choosing a Dog' recommends the mongrel. 'Some of the more fashionable purebred dogs', it says, 'can be highly strung and have hereditary disorders.' Cocker spaniels, GSDs and golden retrievers are the ones most often appearing at Dr Mugford's clinic having bitten their owners.

How is this possible? Mike Stockman is a leading vet; he is also a breeder ('I think 80 per cent of us lose money and I'm a vet – I can get the stuff cheap!'). He points out that the villains of the piece are not show people, but the 'sausage-manufacturers' – puppy farmers who aren't interested in breed standards anyway. They love 'booms', like the 'Dulux dog' boom. 'It becomes easier for the less caring breeders to make a fortune.' Mr Stockman emphasizes, 'Pedigrees don't have a monopoly on things that go wrong, and many breeds have evolved without problems.' But in the veterinary magazine *In Practice* he explains:

> Conditions such as achondroplasia, where the head becomes large but the limb shafts remain stunted, acromegaly, the excessive enlargement of the extremities, and brachycephalicism ... often resulting in protrusion of the lower jaw, are all seen in dogs which are considered typical of their particular breeds.[7]

These are not freak mutants but legitimate show dogs, bred to the standard.

The wording of breed standards in the UK is currently being studied by a working party of vets and Kennel Club authorities, concerned about 'phrases' which could lead to inheritable abnormalities. A preliminary report states, 'The main areas which were pinpointed ... were the head from several viewpoints, forelegs, and hindlegs and the frequent absence of any reference to temperament.' It is hoped that breeders might be helped to avoid excessive skin folds, flews or dewlaps, massive skull size, crooked and foreshortened legs, feet and knees turned in or out, dish faces that prevent normal breathing, giganticism, the use of anabolic steroids, problems of dentition due to 'undershot jaws' and a few other little problems they may have run into following the standard phraseology. Kennel Club Secretary Bill Edmond: 'Generally speaking, I think, almost without exception people who breed dogs love dogs, and the last thing they want to do is to breed animals with problems which are hurtful to them. Unfortunately, when a gene produces a fault, it takes time to eradicate it, but it's just nonsense to think that a breeder sets out to produce a dog with hip dysplasia, or an eye problem or reproduction difficulties that result in vet's bills for Caesarians. Breeders who develop the dogs don't go in for gross exaggeration. It is just that over several decades, something may change imperceptibly.'

It is frequently assumed that most of the problems in purebred dogs are the result of their inbreeding. This is not quite true. Inbreeding (mating father to daughter, brother to sister, etc.) is simply the breeder's computer for fixing traits. Garbage in, garbage out. Former Chairman of the Kennel Club, A. Croxton-Smith: 'It is a truism to say that inbreeding is the shortest road to the fixation of type or characters that we may desire to emphasize. It is equally commonplace, though expedient, to explain that undesirable characters may be firmly implanted with as much certainty as the good.'[8] It is also worth considering that incest, proscribed by the strongest taboos known to mankind, is nevertheless thought good enough for animals, and forced on them if necessary, even by respectable modern breeders. 'It is a good plan,' says one, of the young bitch about to be mated, 'to tie up her muzzle so that she cannot snap, much less bite, and you will also be free to hold the scruff of her neck in your left hand while helping the dog with your right.' How little we must think of the animal kingdom to so despise their natural choice of a mate.

What exactly constitutes 'beauty' in a dog? True, exhibitors no longer go in for the sort of unanaesthetized faking of fifty years ago, tearing and breaking coats, cutting and screwing tendons, frena and muscles to alter ears and noses.[9] But breeders still cull 'unpretty' pups – parti-coloured poodles for example – and ear-mutilation is approved in Europe and America today. Exhibitors everywhere whisk scissors and clippers to dogs' faces and feet even though injuries can take months to heal, and many breeders are still congenitally incapable of leaving tails alone. The tail is an extension of the dog's backbone. It acts as a rudder for balancing, switches with emotion, fans glandular scents at its base and, when tucked under, protects the animal's most sensitive and chemically active organs from other dogs. My own Yorkie often looks behind to see what is no more, though I didn't get him any cheaper for having a bit missing.

Perhaps the tide is turning; in 1983 two new dog events emerged that have nowt to do with fashion or beauty: the first 'Superdogs', at Wembley Conference Centre, celebrating canine services to humanity, and the first 'Scrufts' at Hewitt's Farm, Chelsfield, for mutts, mops and mongrels. But whatever one might think of dog shows, we are all in their debt to an extent. Shows gave pedigree dogs a high value, and leverage to the nineteenth-century animal-welfare movement by improving the dog's legal status in society.[10] Today, even the father of the future Queen of the Realm can have his gamekeepers hauled before a judge for shooting a girl's pet.[11] Exhibitors have helped by forming dog charities such as the NCDL, and shows helped lift the British (and American) dog out of the gutter, where unless his owner was wealthy and wise he commonly resided; and made him a thing of possible class and consideration. Without the power of the exhibitors and Kennel Clubs the anti-dog lobby would undoubtedly crush all dog-owners underfoot as they have done in Iceland. And last, but not least, breeders and exhibitors, by their care, have protected and rescued many doggie races from oblivion. The Shar Pei, that 2000-year-old fellow with the wrinkles, was saved from the woks and fight-rings of provincial Chinese peasants by breed enthusiasts, especially Americans, and shown at Crufts in 1983. I picked up a waiting-room magazine at the time, and someone had been moved to scrawl across the woebegone and exceedingly crumpled features of Shar Pei 'Dandelion': 'You are so lovely'.

Without show people, Dandelion would not be lovely. He would probably be dead.

19

THE UNEMPLOYED

Unwanted. A word capable of reducing human edifices to rubble. Unwanted, unemployed, surplus to requirements. A man on the dole, a woman on the shelf, a dog on the streets, on the motorway, in the river or in the dustbin. Some 10 million dogs are destroyed each year in the US,[1] and a comparably sad number in Britain. In 1982, a modest year, hundreds of thousands of dogs were dumped on the RSPCA, the NCDL, Battersea, the rescue societies, shelters, Blue Cross, police, armed services and vets. Nobody wanted them. 56,645 were humanely destroyed by the RSPCA and 3578 by Battersea alone – a more distasteful job for these animal-welfare workers can scarcely be imagined. The old method was a drop of prussic acid, or carbonic-acid gas and chloroform. Nowadays it's usually an injection with barbiturates or the electrothanator – the electric box. The purpose of this chapter is to see what might be done about the problem, other than buying up all the dogs oneself and living in the Orkneys.

Rescued dogs-home dogs make excellent companions – they know what it is to need a friend. Given the chance, many have served in wartime as messengers, sentries, mine-detection dogs, lifesavers. A few have recently been trained as guidedogs and hearing dogs for the deaf, and who knows what else they could turn their paws to. The tide of wasted talent and discarded devotion is the fault of dog-owners, dealers and breeders, and measures are called for which some may consider harsh. That's a shame. Government contingency plans for dealing with the next rabies' outbreak in Britain are not for the squeamish either, and people who turn dogs out on the streets will get the grandstand seat they richly deserve.

The majority of canines eliminated are mongrels – illegitimate dogs – designated undesirable or unfashionable by human clowns. In 1982 Battersea took in 13,821 of them. (The second highest was GSDs: 837). Charles Dickens, with his sense of outrage at all cruelty, visited the Dogs' Home in the 1860s when it was a small, dying dogs' asylum in London's Hollinworth Street, the butt of jokes in *The Times* ('Why not a home of refuge for all the starving butterflies and caterpillars of the gardens of London?') and the source of constant complaints from local residents. He contrasted the inmates' frantic attempts to catch his eye, as 'worthwhile dogs to have', with the well-fed contestants at the nearby Islington Show, who wouldn't have wetted on him if he'd been on fire. The sight of the mongrel, particularly, upset him.

> Poor beast, with his tail left, not to please Sir Edwin Landseer, but because nobody thought it worthwhile to cut it, with his notched pendant ears, with his heavy paws, his ignoble countenance and servile smile of conciliation, snuffing hither and thither, running to and fro, undecided, uncared for, not wanted, timid, supplicatory – there he was, the embodiment of everything that is pitiful, the same poor pattering wretch who follows you along the deserted streets at night, and whose eyes haunt you as you lie in bed after you have locked him out of your house. . . . I think it is somewhat hard that [people] should turn the whole scheme into ridicule.[2]

It costs 10p to walk round Battersea now, and over £500,000 to run the place. There are eighteen blocks and 456 kennels. If you're just window-shopping you need to move fairly briskly through the serried ranks because if you stop and pay particular attention to a dog his hopes build up. He starts bowing and scraping and confiding whimpering noises, and he says dog swearwords when you walk away. A bullterrier, the tops of his ears snipped off with scissors, caresses your fingers with the side of his head. They're not a bit disillusioned with humanity. They just want to go home. I asked Major Eric Stones, in charge, if it isn't all a bit depressing? 'Well, it's not really, if you have the right frame of mind; if you think what would happen to these poor chaps if there were no Battersea Dogs' Home. And, after all, they do have underfloor heating here, and individual kennels and health lamps, and they're well-fed and loved.

'I have about 500 at any one time, and our intake during the course of the year is 18,000. I collect from the Metropolitan Police stations, for which I have five air-conditioned ambulances. They go out every morning, Monday to Saturday.' The police foot the bill for a stray for seven days, after which it becomes the Home's property. 'Then I resell them. This is very important. We're not here to make money out of the dogs but, on the other hand, we've got to make sure that dogs are not going out either to dealers or for vivisection. The price is pitched at a level where it wouldn't be worth their while.' How much? '£10 and upwards.' More for pedigrees, special rates to OAPs. 'If a dog comes in as a stray we know nothing about it until it's been here for some time. Then, although we can't say whether it is housetrained or not because it's in a kennel, we get to know its temperament. Other dogs are brought in by members of the public because they can no longer keep them.

Then a form is filled in and details taken about the dog. Is it good with children? Is it housetrained? Is it a good guard-dog? And other characteristics that we feel should be transferred to the next owner.' Battersea never closes to dogs. One can be handed in at any hour of the day or night, 365 days a year. In 1982 2736 lost dogs were reunited with their owners and new homes were found for 11,463 other happy souls. They used to go out with a message on their collars:

> Pray have a little patience with me. There are so many of us shut up together here that the keeper has no opportunity to teach us habits of cleanliness. I am quite willing to learn.

If you are thinking of buying a dog, please consider the challenge.

The Dogs' Home, Battersea, 4 Battersea Park Road, London SW8 4AA. Tel. 01 622 3626.

The NCDL takes in over 3000–4000 dogs a year and rehomes 90 per cent. They seem to specialize in before-and-after dogs. When they come in they look skeletal, cowed and covered in sores, and when they go out they look handsome. The kennel staff make a point of building up casualties that have been dragged behind cars on motorways and of restoring their confidence, and they take in boney shivering greyhound failures from flapper tracks, nursing them like children with woolly sweaters on. Elderly mongrels are hard to re-home and have to look their smartest; the younger ones aren't so bad. 'I should think 70 per cent are mongrels; getting on for 10 per cent are greyhounds and the rest are a mixture,' says PR Officer Mrs Clarissa Baldwin. 'We don't like too many strangers wandering round the kennels – it upsets the dogs. They bark like mad. We feel it's best to interview the person first and say, what sort of dog are you looking for? What sort of house have you got? Do you work? have children? etc. and then we go up to the kennels and try to match a dog with that person. We only destroy dogs on veterinary advice. It very seldom happens, thank goodness, but there are some that come in beyond repair and it would be cruel to keep them alive. We don't "sell" the dogs; we ask for a donation for the others left behind. The kennels all make a loss. Shropshire can house 120 dogs; the average is about eighty at each of our fourteen kennels. They're always full.'

The NCDL undertake care of all strays in the areas they serve. 'If, after that, people cannot look after a dog any more and they telephone, we can usually find a bit of kennel space somewhere.' NCDL subscriptions cost £5 per annum (£3.45 to pensioners) and members get free public-liability insurance for their dogs, an advisory service, a collar tag, and a good feeling inside.

The Secretary, NCDL, 10 Seymour Street, London W1H 5WB, Tel. 01 935 5511.

The RSPCA has been rescuing dogs since 1834. They say, 'Dogs suffer more than any other creatures at the hands of men, women and children who invent every imaginable – and unimaginable – abuse and cruelty to inflict on their helpless victims.' They also say sadistic crimes are on the increase, and their records of prosecution read like horror stories. The Society has an inspectorate of 270, and 150 shelters, centres and clinics in England and Wales. In 1982 they found homes for an amazing 51,457 cast-off canines; in 1981, 47,871; in 1980, 48,008. That's an awful lot of dogs. They also had the sickening job of destroying, in their thousands, the halt, the lame and the undesirable. 'We wish desperately there were an alternative.'[3] They use the Huelec electric cabinet, by consensus the most humane method available.

I went along to the RSPCA's Patcham Animal Sanctuary (London Road, Patcham, Brighton BN1 8ZH. Tel. 0273 554218) where boarders help pay for the homeless. Archetypal black mongrels with floppy ears leapt and wiggled impressively, trying to pass themselves off as pups; a greyhound full of sorrow stared out from his plastic bed. 'We have about thirty in now,' said Treasurer and dogsbody Philip Hale. 'In a year the turnover is probably 700–800 or more. It has got worse over the last twelve months but we've had a lot of good publicity over cases of cruelty so we're re-homing more dogs. We don't sell them. We ask for a donation to help meet our running costs. That way the dogs remain our property and if they are ill-treated we can go and take them back.' A photo of what I took to be a greyhound, dreadfully starved, hung from the office wall. 'It's not a greyhound. It's a Great Dane. She collapsed with hunger and exhaustion by the roadside in Crawley. She doesn't look like that now; she's very fit and bold and has gone to a good home.'

The Patcham kennels have a scrupulous pre-visiting and after-care system for dogs rehomed. One RSPCA Inspector I spoke to said, 'There's always the question whether you're actually perpetuating the problem.' Philip Hale: 'Some people bring the new dog back very quickly: they don't seem to realize it has to settle down and adjust to its new surroundings. They think you should hand them a perfect dog. We ought to have a toy one under the counter, and say, "Here you are. Pull it along on a bit of string."' Why do dogs not hate people when they have been hung, tortured, stabbed, stubbed with cigarettes, neglected, starved or abandoned? 'They have an inherent love of man, for what it's worth. I don't think he'll ever knock it out of them.'

Details of local kennels, dogs or donations: RSPCA Headquarters, Causeway, Horsham, West Sussex RH12 1HG. Tel. 0403 64181.

The Stray Problem

Most dogs who end up in charitable dosshouses are ex-strays. They rose to independence on the end of someone's boot. In Britain there are about 6 million dogs; one in four households has one, amid growing restrictions from housing authorities. Dogs can make a noise and make a mess, and though they may not have been expensive to buy, are expensive to keep. Remember Jake, the Jack Russell tied outside Worthing DHSS in April 1983, with a note on his collar? Jake was abandoned by a pensioner who 'couldn't even afford 40p a day to feed him'. At any one time there are approximately 500,000 strays on Britain's streets, 200,000 ending up in police custody and at least 30 per cent of those destroyed. An estimated 220,000 dogs are born each month – (in America it's 2000 pups per *hour*) – and a third of these never see their first birthday. In theory an unspayed bitch can give *rise* to 67,710 offspring in six years.[4]

Many unwanted litters are simply abandoned. Others are bought by dealers, crated and transported for re-sale, often at Christmas and often for children as five-minute wonders. They may also be diseased. Many 'strays' are not ownerless. They are simply shut out and left to wander. They cause approximately 1800 traffic accidents a year, extensive messing of footpaths, worrying of livestock (6000 animals destroyed a year) and they menace children, adults and law-abiding dogs on leads.

Clearly, this will not do.

Restrictions on pedigree breeding are relatively easy to enforce, as happened, for example, during the First World War, though some unscrupulous breeders do 'farm out' brood bitches, and puppy farmers, who rear rather than breed, deal in bulk.[5] In any case because pedigrees are valuable and their sex-lives monitored, they do not commonly roam the streets. Some pedigree breeders, like Major Harding Cox, have even thought up schemes for wiping out the mongrel population as a needless depravity.[6]

Dog-control orders in the past have been swingeing. In Edward III's reign only gentlemen's dogs could tour London and, under the Game Laws, dogs were maimed near forests and restricted by size with a gauge. During the Plague, one enterprising Lord Mayor ordered the destruction of 40,000 mutts, and dog-whippers in churches were a familiar sight, chucking them out by means of forceps clamped on the skull. Beasties at large have been curbed by several schemes, particularly during rabies' outbreaks. One idea was London's annual Dog Whipping Day, on which men and boys set out with clubs and bars at dawn and bludgeoned all the dogs they could find, leaving the carcases strewn in every alley and doorway.[7]

Abroad, even today, there are punitive measures. In the US, with its dog deluge and rabies, there are stringent state leash and muzzling orders, curfews and quarantines, and strays are sent en masse to decompression chambers. Dog catchers operate with lassoos, nets and vans. In poorer New York areas, the ASPCA can scarcely cope. In Buffalo and New York there are state laws regarding 'fouling' and 'pooperscooping' – clearing it up with a device like a minute mop. In Iceland dogs are banned altogether from cities and towns, and the ban is quite ruthlessly enforced. Finance Minister Albert Gudmundsson, reported to the police over his mongrel Lucy, said he would emigrate to keep his dog. In the USSR there are stern laws concerning fouling of footpaths, and dog-owners have to take their pets for regular free veterinary check-ups and inoculation. They are sent reminder cards. Peking's dogs, by the time you read this, will be dead. France's 9 million dogs are being silenced by high-frequency anti-bark collars and curbed by spiked chains, but they are allowed in cinemas and bistros, and Paris street sanitation department has carts that whisk dog-droppings from view.

In Britain we have a ludicrous system whereby it costs about 60p to process licences costing 37½p. Most dog-owners don't bother to buy a licence in the first place, which saves on administrative costs. Originally the dog licence was a variable revenue-raising tax, levied first in 1796. In 1867 this was suddenly replaced by a fluctuating excise duty of 5s; 3s; 14s; and lastly 7s 6d in 1878. It has been '7s 6d' ever since. Successive governments have been reluctant to interfere with it. In 1867, when the duty was introduced, there were unforeseen consequences. 'The public, in whose name all this had been done, killed their dogs rather than pay the tax, and in every large town dogs lay dead in the roads.'[8] Every 1 January, when licences were renewable, a new lot of strays stood bleakly in the snow. A recent Private Member's Bill, intended to raise the licence to £10, seems to have died a merciful death.

Two reports on Britain's dog problem have recently been compiled: one in 1975 by the Joint Advisory Committee on Pets in Society (JACOPIS), with the support of the RSPCA, NCDL and other pro-dog groups, and one by a Department of the Environment Working Party in 1976, following from those recommendations. The JACOPIS idea, put simply, is to raise the dog licence to £5 in order to finance a national dog-warden scheme (there are at present 150 local-authority wardens, but these are on the rates). The said wardens, after rudimentary training in dog-handling and first-aid, would pick up strays in vans and either return them to their owners or take them to a pound for reclamation or destruction after a few days. Some local authorities would have their own kennels, but most would use existing animal-welfare shelters. Police responsibility for capture, custody and disposal of strays would devolve upon local authorities. This was tried at the end of the nineteenth century, with disastrous consequences.[9] JACOPIS proposes to reconcile the dog-owner with the anti-dog lobby by means of a Code of Practice for owners regarding control, fouling, etc., and guidelines to local authorities, suggesting they provide exercise areas and dog loos. (This would upset Burnley District Council who, in 1978, fought an action in the High Courts over banning dogs from parks.) JACOPIS does not foresee any additional difficulty in getting dog-owners to cough up a fiver, though many dodge paying 37½p. It recommends licensed dogs wear tax discs, like cars.

With the greatest respect for the motives behind both the JACOPIS scheme and the humane and surprisingly pro-dog Government report of 1976, I believe any plan based on an annual licensing system for dogs is unworkable. So does Battersea's Major Eric Stones. 'Dog wardens and increasing the licence are not going to stop the problem. After all, large numbers of people don't buy a television licence, or pay 37½p for the dog licence we have now.' As a direct result of the JACOPIS initiative we have the Draft Dogs (Northern Ireland) order threatening to get on the statute books; this is condemned in its present form, even by the BSAVA President, as 'draconian', a mandate to euthanize harmless and healthy dogs.[10]

Besides, the £5 licence fee is contingent on a warden salary of £2500. If the revenue necessary to provide wardens and discs is to come from a licence increase, owners will either not comply or, if there are stiff sanctions, throw out their dogs. The animal shelters are already bursting at the seams. Animal-behaviour consultant Roger Mugford: 'The problem of free-roaming dogs is not going to be solved by a lot of unsophisticated characters running around in Ford vans telling people off.' Even with the wardens we have already, there is sometimes overzealousness. Dogs turn up repeatedly at certain NCDL kennels with name tags on to 'teach the owner a lesson'.

My own scheme, simple and drastic, is as follows. Abolish the licence. Replace it with a Value Added Tax at the point of sale. The real cost of the dog should be included in the purchase price, commensurate with its value and with the cost of looking after it properly throughout its life. The cost of neutering at an approved clinic (recommended by animal-welfare groups and by JACOPIS) is prohibitive to most dog-owners once they get the pup home. It should be included in the purchase price. The cost of inoculation against hardpad, distemper, canine hepatitis, leptospirosis, canine parvovirus and worming – all avoidable expenses once the dog gets home – should be included. So should the cost of such facilities, exercise areas, dog loos, wardens and drinking troughs as are deemed necessary for the proper care and control of the dog population.

When this new dog VAT began to bite, existing dogs would not be thrown out, but less new dogs would be purchased. OAPs and the less well-off who could not afford to buy a dog at the going rate could get excellent second-hand ones more cheaply from the dogs' homes. An estimated 26 per cent of pups would still be obtained from the litters of friend's dogs.[11] As an increasing proportion of the dog population was neutered, these litters would diminish. The puppy farmers and the dealers crating pups across the country would look for alternative employment because the price rise would not benefit the retailer. All dogs, mongrels included, would be considered valuable and the threat of theft would deter owners from letting their animals stray, just as it leads to concern for inanimate valuables. In its original report, JACOPIS considered it morally wrong 'to ration dogs by the purse'.[12]

I consider it morally right. Those who cannot afford to keep a dog all its life, relatively free from danger and disease and from incurring the wrath of the public by foraging about, should not be permitted to buy one. They should be given a toy from under Philip Hale's counter and told, 'Here you are. Pull it along on a bit of string.' Remember Jake?

Feral Dogs: the Unclean

Hebraic and Moslem traditions have marked the dog for centuries as 'unclean'. Just how unclean is he?

After thousands of years of domestication, the dog retains the ability to revert to the wild: to become feral. Dingoes, like the pariah dogs of Asia, are almost certainly ex-domesticates. Studies of feral dogs in the US, in Mexico and India carried out by dog scientists like Alan Beck and Michael Fox, make sad reading. Lady and The Tramp live in dilapidated buildings and scavenge at dawn and dusk. 'Packs' tend to be of limited duration, forming round the nucleus of a bitch on heat. It's easier to forage alone. But little groups do stick together, like the trio in St Louis, Missouri studied by Michael Fox in the 1970s. The group consisted of a female mongrel, a large mutt with a bad hip, and a GSD who seemed to be the gooseberry, following the other two about. Feral dogs are distinguishable from free-roaming dogs: the former are more scabby, skinny and scared. The trio ranged for up to a mile, scavenging in parks and refuse dumps, chasing squirrels without catching any, and keeping in contact by marking, wagging and looking at one another. 'They avoided people, especially children,' says Fox. 'This study underlines the tragic consequences (to the dogs) of irresponsible ownership.'[13]

Health hazards to humans from dogs in the UK have been grossly exaggerated in the Press. Dogs don't have lawyers. The following are findings from the 1976 Government Working Party report:

(14.2) dogs which are correctly managed and cared for constitute only a small hazard to human health.

(14.5) so far as the Working Party could discover there is no recorded instance where infection has been transmitted from dogs to humans through contamination of food in shops. Any feeling against allowing dogs into food shops is largely aesthetic.

On *Toxocara canis* being transmitted to humans:
(14.3) it should be emphasised that infection with overt symptoms is rare.

Toxocara canis is a nematode parasite found in dogs, the equivalent of *Toxocara cati* in cats, and similar parasites in other species. The *T. canis* scare, orchestrated by the anti-dog lobby and one London campaigner well known for crouching behind bushes on Hampstead Heath counting dog droppings, has caused needless anxiety to parents of young children afraid that they might ingest *T. canis* eggs from the faeces and get an extremely rare disease called *Toxocariasis* (most doctors have never even seen a case). Here are two leading vets on the subject. Douglas Brodie (crossly): 'There's so much rubbish coming from the anti-pet lobby it's about time somebody stood up and articulated clearly the facts.' Mike Findlay: 'The parasite affects all the canidae in this country – dog, fox, badger, the domestic cat and presumably the wild cat. The reason the cat has been held less to blame is that it buries its faeces, whereas the dog, the badger and fox leave them on the surface.' Can't the problem be solved by a child washing its hands? 'Elementary hygiene education is always very high on our list of priorities.'

Children are statistically in far more danger from human filth, chemical sprays and refuse than they are from dog droppings, however unsightly.

One health risk definitely not exaggerated, though, is that of rabies. In July 1983 an Irish wolfhound, imported from the US, died in quarantine in Rugby, the first case of a rabid dog in the UK since 1970. Shortly before, a woman from Stroud, returning home from India, died of the disease. Britain continues to fend off an outbreak by stringent quarantine measures but, between 1979 and 1981, there were 227 prosecutions against persons attempting to circumvent them, with 176 dogs, ninety-five cats and 817 other mammals landed illegally. Rabies is a disease of the central nervous system transmitted in saliva by the bite of an infected animal. Most warm-blooded mammals can become rabid; in Britain the most likely vector among wildlife is the fox, and cats and dogs domestically. A particular hazard is that wild animals which are normally timid, once rabid, will approach humans brazenly.

Under the Rabies (Control) Order of 1974, in an area declared infected, the Ministry of Agriculture, Fisheries and Food (MAFF) would confine and control dogs, cats and other mammals, seize, detain and destroy all strays, compulsorily vaccinate pets and destroy the fox population. Owners would receive only 'nominal' compensation for animals put down. Holding facilities are available at West India Dock; carcases would be incinerated.

Rabies is a nightmare disease and people are understandably afraid of it. Outbreaks in Britain have led to panic and the indiscriminate brutalizing of dogs on the streets. In 1843 police and public set to battering London dogs, rabid or otherwise. Similar scenes occurred in 1877 and 1896. In 1886 Queen Victoria protested angrily when a gentlewoman's little spaniel, squealing, muzzled and completely harmless, was beaten for over twenty minutes with a policeman's truncheon despite the owner's hysterical pleas. In 1919 a severe outbreak, believed to have begun with a serviceman smuggling back a dog from the Continent, resulted in 319 confirmed cases in five years.

People who allow their dogs to roam the streets are like those who attempt to smuggle animals into the country. Mad, bad and dangerous to know.

20

THE COMPANION

People campaigning to sanitize the country of dogs should really be made to do their own dirty work. Let them go along to the council estate, hospital ward or old people's accommodation from which dogs have been banned, and remove the offending pets with their own hands from the child, the childless and the pensioner. Perhaps then they would realize the suffering they cause. They'd have to be careful, of course. Not all dog-owners are children or harmless old ladies. Lord Byron will never rest in his grave. He wanted to be buried in a vault he had commissioned at Newstead Abbey beside a tomb bearing the inscription, 'To the memory of Boatswain, a Dog' who 'possessed beauty without vanity, strength without insolence, courage without ferocity, and all the virtues of man without his vices'. Sir Walter Scott, when his favourite dog died, excused himself from a dinner engagement because of 'the death of a very dear friend', and Alexander Pope exercised his beloved dog Bounce with pistols in his pockets, especially after *The Dunciad.*

These days, fewer marriages than ever last 'till death do us part'. People have to make do. In the US, 33 million women, many of them single and professional, now own one or more dogs. In Paris, owners were asked to respond to a survey on the reasons for having a dog. To 'the dog gives me love and affection' 93 per cent agreed completely; 5 per cent with reservation. To 'the dog gives me someone to lavish love on' 63 per cent agreed completely, 19 per cent with reservation. Another study, in Australia, found that the most important function of the dog was 'companionship'. Second was 'protection'. Professor Alan Beck, referring to American research, says, '99 per cent of all owners admit to talking to their dogs. And the other 1 per cent lie'. Ninety-four per cent address the dog as they would a person; 28 per cent impart confidences. A world authority on the subject is Dean Leo Bustad, Professor of Veterinary Medicine, Washington State University. Dean Bustad told the BSAVA's twenty-sixth Annual Congress: 'I've seen people living in pathological grief for years after a pet has died, or who have had their animals taken away from them and been warehoused in a nursing home. For some of these people, I was the only visitor they saw. They were just staring at bare walls. I have many letters saying, "There's nothing to live for, but my animal gave me the need to live. It regulated my life. It made me exercise. Now all I do is sit and smoke and watch the boob tube and wait to die." That's a great condemnation on society.'

In some US states there is now legislation to prevent such callousness, and allow the aged to keep their pets, and in France an animal companion is allowed to live in any dwelling.[1] Not so in Britain. Apart from 75 per cent of landlords imposing restrictions, so do most local authorities, especially in 'sheltered accommodation' for old people. Yet research has shown that the elderly, in particular, think of their pets as members of their families, specifically as children under the age of three. Des Thompson, BSAVA President: 'I think it is tantamount to criminal. For many people their life ends when their animal is taken away from them.'

The final and most important of all the dog's jobs is to be a companion. Of all living things, he seems best qualified for it. One canine chronicler has collected 784 cases of faithfulness and devotion, of dogs following their owners to war, the grave and the scaffold.[2] A seventeen-year-old Italian rickety mutt called Fido plods every evening, in all weathers, to meet his owner at the bus stop. Years ago his master was killed, but Fido continues to wait for the bus, just in case. He has been decorated, for reasons he does not know or care about, by the Italian government. Authenticated stories of dogs journeying hundreds of miles to find lost owners, or having premonitions of the owner's death, are not uncommon. Nor are dog hauntings. Ethologist Konrad Lorenz grieved over a dog called Bully: 'The constant sound throughout years of the dog trotting at my heels had left such a lasting impression on my brain – psychologists call this an "eioletic" phenomenon – that for weeks afterwards, as if with my own ears, I heard him pattering after me.'[3] Cases of canine apparition, reported to the British College of Psychic Science in the 1920s, included one with photographic evidence from a Lady Hehir, pictured with a wolfhound. She'd had a cairn puppy who died in her arms, which appears, curled up, on the wolfhound's rump.[4] Pythagoras believed in reincarnation. When a friend died he thought it a good idea to hold a dog near the mouth of the departed, to receive his spirit. The Egyptians had no doubt that the dead were guided in the afterworld by a dog- or jackal-headed god, Anubis, and myths and legends connecting man and dog in some death-defying way abound in many cultures.

The depth of friendship between human and dog companions often goes unnoticed until one of them dies. In 1983 Mrs Hilda Harris left £27,000 to her mongrel Trix. Her brother is reported to have said, 'It is an insult. If the money had gone to a medical charity I would have said good luck.'[5] Such wills are generally contested. At Blackpool early in 1983 a holidaymaker died trying to save his dog from the sea, and three policemen were drowned trying to rescue the holidaymaker. Banner headlines blamed the animal for four lives tragically wasted. One or two suggested the dog had killed them all. On the other side, British and American vets are increasingly concerned about human grief after euthanasia, which they perform three or four times in every 200 consultations. One recent study carried out by a vet, Dr Mary Stewart, compared grieving for a companion animal with human bereavement. She found that lonely and childless people who depend on their animals were often completely broken by the experience. 'I had to put down a dog for one of our neighbours, who went into a really bad state for a month. He wouldn't go to work or talk to his wife. He said he didn't want another dog, but in the end his wife brought home a pup and that was the best possible therapy.' Vet Douglas Brodie: 'If the animal in question has some very strong role in the owner's mind, such as a substitute sibling or spouse, there may be pathological mourning, and the owner may become very distressed and even be hospitalized.' The owner is often asked to sign a release slip. 'To me that's an horrific concept, to ask a person to sign away the life of a close friend for perhaps fifteen years.' American vet Dr Bruce Fogle, author of *Pets and Their People*, wrote his book out of concern for those like the owner of an emergency case he treated in London, who went home and tried to kill herself. 'Veterinarians should be aware that the owner's anger and crying are normal early stages of grief. We aren't trained to cope with these things. When a pet dies, people are embarrassed to commiserate. The family routine is expected to continue, with simply a void where the pet used to be.'

How can such a relationship, older than history and so important and binding on either side, have been so long neglected by scientists? Well, now it isn't. Because of the volume of important research coming out of the universities of Washington state, Pennsylvania, Minnesota, Purdue and Edinburgh, showing the enormous benefits of pets to both mental and physical health, scientists are now very busy studying the Human-Companion Animal Bond. Symposia have been held in Paris, London, Philadelphia and, most recently, Vienna, to pool international findings. Two studies in particular have awakened interest. One revealed that, a year after heart attack, survival was much higher among pet owners. The other showed that, whereas greeting another person raises blood pressure, greeting a dog lowers it, significantly beneath either reading or resting. Some scientists believe the companion animal somehow provides a link between man and the old instinctive paradise before we became intellectual: the Garden of Eden, if you like. Man and dog had the same shrew-like ancestors way back in the prehistoric forests, and their development was analogous. Both became social hunters. Konrad Lorenz reserves days when he goes 'to the dogs' and returns to that unthinking paradise, watching his dog's tremendous mouse-leaps and stalking behaviour. It's very therapeutic. Dr Peter Messent is an animal behaviourist and Honorary Secretary of the Society for Companion Animal Studies (SCAS) whose membership from fourteen countries includes doctors, psychiatrists, community workers and vets (and authors of dog books), and I am indebted to Dr Messent and SCAS for much of the research material in this chapter. Dr Messent refers to American research on childhood dreaming: the younger the children, the more they have animals in their dreams. 'The pet fills a gap between our own lives and nature outside. In very young children, something like half their dreams contained an animal of some sort, commonly the dog.'

Dr D. Abrahamson is a psychiatrist who used to be a vet. 'One of the first of the humane mental hospitals, the eighteenth-century retreat at York, made a practice of introducing animals into the milieu, and after that most mental hospitals had animals as a prized feature, seen in terms of occupation of the patient. Psychiatrists saw that mental illness had something to do with alienation from nature.' The hospital farms died out in the 1940s; now there is so-called 'pet-facilitated psychotherapy', begun by New York psychiatrist Boris Levinson in the 1950s, using animals to break the ice and facilitate contact with disturbed children and adults. 'In fact', says Dr Abrahamson, 'Freud usually practised with a dog in the room, but this has been almost hushed up.' Boris Levinson was the first psychiatrist actually to acknowledge a canine assistant. In the late 1950s he began bringing in his own dog, Jingles, as 'consultant' to a withdrawn boy, who was cured by their joint ministrations. Levinson later dedicated a book to Jingles, 'my co-therapist'.[6]

Animals are now being allowed into old people's homes, hospitals for the criminally insane, prisons and convalescent homes. In the UK the DHSS leaves such policy decisions to the local authorities. Goodmayes has hospital pets; Shelton Psychiatric Hospital in Shropshire has admitted pets to ward D after an elderly patient was found to be pining away for his sheepdog, Nell. In Derbyshire volunteers are sharing their dogs with people in residential care. 'Pro-Dogs Active Therapy Dogs' – PAT Dogs for short – are visiting children and old folk in nursing homes and similar institutions where there are no pets to cuddle. In Australia a black labrador introduced into a geriatric hospital ward acted as a social catalyst. Time spent alone by the patients was reduced from eighteen hours a day to eleven as they began talking not only to the dog but to other people. 'It worked for Schweizer', says Dean Bustad. 'I think it'll work for us.' Professor Bustad reckons that, by the end of the decade, doctors will routinely prescribe a dog rather than a drug for disturbed patients, 'and we owe it to the dog to pick one that can mentally withstand it'. He thinks patients should not in any case be separated from beloved pets. 'I could give you several examples of people hauled off to hospital, maybe after an accident, and they've actually been poor surgical risks because they were still mentally alert, worrying about their pets back home and who would take care of them. A lot of people exaggerate the risk of disease from animals. If you have a healthy pet with veterinary care and you place it in a home or a hospital, the big health hazard is not the animal but the person next door.' Dr Fogle: 'There is a children's hospital in London, for example, where the administrator encourages parents to bring small pets to visit. His contention is that there is less chance of the children picking up diseases from their pet dogs and cats than from their brothers and sisters coming to visit them.

Those wishing to look into this companion animal business should contact:

SCAS (Society for Companion Animal Studies), Hon. Sec. Dr P. R. Messent, Animal Studies Centre, Freeby Lane, Waltham-on-the-Wolds, Melton Mowbray, Leicestershire LE14 4RT. Tel. 0664 64171.

The Delta Society of North America, NE 1705 Upper Drive, Pullman, Washington 99163, USA.

JACOPIS (Australia), 117 Collins Street, Melbourne 3000, Australia.

Killed with Kindness

After all the dog has been through doing cruel and hard jobs for mankind, and considering the RSPCA's evidence of growing sadism by awful owners, it seems ironic that, as a twentieth-century companion, the dog is sometimes killed with kindness. Vets estimate that one in three British dogs is obese.[7] Elderly and overweight people tend to have fat, under-exercised dogs. They suffer from heart disease, liver disease, respiratory problems, joint and locomotive disabilities, lowered resistance to infection, diabetes, digestive upsets and a higher mortality rate than slimmer canines. Petting the dog leads to other problems too. Dr Bruce Fogle: 'The smothering overprotective care of some owners, their love and concern, can produce a neurotic dog. I'm not saying it's wrong. I'm just saying it's a fact.' In Britain and the US a high proportion of dogs thrown out or euthanized have what are called 'behavioural problems'.

Dr Roger Mugford, UK and Paris consultant in animal behaviour, is one of a dozen or so specialists worldwide now dealing professionally with loony companion animals (most of the others are in the US; Professor Michael Fox of the American Humane Society has even made a record, 'Dog Talk', to explain weirdo syndromes). Dr Mugford: 'Many of the cases I see are due to inherent factors within the animal, rather than a lack of competence or willingness to try on the part of the owner. The owners are often nice, normal people who have had a dog successfully in the past and have reasonable expectations of the present one.' Dr Mugford believes that the JACOPIS idea of legislating against irresponsible owners is misguided, and that many dogs chucked out of doors are destructive. They chew, howl and defecate on the duvet, and the owner doesn't know what else to do. The correct solution is to send for Dr Mugford. He sees patients by referral from local vets and either visits or invites them for consultation in Bayswater or Paris. This is followed by a report and treatment plan. Eighty per cent of his patients are dogs. Neuroses in the dog frequently do not respond to chemotherapy, Valium, Epanutin and mysolin, prescribed by the vet, so he gets a lot of neurotics. No, they don't lie on a couch and no, he doesn't hypnotize them. I spent the day at the Bayswater clinic watching Dr Mugford at work with a typical batch – all pedigree dogs and all unspeakably badly behaved.

To give you a taster, meet little Lulu, a black cocker spaniel. She came first class on the train, spayed and bearing her pedigree certificate ('A lot of those we have investigated turn out to be faked') and good credentials from training classes. Many of Dr Mugford's clients have tried training classes of the 'show it 'oos boss' type which exacerbate their problems. Lulu, a seemingly charming creature, was, at home, more exciting. She would start barking at dawn in her comfortable room and if anybody came down to scold or punish, her eyes turned to two little red coals and she would attack with a continuous snapping movement, rather like a hedgemower. Left alone for even five minutes she would gnaw the carpet and all the wood round the door. She had recently staged a *putsch*, climbing her mistress's back and seizing her master's tie in lieu of his face. She had also bitten the vet's bottom in revenge for an injection. The family had tried pleading, remonstrating and whacking without success. Dr Mugford, an eminently sensible chap with a tranquil sense of humour, had seen it all before. He showed the family diversion tactics, using a rape-alarm. At the sound of the peep, Lulu must rush to a mat and be given a nourishing titbit. Switching the dog into another routine at the start of a dotty turn is often more effective than punishment. On close examination Lulu wasn't really malicious, just very possessive of her owners and desperate when left. Her attacks occurred when someone was about to leave her all alone. Dr Mugford recommended 'a less affectionate relationship', being more offhand before they went out and leaving the radio on.

'My clients run at an 83 per cent satisfaction level: I try to monitor it,' says Dr Mugford. 'I'm professionally accountable to the Royal College.' He avoided blinding the owners with science, or rather, 'unsupported crap about dominance theory, etc.', and kept the consultations practical and humane. There was Rum, a golden retriever who'd started attacking strangers. We all walked him round Bayswater to diversify his affections, while Dr Mugford appeared from side turnings affecting a limp and a strange voice. Rum cleverly ignored this but obligingly attacked him when we got back to the surgery. Rum was tried with the rape-alarm routine and a flexi-lead instead of a check chain to defuse the physical link between dog and walker. He must be encouraged to like visitors taking him for little walks and bearing titbits, not pulled away from them in panic. Another patient, Dottie, a tiny Border collie, would snap every time 'Dad' moved to get his reading glasses or turn the television on. She went into a barking set-out when the phone rang – or anything occurred which might put her out of the limelight. She also hated people leaving the room and would take it out on the last one. Various options were open, including a water pistol and an automated bark collar that echoes barks with peeps. But the main thing was to get her gradually used to being alone for set periods on a time chart.

It was recommended to all these clients that they lower the temperature of their relationship with the dog, especially while the treatment plans were underway. You could see the owners' faces drop: affection is what most people get a dog for. 'Exactly, and thank goodness for that: long may it continue. But in particular problem situations, owners have to manipulate that variable. Love the dog but realize that love is a potent weapon for overcoming specific irritating habits. People find it strange that asking them to do *nothing* can be as effective as asking them to do *something*. It's very easy and comforting to be able to say, "Well, your problem is that you've been indulgent with the dog," which would be the obvious thing to say to these people. In fact the problem is that the dog is in a high league mentally, and very resourceful at developing a whole series of attachment-promoting activities. Many of my referrals are showing some form of distress due to their great attachment to their owner, as, for instance, when left on their own. These problems are very upsetting for the owners because they love the dog so much, which makes the decision about re-homing or euthanasia such an unpleasant one, and I would say an unnecessary one because the problems are relatively simple to overcome. The owners must detach themselves from the dog and make it more independent. There's about an 80 per cent success rate in all the attachment problems that I see.'

Dr Mugford believes his work will not really make an impact on Britain's dog problem unless a responsible body like the veterinary profession involves itself in a big way. Fortunately, this is increasingly likely. Therapists will also need a genetic data-base on breeds and temperament from which to work, because fundamentally most of the personality defects are inherited. 'All it needs is a commitment on the part of the breeders to produce the sort of animals that people want to have as companions.'

Indeed, of all the jobs the dog has been bred to do, 'friendship' is his last and greatest vocation.

NOTES

1 The Dogfather

1 *Umschau*, 79, 1979, p. 19.
2 The small Asiatic wolf, *Canis lupus pallipes*, is a favourite suspect. A wolf dogfather seems to be the official line at the British Museum of Natural History, at Tring Museum, and at the London Zoo (*vide* their Guide Book). Dr Jewel, née Clutton-Brock, author of *Domesticated Animals from Early Times*, favours the wolf. So does canine genealogist John McLoughlin, US author of *The Canine Clan*. German experts like Prof. B. Klatt of Halle, Prof. Wolf Herre of Kiel, and Erik Zimen all support the wolf.
3 See Konrad Lorenz, *Man Meets Dog*, Penguin Books, 1953, pp. 10–23, and *King Solomon's Ring*, Methuen, 1952, p. 114.
4 Michael W. Fox, *The Dog: Its Domestication and Behavior*, Garland STPM Press, 1978.
5 Erik Zimen, *The Wolf; His Place in the Natural World*, Souvenir Press Limited, 1981, p. 9.
6 Capt. A. H. Trapman, *The Dog: Man's Best Friend*, Hutchinson Publications, 1929, p. 43.
7 R. Schenkel, 'Submission: Its Features and Functions in the Wolf and Dog', *Am. Zool.*, 1967, VII, pp. 319–29; 'Expression-Studies of Wolves', *Behaviour I*, 1947, pp. 81–129.
8 J. P. Scott, 'Evolution and Domestication of the Dog', in T. Dobzhansky *et al.* (eds.), *Evolutionary Biology II*, Academic Press, NY, 1968.
9 L. David Mech, *The Wolf: the Ecology and Behavior of an Endangered Species*, Doubleday, NY, 1970.
10 Zimen, op. cit., p. 100.
11 The Linda Chamberlain case. Chamberlain was jailed for the murder of her daughter Azaria after claiming the baby had been taken by a dingo. The case has since been reopened. In 1983 two investigators alleged that a campsite dingo called Scarface took the child after all.
12 Catherine Fisher, *The Pan Book of Dogs*, Pan Books, 1958, p. 180.

2 The Taskmaster

1 The first of these types is Konrad Lorenz's 'little Spitz-like Turf dog', *Canis familiaris palustris* – some taxonomists call this group *C. f. Leiner*. Second comes the medium-sized European type, *C. f. intermedius*. Third is the sort believed to have been the ancestor of sheepdogs and collies, *C. f. matris optimae*, and fourth is *C. f. inostranzewi*, the prototype heavy-duty draught dog.
2 Juliet Clutton-Brock, *Domesticated Animals from Early Times*, Heinemann/ BMNH, 1981, p. 44.
3 Edward C. Ash, *This Doggie Business*, Hutchinson, 1934, p. 29.
4 A. Sloan and A. Farquhar, *Dog and Man: the Story of a Friendship*, Hutchinson, 1925, p. 44.
5 Ash, op. cit., 31.

3 The Accomplice

1 Andrew Alexander, *Daily Mail*, 25 April 1983.
2 Major Harding Cox, *Dogs and I*, Hutchinson, 1923, p. 37.
3 ibid., p. 13.
4 A. H. Trapman, *The Dog: Man's Best Friend*, Hutchinson, 1929, p. 284.
5 E. C. Ash, *This Doggie Business*, Hutchinson, 1934, p. 199.
6 A. Sloan and A. Farquhar, *Dog and Man: the Story of a Friendship*, Hutchinson, 1925, p. 76.
7 Philip Windeatt, *The Hunt and the Anti-Hunt*, Pluto Press, 1982, p. 17.
8 Harding Cox, op. cit., p. xxiv.
9 ibid., pp. 282–3.
10 Miss A. K. Galbraith in Windeatt, op. cit., p. 24.
11 W. H. Hudson, *A Shepherd's Life*, MacDonald Futura, first published 1910. This edition 1981, p. 84.
12 Windeatt, op. cit., pp. 52, 32.
13 ibid., p. 41.
14 ibid., p. 43.
15 Hudson, op. cit., p. 87.
16 R. V. Denenberg and Eric Seidman, *The Dog Catalog*, Grosset and Dunlap, NY, 1978, p. 21.
17 A. Croxton Smith, *About Our Dogs*, Ward, Lock (undated), p. 103.
18 Aneurin. See Trapman, op. cit., p. 286.
19 Ash, op. cit. p. 151.
20 Harding Cox, op. cit., p. 271.
21 J. Wentworth Day, *The Dog in Sport*, George Harrap, 1938.
22 Sloan, op. cit., p. 104.

4 Hairs to the Throne

1 Fiorenzo Fiorone, *Encyclopedia of Dogs*, Hart-Davis MacGibbon, 1973, p. 1.

2 Dorothy Laird, *How the Queen Reigns*, Hodder and Stoughton, 1959, p. 130.
3 A. H. Trapman, *The Dog: Man's Best Friend*, Hutchinson, 1929, p. 67.
4 A. Sloan and A. Farquhar, *Dog and Man: the Story of a Friendship*, Hutchinson, 1925, p. 90. (They refer to Henri III of France. Navarre was his successor.)
5 ibid., pp. 102–3.
6 Trapman, op. cit., p. 65.
7 There are many accounts of this duel, the most authentic source being J. de la Taille's in 'Discours notable des duels'.
8 C. Fisher, *The Pan Book of Dogs*, Pan Books, 1958, p. 124.
9 Gordon Carter, *Dogs and People*, Abelard-Schuman, 1968, p. 106.
10 Mary Forwood, *The Cavalier King Charles Spaniel*, Popular Dogs, 1967, p. 19.
11 Harding Cox, *Dogs and I*, Hutchinson, 1923, p. 31.
12 ibid., p. 32.
13 ibid., p. 33.
14 Macdonald Daly, *Royal Dogs*, W. H. Allen (undated).
15 E. C. Ash, *This Doggie Business*, Hutchinson, 1934, p. 215.
16 Harding Cox, op. cit., p. 34.
17 Robert Lacey, *Majesty*, Hutchinson, 1977, p. 326.
18 R. V. Denenberg and E. Seidman, *The Dog Catalog*, Grosset and Dunlap, NY, 1978, p. 243.

5 The Seven Dwarves

1 John C. McLoughlin, *The Canine Clan*, Viking Press, NY, 1983, p. 124.
2 Tring Zoological Museum; notes referring to two exhibits in their collection.
3 McLoughlin, op. cit. p. 125.
4 E. C. Ash, *This Doggie Business*, Hutchinson, 1934, p. 181.
5 Erich Tylinek, *Introducing Dogs*, Golden Pleasure Books: Artia, 1962, p. 78.
6 Johannes Caius, *De Canibus Britannicis*.
7 De Maulde.
8 A. Croxton Smith, *About Our Dogs*, Ward, Lock (undated), p. 331.
9 J. Clutton-Brock, *Domesticated Animals from Early Times*, Heinemann/BMNH, 1981, p. 39.
10 Croxton Smith, op. cit., p. 349.
11 See, for example, Ash, op. cit., p. 177.
12 A. H. Trapman, *The Dog: Man's Best Friend*, Hutchinson, 1929, p. 216.
13 Ash, op. cit., p. 178.
14 Croxton Smith, op. cit., p. 348.
15 Attributed to Dame Julyana Berners. See Katharine Tottenham's *The Jack Russell Terrier*, David and Charles, 1982, p. 129.
16 R. V. Denenberg and E. Seidman, *The Dog Catalog*, Grosset and Dunlap, NY, 1978, p. 79.
17 R. Lacey, *Majesty*, Hutchinson, 1977, p. 167.
18 McLoughlin, op. cit., p. 118ff.
19 Harding Cox, *Dogs and I*, Hutchinson, 1923, p. 217.

20 Ash, op. cit., p. 74.
21 Croxton Smith, op. cit., p. 345.
22 Trapman, op. cit., p. 300.

6 The Gladiators

1 *Sunday Times*, 1 September 1974.
2 *Sunday Times*, op. cit.
3 R. V. Denenberg and E. Seidman, *The Dog Catalog*, Grosset and Dunlap, NY, 1978, p. 208.
4 *Sunday Telegraph*, 5 November 1978.
5 *Daily Mirror*, 4 December 1978.
6 A. Sloan and A. Farquhar, *Dog and Man: the Story of a Friendship*, Hutchinson, 1925, pp. 60–61.
7 Denenberg, op. cit., p. 214.
8 E. C. Ash, *This Doggie Business*, Hutchinson, 1934, p. 17.
9 Sloan, op. cit., p. 80.
10 Ash, op. cit., p. 99.
11 ibid., p. 100.
12 ibid., p. 109.
13 Barbara Woodhouse, *Just Barbara*, Michael Joseph/Rainbird, 1981, pp. 114–15.
14 Vol. 4, No. 6, November 1982.
15 Harding Cox, *Dogs and I*, Hutchinson, 1923, p. 5.
16 *Daily Mirror*, 4 December 1978.
17 *Sunday Telegraph*, 5 November 1978.
18 *Daily Mirror*, 4 December 1978.
19 Published by the National Canine Defence League (undated).

7 Good Shepherds and Heelers

1 W. H. Hudson, *A Shepherd's Life*, MacDonald Futura, first published 1910. This edition 1981, p. 216.
2 ibid., p. 215.
3 G. O. Willison, *The Bearded Collie*, Foyles' Handbooks, 1971, pp. 9–10.
4 ibid., p. 10.
5 Tony Iley, *Sheepdogs at Work: One Man and His Dogs*, Dalesman Books, 1978, p. 67.
6 Johannes Caius, *De Canibus Britannicis*.
7 E. Tylinek, *Introducing Dogs*, Golden Pleasure Books: Artia, 1962, p. 14.
8 B. Woodhouse, *Just Barbara*, Michael Joseph/Rainbird, 1981, p. 118.
9 Hudson, op. cit., p. 186.
10 Evliya Effendi, in Lt.-Col. E. H. Richardson's *British War Dogs*, Skeffington and Son (undated), ch. 1.
11 A. Sloan and A. Farquhar, *Dog and Man: the Story of a Friendship*, Hutchinson, 1925, p. 38.

12 C. Fisher, *The Pan Book of Dogs*, Pan Books, 1958, p. 174.
13 Hudson, op. cit., p. 10.
14 ibid., p. 187.
15 Iley, op. cit., p. 35.
16 ibid., p. 58.
17 Hudson, op. cit., pp. 180–81.
18 Iley, op. cit., p. 59.
19 ibid., p. 56.

8 Transport and General Workers

1 Apsley Cherry-Garrard, *The Worst Journey in the World*, Chatto & Windus, 1965, p. 453.
2 R. F. Scott, letter to Maj.-Gen. Sir D. Haig, Winter Quarters, Cape Evans, 22 January 1911, MSS 739.D.
3 A. G. E. Jones, 'Scott's Transport 1911–1912', in *Polar Boken*, Scott Polar Research Institute, 1977–8.
4 Leonard Huxley (ed.), *Scott's Last Expedition*, Smith, Elder and Company (undated), Vol. I, p. 7.
5 Jones, op. cit., p. 77.
6 Letters (69) to R. W. Skelton, MSS 342/28/1–69.D.
7 'The Sledging Problems in the Antarctic: Men *v.* Motors' (undated).
8 Jones, op. cit., p. 77.
9 Roland Huntford, *Scott and Amundsen*, Hodder and Stoughton, 1979.
10 Robert Peary, *Northward Over the Great Ice*, Pan Books, p. 176.
11 Many such sources can be found in *Researches into the History of the British Dog* by George Jesse (2 vols.), Robert Hardwicke, 1866.
12 See, for example, Grahame Clark's *World Prehistory*, Cambridge University Press, 1961, pp. 149ff, 420ff.
13 A. Sloan and A. Farquhar, *Dog and Man: the Story of a Friendship*, Hutchinson, 1925, p. 151.
14 E. C. Ash, *This Doggie Business*, Hutchinson, 1934, p. 64.
15 Sloan, op. cit., pp. 112–13.
16 Ash, op. cit., p. 120.
17 A. Croxton Smith, *About Our Dogs*, Ward, Lock (undated), p. 301.
18 Ash, op. cit., p. 120.
19 Croxton Smith, op. cit., p. 301.
20 R. V. Denenberg and E. Seidman, *The Dog Catalog*, Grosset and Dunlap, NY, 1978, p. 29.
21 Ash, op. cit., p. 122.
22 ibid., p. 123.
23 Denenberg, op. cit., p. 29.
24 A. H. Trapman, *The Dog: Man's Best Friend*, Hutchinson, 1929, p. 87.
25 Ash, op. cit., p. 17.

9 Come On My Son

1 A. Sloan and A. Farquhar, *Dog and Man: the Story of a Friendship*, Hutchinson, 1925, p. 57.
2 E. C. Ash, *This Doggie Business*, Hutchinson, 1934, p. 154.
3 G. Carter, *Dogs and People*, Abelard–Schuman, 1968, pp. 27–8.
4 Ash. op. cit., p. 168.
5 H. Edwardes Clarke, *The Waterloo Cup 1922–1977*, Spur Publishers, 1978.
6 Harding Cox, *Dogs and I*, Hutchinson, 1923, p. 179.
7 ibid., p. 177.
8 Larry Freas, writing in Beverly Pisano's *Siberian Huskies*, T F H Publications Inc, 1979, p. 30.

10 The Earth Dog

1 Katharine Tottenham, *The Jack Russell Terrier*, David and Charles Publishing Company, 1982, p. 128.
2 A. Croxton Smith, *About Our Dogs*, Ward, Lock (undated), p. 113; Tottenham, op. cit., p. 128.
3 Attributed to Dame Julyana Berners; see Tottenham, op. cit., p. 129.
4 Croxton Smith, op. cit., p. 200.
5 Tottenham, op. cit., p. 12.
6 W. H. Hudson, *A Shepherd's Life*, MacDonald Futura, first published 1910. This edition 1981, p. 187.
7 Croxton Smith, op. cit., p. 201.
8 ibid., p. 202.
9 ibid., p. 212.

11 Sniffers and Trackers

1 This theory of the neopallium is explained in John C. McLoughlin's *The Canine Clan*, Viking Press, NY, 1983, pp. 8–9.
2 This well-authenticated story appears in many canine histories, e.g. A. Sloan and A. Farquhar, *Dog and Man: the Story of a Friendship*, Hutchinson, 1925, p. 194ff; A. H. Trapman, *The Dog: Man's Best Friend*, Hutchinson, 1929, p. 131ff.
3 G. R. Jesse, *Researches into the History of the British Dog*, Vol. I, Robert Hardwicke, 1866, p. 158.
4 E. H. Richardson, *British War Dogs*, Skeffington & Son, p. 4.
5 *History of the Antiquities of Westmoreland and Cumberland*, Nicolson and Burns, 1777.
6 E. C. Ash, *This Doggie Business*, Hutchinson, 1934, pp. 89–90.
7 A. Croxton Smith, *About Our Dogs*, Ward, Lock (undated), pp. 104–5.
8 Jesse, op. cit., p. 160ff.

12 War and Patrol

1 *Julius Caesar* III, i, 273.
2 Clara Bowring and Alida Monro, *The Poodle*, Popular Dogs, 12th edn 1980, p. 29.
3 Max Halstock, *Rats: the Story of a Dog Soldier*, Victor Gollancz, 1981.
4 R. V. Denenberg and E. Seidman, *The Dog Catalog*, Grosset and Dunlap, NY, 1978, p. 80.
5 A. H. Trapman, *The Dog: Man's Best Friend*, Hutchinson, 1929, p. 241.
6 Lt-Col. C. E. W. Beddoes, in L. G. Cashmore's (ed.) *A Tribute to the Dogs That Serve*, George Ronald Publishers, 1960, p. 83.
7 Denenberg, op. cit., p. 34.
8 Trapman, op. cit., p. 49.
9 Gloria Cottesloe, *The Story of Battersea Dogs' Home*, David and Charles 1979, p. 99.
10 G. Carter, *Dogs and People*, Abelard-Schuman, 1968, pp. 86–91.
11 A. Sloan and A. Farquhar, *Dog and Man: the Story of a Friendship*, Hutchinson, 1925, p. 198.
12 Cottesloe, op. cit., p. 97.
13 E. H. Richardson, *British War Dogs*, Skeffington & Son.
14 Cottesloe, op. cit., p. 129.
15 Letter to the Kennel Club Secretary.
16 Arthur Moss and Elizabeth Kirby, *Animals Were There*, Hutchinson, 1946.

13 The Dog in Blue

1 E. C. Ash, *This Doggie Business*, Hutchinson, 1934, pp. 131–2.
2 See, for example, Erik Zimen, *The Wolf*, Souvenir Press, 1981.

14 The Big Time

1 Clara Bowring and Alida Monro, *The Poodle*, Popular Dogs, 12th edn 1980, pp. 25–6.
2 The *Spectator*, October 1914.
3 A. H. Trapman, *The Dog: Man's Best Friend*, Hutchinson, 1929, p. 81.
4 *Woman's World*, July 1982.
5 Patricia Poleskie of Animal Talent Scouts Inc., quoted in R. V. Denenberg and E. Seidman, *The Dog Catalog*, Grosset and Dunlap, NY, 1978, p. 265.
6 William Shatner, Sondra Marshak and Myrna Culbreath, *Shatner: Where No Man*, Tempo Star Books, 1979, p. 31.
7 Eric Knight, *Lassie Come Home*, Cassell, 1942.

15 In Death and Darkness

1 A. Sloan and A. Farquhar, *Dog and Man: the Story of a Friendship*, Hutchinson, 1925, p. 219.

2 E. C. Ash, *This Doggie Business*, Hutchinson, 1934, p. 128.
3 G. Carter, *Dogs and People*, Abelard-Schuman, 1968, p. 80.
4 A. H. Trapman, *The Dog: Man's Best Friend*, Hutchinson, 1929, p. 88.

16 The Protection Racket

1 E. Zimen, *The Wolf: His Place in the Natural World*, Souvenir Press, 1981, p. 158.
2 K. Lorenz, *Man Meets Dog*, Penguin Books, 1953, p. 47.
3 This was 'Lulu', a flop-eared male. See Wilfred Sheard, *The Glory of the Dog*, Hutchinson, 1935, p. 106ff.
4 Harding Cox, *Dogs and I*, Hutchinson, 1923, p. 273.
5 R. V. Denenberg and E. Seidman, *The Dog Catalog*, Grosset and Dunlap, NY, 1978, p. 76.
6 G. Cottesloe, *The Story of Battersea Dogs' Home*, David and Charles, 1979, p. 137.
7 Department of the Environment, 'Report of the Working Party on Dogs', HMSO, 1976, 18.5.
8 Fred Curnow and Jean Faulks, *The Dobermann*, Popular Dogs, 6th edn 1983, pp. 152ff.
9 Denenberg, op. cit., p. 236.

17 Brutes of Science

1 *NCDL News*, spring 1983.
2 See National Anti-Vivisection Society (NAVS), *Animals' Defender*, September/ October 1983 for detailed analysis of White Paper. Changes remove existing safeguards.
3 NAVS Annual Report, 1982.
4 R. V. Denenberg and E. Seidman, *The Dog Catalog*, Grosset and Dunlap, NY, 1978, p. 35.
5 *RSPCA Today*, autumn/winter 1982.
6 See Spence's *Anecdotes*, and Pope's paper in the *Guardian* on animals, 21 May 1713.
7 NAVS revised edition, 1983.
8 Denenberg, op. cit., p. 36.
9 G. Zbinden and Flury-Roversi, *Archives of Toxicology*, 1981, Vol. 47, pp. 77–99.
10 Colin Smith, *The Moral and Social Aspects of Vivisection*, International Association Against Painful Experiments on Animals, p. 7.
11 I. P. Pavlov, *Conditioned Reflexes*, Oxford University Press, 1927.
12 *Encyclopaedia of Medical Science*, published in Russia, 1893.
13 Reprinted in NAVS, *Animals' Defender*, May/June 1983.
14 ibid., p. 46.

18 Dogs for Show

1 E. C. Ash, *This Doggie Business*, Hutchinson, 1934, p. 117.

2 Harding Cox, *Dogs and I*, Hutchinson, 1923, pp. 44–6.
3 ibid., pp. 48–9.
4 ibid., p. 28.
5 K. Lorenz, *Man Meets Dog*, Penguin Books, 1953, pp. 87–9.
6 Harding Cox, op. cit., p. 57.
7 Vol. 4, No. 6, November 1982.
8 A. Croxton Smith, *About Our Dogs*, Ward, Lock (undated), p. 67.
9 Harding Cox, op. cit., p. 67.
10 See, for example, R. V. Denenberg and E. Seidman, *The Dog Catalog*, Grosset and Dunlap, NY, 1978, p. 202.
11 *Daily Mail*, 26 April 1983, referring to Earl Spencer's gamekeepers before Northampton County Court.

19 The Unemployed

1 J. C. McLoughlin, *The Canine Clan*, Viking Press, NY, 1983, p. 133.
2 *All the Year Round*, 2 August 1862.
3 *RSPCA Today*, spring 1983.
4 *Dogs in the UK*, Report of the Joint Advisory Committee on Pets in Society (JACOPIS), 1975, p. 12.
5 Department of the Environment, 'Report of the Working Party on Dogs', HMSO, 1976, 19.2.
6 Harding Cox, *Dogs and I*, Hutchinson, 1923, p. 75ff.
7 E. C. Ash, *This Doggie Business*, Hutchinson, 1934, p. 200.
8 ibid., p. 202.
9 G. Cottesloe, *The Story of Battersea Dogs' Home*, David and Charles, 1979, p. 89.
10 BSAVA Press Release, 7 April 1983.
11 *Dogs in the UK*, JACOPIS report, p. 28.
12 ibid., p. 2.
13 Michael W. Fox. *The Dog: Its Domestication and Behavior*, Garland STPM Press, 1978, p. 1.

20 The Companion

1 *Dogs in the UK*, JACOPIS report, p. 3.
2 A. H. Trapman, *The Dog: Man's Best Friend*, Hutchinson, 1929, p. 196.
3 K. Lorenz, *Man Meets Dog*, Penguin Books, 1953, p. 196.
4 W. Sheard, *The Glory of the Dog*, Hutchinson, 1935, p. 113.
5 *Daily Mail*, 16 May 1983.
6 Boris Levinson, *Pet-Oriented Child Psychotherapy*, Charles C. Thomas, 1969.
7 *Veterinary Practice*, 4 April 1983.